Know Law
A Guide to Understanding U.S. Law

By

T.C. Dreyer, Esq.

Know Publishers

Jacksonville Beach, Florida

Know Publishers produced this book to educate you about United States law. It provides a general overview of law without specific authority applicable to any particular issue in any state. It contains commentary about the law that is not legal authority. The information in this book is presented as an accurate account of the law, but it was not written by a person admitted to the practice of law in all jurisdictions. The book does not give legal advice and should not be relied upon as authority for any particular legal issue. The book is not a substitute for legal advice from a licensed attorney in your location. If you need legal advice, seek a competent attorney.

The examples and stories (i.e., Stories from the Real) in this book are primarily based on actual tried cases that are in the public record. In some of these, the author changed the names and omitted facts to allow easier reading. Other examples and stories are fiction created by the author to make or illustrate points of law. They are not based on actual persons or historical events. Any similarities are purely coincidental.

Copyright 2017 by T.C. Dreyer
Copyright 2017 by Know Publishers
3948 3rd St. S. #113
Jacksonville Beach, FL 32250

ISBN-13: 978-1977731210
ISBN-10: 197773121X

ACKNOWLEDGMENTS AND DEDICATION

I wish to acknowledge the thousands of students I had the pleasure to educate over the past 20 years. It is their questions, comments, and contributions in the classroom that led to my better understanding of our law.

I dedicate this book to those who want to know.

Know Law
A Guide to Understanding U.S. Law

Contents

Preface

I wrote this book based on interactions with people during 20 years of teaching college courses, and a 40+ year career in tax, law, and finance. It was evident to me that many Americans, too many Americans, did not really understand the law or its impact on their lives or the businesses in which they worked.

We are expected to know and understand the law, but we are not taught much about it. Many go through school, sometimes to graduate level degrees, without even an introduction to the very rules that govern our society. And too many acquire their knowledge of the law from rumors, media stories that do not contain all of the facts, or from tales of woe presented by friends, business associates, and news articles.

So I wrote this book to familiarize everybody with the law and its reaches into our lives. I wanted to provide an easy to read and understandable explanation of what the law is and how it works in our world. This is not a legal textbook, nor is it meant to provide legal guidance for a particular set of facts.

The U.S. has a unique legal system because of our republic form of government. Each of the 50 states and each of the territories of the U.S. has its own law that is unique to it. Also, many of our counties, cities, and towns also have their own sets of laws. Finally, the laws of the federal government supplement, augment, and in some cases supersede the laws of the various states. A specific discussion of the law is necessarily restricted to the locality in which it is applied. This book is intended to give an overview of the law, bringing together its common features and discussing them in a general way.

You will not find many references, citations, or even many quotation marks or italicized words in this book. It is written from my personal understanding of the law and highlighted with real stories from case law and the world around us. The intent is to remove much of the complexity of real world law and provide a clear presentation of how it should and does work. The book contains some opinions about the law, not in a way to censure or question it, but rather to expose and discuss many common perceptions that should be in the forum of public knowledge and conversation.

Read this book as you would read a book about gardening. The gardening book will not make you a botanist, but it may help you grow a more beautiful garden. Reading this book will not make you a lawyer, but it will help you have a better life through knowledge and understanding. It may improve your ability to contribute to workplace dialogue. It might help you evaluate risks in your life or business activities. And, it could help you make better decisions. But it will not make you an attorney or provide definitive legal answers.

Again, this is not a legal guide or statement of the law in any particular topic or locale. It is a book of understanding. If you need legal guidance, there are many resources available to research your particular situation. Or better still, consult with an attorney.

T.C. Dreyer
Jacksonville Beach
August, 2017

Know Law
A Guide to Understanding U.S. Law

Chapter 1
Introduction to Law

(The Emanation of Our Law)

This book introduces United States (U.S.) law and the impact it has on our lives. We all encounter the law every day, and it guides our goals, relationships, and behaviors.

We will explore together many legal areas that affect our lives, including the basis of U.S. law itself.

The study of law must start with understanding some basic concepts:

- Law reflects society.
- Law is created by society's institutions.
- Law changes as society changes.

Law is a Reflection of Society

Law is quite simply the rules that a society sets and enforces. There are different concepts of law. Natural law theory derives from our humanity - we know it is wrong to murder. Positive law comes from the authority of the state - it is wrong because the government so declares. But law is something much simpler, especially in democracies, but perhaps in all societies.

Law is what a society wants the rules to be. In the U.S., we can propose that every law we have reflects the wishes of the majority. Consider that. What law do we have, that if put to a vote of the entire population, would not receive a majority? You may think of some that are near 50/50, but it is very difficult to find one that would not carry a majority.

Law is the best expression of democracy because it reflects the will of a pure majority. The majority cuts across classes of society; it ignores race, religion, social status, wealth, and political status. It simply reflects the will of a majority - more than 50 percent - of our population. There are numerous examples of how law reflects the majority opinion. Some are very recent and dramatic.

Before 1972, abortion was illegal and any public opinion poll taken a few years before that would have shown that a majority of the population opposed abortion. But in the 1960s, this public sentiment changed. A majority wanted legalized abortion. The law changed to reflect this. Today, we see a much divided population regarding this topic, but the polls show that a majority favor legalization. If the public opinion changes, I suggest that abortion will become illegal again. But the change will not occur until a majority supports a change.

Capital punishment is another example of changing public opinion reflected in changing law. In the 1970s capital punishment was banned in the U.S., but was revived as the majority attitude shifted.

Another not too ancient example of change influenced by the public is the 55 mph speed limit - popular with the citizens during the 1970s oil shortages - unpopular and repealed as the crisis ended.

The law, like it or not, reflects the morals and principles of a democratic society. Morality changes and so do the rules of society. The law is us. Those who do not like the law as it stands cannot change it until they convince a majority of their fellow citizens to agree. Efforts by the minority to force standards on the majority are not successful. The minority does not make the law.

Law is Created by Society's Institutions

We make our law through our government and the court systems established by our government. Our Constitution sets a framework of rights, obligations, and limitations on government. Read it; it is not very long and does not contain very much in the way of complicated legalese. It simply provides an overall framework for our law.

The U.S. Constitution and the various state constitutions provide authority for elected officials to make law. Congress, state legislatures, and county and local government bodies pass statutes, codes, and ordinances that establish the formal rules. These rules regulate behavior among all citizens (criminal law) and between individual members of society (civil law). And, they provide consequences or sanctions for not following the rules.

A violation of a criminal statute is an affront to societal standards of conduct and is prosecuted by the state. If the prosecution results in a conviction, the party committing the act is subject to confinement, fines (that go to the state), or even death. Sometimes, the criminal will also be ordered to pay restitution. (Pay the victim for injuries or property damage caused by the crime.)

Civil law allows for disputes between individuals to be resolved in an orderly manner. An aggrieved party has a society sponsored set of rules (the law) and forum (the courts) to seek damages (usually monetary) for the misconduct of another. The aggrieved party brings the action and receives the award if successful.

The legislative bodies delegated some of their law making authority to governmental agencies and in so doing created a new area of law commonly referred to as administrative or regulatory law. This law is created, enforced, and in many cases adjudicated by administrative agencies through their rule making authority.

Administrative law probably has the greatest impact on modern business operation. Agency rule making at the federal and state levels has dramatically increased government involvement in business operation and costs, and in the lives of all of us. Consider just a few of the many federal agencies that control business operation - EPA, OSHA, IRS, FCC, EEOC, ICE, FDA, CPSC, FTC, SEC (all discussed later is this book) - the list is very long. There are literally thousands of administrative agencies making rules for us.

What caused regulatory law? As our society changed in the industrial revolution from one primarily engaged in agriculture and small business into one dominated by large, complex manufacturing and transportation businesses, legislators found themselves without the expertise to control the impact of these businesses on the general welfare of the citizens.

Congress, therefore, created agencies to oversee these complex new business operations. The agencies were expected to have the subject matter expertise to understand, and control for the public good, the activities of these large enterprises. Congress gave the agencies authority to make rules, enforce them, and provide for hearings of disputes that arose under them.

The court system is the final component of our law creation system. Courts do make law and are often the leaders in changing the law. How do courts make law?

Our legal system is based on the "common law" of old England. Common law arose as the King delegated his dispute resolution authority to magistrates throughout the kingdom. The magistrates started from a base without rules or structure. To facilitate the resolution of disputes, and to provide a degree of predictability in the system, magistrates began to honor and follow the decisions of other magistrates. Over time, they established a body of law that was followed by all. The concept of "precedent" means that a decision by one court will form the basis for decisions by others.

Under the common law ability to set rules, the courts interpret and apply the law to new and changing facts. As society evolves and changes, the law changes with it. Once the Supreme Court, as the final court of the land, rules on a matter of law, it becomes the law that all other courts must follow under the concepts of common law precedent.

While the courts have the authority to make law in this way, the statutory law made by the legislative branch is superior. Once the legislative branch enacts as law, the courts must follow it. Courts, therefore, generally only make law when there is no statutory law in place to cover the situation presented, or when the statute that applies is not clear and needs interpretation. The legislative branch can always overrule court-made law by passing legislation.

But, the courts also have the authority to define our rights under the Constitution. If a particular statute or rule of law conflicts with one of our rights, the courts can find the law "unconstitutional" and thus unenforceable. By expanding, or contracting, the interpretation of our rights, courts also make or change the law.

The layers of laws in the U.S. are presented and prioritized below, from highest law down:

The Constitution – No other law can supersede the Constitution.

Treaties – These are agreements between the U.S. and other countries. They override all laws except the Constitution.

Statutes (also called Codes and Ordinances) – These are laws passed by legislative bodies such as Congress, state legislatures, county and city councils, and elected boards.

Regulations of federal and state agencies – These written rules have the same level of authority as statutes.

Executive orders – The President and the Governors of states have the authority to make law by orders - these are simply written directives that have the force of law. This power to make is law is limited. Most of the executive order power comes from authority granted to the executive branch by the legislative branch.

Case law – The courts can and do make laws, but courts are bound to follow all of the laws above, and court-made law cannot supersede a statute unless it finds the statute violates a Constitutional right. Judicial review, at the Supreme Court level, can nullify any other law if it violates a provision of the Constitution.

Rulings, opinions, and directives issued by federal and state agencies – These rules give guidance, but do not have the force of law. They can be disregarded by the courts.

Legal Treatises – topical law summaries, scholarly explanations of the law, and legal manuals written by legal experts are good sources for information, and are sometimes referenced by the courts. They are not, however, law and they do not provide any legal authority.

Federal law always supersedes conflicting state law – States can have laws that are stricter than federal laws, but state laws that are more lenient do not change the rule or enforcement of the conflicting federal law.

Law Changes as Society Changes

Several examples above discuss some areas of law that have changed in recent times. Certainly, if we look over the history of the U.S., we can find many examples, from the inane (dueling used to be legal) to the very significant (abolishment of slavery). Every change that has occurred reflected the changes in attitudes of the society as a whole. This change in thinking developed from several factors, including changes in technology, communications, religious beliefs, and ethics. The process continues today.

How do we change our law? We can and do amend our Constitution. We can provide substantial rights, or remove them by amendment. This is a difficult and perhaps drastic process, but it has happened 27 times so far. Granting women the right to vote (19th Amendment) is a very clear example of a Constitutional amendment substantially changing our law. Amendment of the Constitution also provides the only way to change an interpretation of the law issued by the Supreme Court or to limit or expand the role of the Congress or the President.

We can and do change our statutes, codes, and ordinances. This is the most recognized way to change the law. We elect representatives who see things as we do and we expect that the laws they pass or remove reflect our collective wishes.

Federal and state agencies likewise change the law based on the input they receive both in the legislation that established them and from the industries and businesses they control. Agencies are continually changing the regulations they issue based on this feedback that reflects the will of society.

Finally, the courts will change the law when the legislatures fail to act. Judges can make laws by deciding a new issue brought before them (or expanding on an existing precedent), or by statutory interpretation (interpreting the words of statutes that are relevant to the case).

It is a fact that our elected representatives may be politically incapable of making changes, or may not reflect the will of the majority for various reasons, including the failure of many to vote. The courts have become the unwitting conscience of society changing the law to reflect the will of the majority.

In Conclusion

Our legal system produces rules and sanctions that reflect the will of society. That does not mean that a law reflects the will of all of society. There can be, and frequently are, substantial minorities who disagree with a law. They can and do, of course, try to change the law by convincing and creating a majority.

More importantly, however, our system provides protections to the minorities. They have the right to try to change the law. They have the right to speak out. In many situations, they have the right to make choices so long as they do not interfere with the rights of others.

Remember as we explore the law and its sometimes heavy-handed impact, that the law is us. Perhaps the law does not reflect you personally and perhaps not your friends personally, but rather it does represent the majority of us all. When we complain about the law, we are complaining about the character of the society in which we live!

A Story from the Real

We are all familiar with the "terms and conditions" tabs that we must accept or refuse when making online purchases of many different products. These "check the box" acceptances of the sellers' limitations and conditions are legally binding. They are typically used to disclaim warranties, limit the seller's liability to the price of the product, restrict uses, provide a location of the law (i.e., the law of a particular state) for resolving a dispute, require arbitration, and prohibit copying of the software or any data included in it.

Do statutes passed by a state or the federal government make these "contracts" enforceable? Not really; at least not at the time when the enforcement of these click-on contracts became an issue. Although the Uniform Commercial Code provides the necessary steps to create a commercial contract, it was drafted before the invention of computers.

Sometimes the conditions in these online contracts are not even presented on the screen until after the money has been paid. Many similar issues have arisen in computer contracts. For example, is that "electronic signature" button you push when ordering from Amazon enough to form an enforceable contract?

Although statutes were passed by the states and the federal government in 1999 and 2000 (The Uniform Electronic Transactions Act and the E-SIGN Act), these issues were left to the courts until the legislative branch got its act together.

Judges made decisions based on the cases brought to them, and there were various opinions issued based on the facts in each case. Even 150 years ago, judges decided that legally binding contracts could be made over the telegraph lines using Morse code! The internet, however, vastly expanded the questions and issues. By 1996, it was clear that the courts were going to enforce these click-the-button contracts, so long as they were not abusive.

The courts found legal reasons for their decisions, but they also recognized the changes in commerce that the internet was imposing on society and the law. They dealt with it. The courts may have created law by deciding this new issue brought to them, or they may have been interpreting the words of the Uniform Commercial Code, but either way, they were legitimately making law under our common law system.

This is a good example of the common law approach where courts actively make law when the statutory law is either not available or not clear. Non-common law (civil law) countries struggled with the concept of electronic contracts, and they required legislation (new statutes) before electronic signatures, or electronic contracts could be accepted. Perhaps, though, this led to faster legislation. The German electronic signature act, for example, was passed in 1990.

Chapter 2
The Constitution

(The Foundation of our Law)

The U.S. Constitution is a remarkable document that lends itself to a changing society. It is flexible and adaptable as our economy changes and our moral perspective changes. We can argue whether or not the founding fathers designed or intended their document to allow its instructions to be modified by future developments in business, technology, and societal norms, but it might give us all comfort to at least think they meant this result. Our society is much different today than it was when the Constitution was written. Without adaptability, our nation could not have survived.

The Constitution was written to form a basis and framework for a new government after the 13 original colonies succeeded in winning independence from Great Britain. It was completed in 1787. But, before the Constitution could become effective at forming a new nation, it had to ratified, or approved, by at least nine of the states. This occurred in 1788 after an interesting and informal agreement.

New Hampshire was the ninth state to ratify, and the politicians in New Hampshire, like those in some of the other states, were fearful of a too powerful federal government that could limit the rights of their citizens. They wanted the Constitution to guarantee certain basic rights to the citizens of the new nation. England and several of the American states had "bills of rights" already in their constitutions. To ratify, New Hampshire wanted a bill of rights in the new federal Constitution as well.

An informal agreement was made between those favoring the new Constitution and the concerned legislators in New Hampshire. They agreed that if the Constitution was ratified and became effective, these rights would be added. New Hampshire ratified, creating the United States of America, and the founders kept their promise to amend the

Constitution. The first ten amendments, which we refer to as the Bill of Rights, were added in 1791. It was perhaps a different time; when politicians kept their promises!

What Does the Constitution Do?

The Constitution creates a centralized national government that brought the original 13 colonies into a union that could operate in the international arena and could work together economically. It designed a government based on three centers of power - an executive branch and the President, a two house Congress, with one house speaking for the people (the House of Representatives) and another speaking for the states (the Senate - which was originally elected by the state legislatures). And a third branch, the judiciary branch, headed by the Supreme Court.

The Constitution provides the powers of each branch of the government. These stated powers are very succinctly listed. The original hand written Constitution was only four pages long.

Article 1 - The Powers of Congress – It was intentional that the Congress was created and empowered in the first section of the Constitution. Representative government was vital to the authors, and they made it clear that the power of the government rested in the hands of the people through their representatives in Congress.

But Congress is not all-powerful. Its powers are limited very specifically in the Constitution:

- To levy taxes (that must be uniform among the states).
- To provide for the defense and the general welfare of the country.
- To borrow money.
- To regulate commerce with foreign nations, and among the several states, and with the Indian tribes.
- To pass laws allowing naturalization.
- To pass laws allowing bankruptcy.

- To print money.

- To establish Post Offices.

- To issue copyrights and patents.

- To create courts below the Supreme Court.

- To pass laws controlling the high seas and interactions with foreign governments.

- To declare war and to raise and support armies and a navy and call up state militias for federal service.

- To create a separate area for the seat of government (i.e., the District of Columbia).

- To make all laws necessary for carrying out any of its authority.

- Congress is also specifically prohibited from passing laws that allow for people to be held without being charged, convicted without a trial, or convicted of a crime that was only later made illegal. Congress is also not permitted to make laws that levy export taxes, give preferences to the laws of one state over another, or to spend money without proper laws permitting it.

The power to regulate trade, known as the "Commerce Clause" is perhaps the most significant few words in the Constitution from an "impact of government" standpoint.

It is the authority granted to the federal government in this clause to "regulate interstate commerce" that has allowed federal control and oversight of business activity. All of the federal laws that impact business, from national pollution limits to OSHA, have their authority in the Commerce Clause.

This federal control is derived from the findings of the courts that almost all businesses operate in "interstate commerce." Try to think of one that does not somehow have a connection to another state - even if only through the products it sells, the tools it uses, or the location of its suppliers and customers.

Interestingly, Article 1 also contains a limitation on Congressional power that is an important part of the balance of powers between the three branches of the federal government. Article 1 provides that the President can veto, or reject, a law passed by Congress. However, the article also permits the Congress to override a Presidential veto with a two-thirds vote in both the Senate and the House of Representatives.

Article 2 - The Executive Branch – Article 2 places the executive powers of the government in the President. Because of the perceived abuses of the King that led to the revolution, the executive powers granted are very much limited. In fact, many of the presidential powers exercised today are not mentioned in the Constitution, but have arisen by necessity and with the implied permission of the Congress and courts.

The specific Presidential powers granted by the Constitution include commander-in-chief of the armed forces, the power to grant pardons from crimes, to make treaties with other countries, and the right to appoint judges, ambassadors, and other officers of the U.S. government.

The Constitution states that the President is the chief executive officer of the U.S. This statement is construed to mean that he has the power to manage all government operations, including enforcing laws, managing the budget and assuring the completion of all government programs and missions. Legislation with court approval has also given him the authority to manage federal regulatory agencies and law enforcement operations.

Article 3 - The Judicial Branch – Article 3 states judicial powers in just one paragraph. The powers are very broad and include "all cases" arising under the Constitution and federal law, as well as all disputes between citizens of different states. It was assumed and intended by the authors of the Constitution that the legal system it created was a common law system like that in Great Britain that allowed courts to make law when statutes were silent and to set precedents in the creation of law and the interpretation of law. The Seventh Amendment shows the intention when it uses the phrase "common law."

The Constitution creates just one court, the Supreme Court, and provides that it has sole jurisdiction over matters relating to Ambassadors and disputes between the states. For all other matters, the Supreme Court has appellate or review jurisdiction.

Interestingly, the Constitution places the creation of all other federal courts and their powers to Congress. In both the powers granted to Congress in Article 1, and in Article 3, the Constitution provides that Congress will create courts and give them the authority to decide cases as it deems appropriate.

Article 3 also guarantees a right to trial by jury in all criminal cases.

Article 4 - The States – The Constitution also provides powers and limitations to the states. States are required to honor the contracts, official actions, and court decrees of all the other states and the citizens of each of the states have the same legal protections in all of the states.

The provisions above are the critical contents of the original Constitution. The powers of the federal government and its restrictions are limited. There are additional provisions that provide for the qualifications of Congresspersons and the President, and that explain the procedures for government operations and elections, including the Electoral College that has become very controversial in recent elections. But it is amazing that just four handwritten pages designed the structure of the U.S. government!

The Constitution provides that it can be amended, or changed, and a process for doing so. Any amendment requires approval by two-thirds of both houses of Congress and three-fourths of the state legislatures. There are also provisions for Constitutional Conventions to be called in the states to start the amendment process. The process requires very substantial agreement in both the Congress and the states for changes, but so far there have been 27 amendments made.

Amendments

As mentioned previously, the first ten amendments were all made together, and we know them as the Bill of Rights. They provide a list of rights granted to the people and can be summarized as follows:

Amendment 1 – Grants the freedoms of religion, press, expression, and assembly.

Amendment 2 – The right to bear arms.

Amendment 3 – Limits quartering of soldiers in private property.

Amendment 4 – Limits government searches and seizures and requires warrants issued by the courts and based on probable cause before searches or seizures are made.

Amendment 5 – Provides that a capital crime indictment must arise from a Grand Jury, that a person cannot be tried twice for the same crime or be forced to testify against himself, and due process is guaranteed (due process is a broad term that means both legal rights must be protected and the normal rules of legal procedure followed). This amendment also requires that the government pay just compensation for government taking of private property.

Amendment 6 – Gives the right to a speedy criminal trial, and to confront witnesses. Also requires an explanation of the charges brought against a person, a public trial in the place where the crime was alleged to be committed, a right to an attorney, and the right to call witnesses.

Amendment 7 – Provides trial by jury in civil cases.

Amendment 8 – Prohibits cruel and unusual punishment, excessive bail, and excessive fines.

Amendment 9 – This amendment states that the rights protected by the Constitution do not grant the federal government authority to deny any other rights not listed. It protects all citizen rights from federal government interference.

Amendment 10 – States the authority of the federal government is limited to the specific authorities granted by the Constitution; all other powers remain with the states and the people.

The other 17 amendments to the Constitution cover a variety of limitations and expansions of federal authority. They further define the powers granted in the Constitution and they expand the operations of the federal government.

Amendments 11 through 27 abolish slavery, provide civil rights and equal protection of the laws to all, apply bill of rights protections to all state laws, give the right to vote to women, change the federal voting age to 18, create and then abolish prohibition, limit the terms of the president, change the way Senators are elected, provide for succession in the case of disability of the President, and allow an income tax.

The Constitution, perhaps because it is so brief, is subject to change based on changes in societal norms. The very early Supreme Court case of *Marbury v. Madison* in 1803 gave the courts the power to review laws and interpret the Constitution. Using this authority, the federal courts, and ultimately the Supreme Court have construed the minimal language in the Constitution to apply it to a society and economy that could not be foreseen by the original authors. The meaning of Constitutional provisions changes in light of altering culture, beliefs, and economic development within the country. Some protest this continual "adjustment" of the Constitution, but it has become our law. A Constitutional amendment, however, could prevent such change.

The Constitution and its amendments, including the Bill of Rights, generally apply to business organizations, operations, employees, and business publications such as advertising. Some business protections include the equal protection clause that grants equal legal protection to citizens of all states, the contract clause that requires all states to recognize contracts formed in other states, and the privileges and immunities clause that prohibits states from protecting or promoting its own citizens and their businesses over those from other states. Corporations and other business entities generally have all the same Constitutional protections as those afforded natural persons. Two notable exceptions are the right to vote and the right against self-incrimination in a court action.

In Conclusion

In the U.S. legal system, the Constitution is the ultimate authority. No law, treaty, regulation or court decision can violate any of the provisions of the Constitution.

A Story from the Real

Remember the 2000 presidential elections? If you don't, let's review what happened. The election was close, with Al Gore actually receiving the most popular votes nationwide. But the Electoral College vote and the presidency ultimately went to George Bush. The State of Florida determined the Electoral College vote. The popular vote in Florida was very close with George Bush originally winning by less than 2,000 votes out of over 6 million cast. Al Gore demanded a recount. The initial automated recount reduced George Bush's margin to 900 votes. Under Florida law, Al Gore could demand a manual recount in four counties and then, if inconsistencies were discovered, he could demand a statewide recount.

There were problems with some of the ballots across the state. Where voters used punch card type ballots, on some ballots, the punch did not push out the chad but merely marked it with an indentation (so-called "pregnant chads"). On other ballots, voters punched out more than one chad, many times because the ballots were confusing. And on still others, the chads were left partially punched ("hanging chads"). There were also allegations that some voters were confused by the ballots and voted for the wrong candidate. As in most elections, there were also uncounted ballots; many were from overseas military.

The local voting boards in the four selected counties filed suits requesting extensions of the statutory time for the recount because of the many issues that required manual handling of the ballots. A court granted the extension in one case, but other local courts made different rulings about both the time extension and the manner for counting the votes. Al Gore appealed to the Florida Supreme Court. The Florida Supreme Court ordered a recount statewide under an extended time frame.

George Bush appealed to the U.S. Supreme Court alleging the recounts violated the U.S. Constitution. In perhaps the quickest Supreme Court appeal in history, the Court issued its ruling just 11 days later. Instead of just a majority opinion and a dissenting opinion as is normal, in their haste to issue a ruling, the nine Supreme Court Justices wrote five different opinions. When its ruling was released, observers and commentators were confused by the multiple opinions, and the decision of the Court was not immediately clear. But within an hour, the different opinions had been sorted out. Bush won. With a five to four vote, the Supreme Court returned the case to the Florida Supreme Court for further action.

Seven of the Justices found Constitutional issues with the Florida Supreme Court ruling; specifically, that it violated the Equal Protection Clause. The Equal Protection Clause is part of the Fourteenth Amendment to the U.S. Constitution. The clause provides that no state shall deny to any person within its jurisdiction "the equal protection of the laws." The U.S. Supreme Court decided that because the Florida Supreme Court had ordered a recount, it also had a duty to instruct the various county voting boards on the correct way to count the ballots given the types of issues present (e.g., did a pregnant chad count as a vote or not). By not providing this statewide guidance the votes would be counted differently in different locations denying the voters equal protection under the law.

Four of the Justices believed that the Florida court should have been ordered to make a correct recount and extend the time limits that were provided by statute. Five did not find justification to overrule the state's statutory time limits. Therefore, the U.S. Supreme Court returned the matter to the Florida Supreme Court with directions to comply with the order. But the extended time for counting the votes was at hand, and the lack of time effectively stopped the recount.

Note: In the final count certified by the State of Florida, George Bush won by just 534 votes! It is interesting to note that a group of news outlets did recounts counting the derelict punch cards in a number of ways. George Bush still won. However, if punch cards with multiple votes were recounted to allow votes where more than one candidate was punched, but the voter wrote a name on the ballot, Al Gore won by a few hundred votes. Florida has since done away with punch card voting.

Chapter 3
The Courts

(The Forum for Resolving Legal Disputes)

We know that the courts in the U.S. are formal and powerful extensions of government power. We understand that they try criminal cases and find defendants guilty or not guilty; they then impose sentences ranging from parole to death. We also know that courts provide a forum for resolving disputes between private parties with the prevailing party receiving "damages" that we commonly understand to be money. We often hear that courts make law. We know that they enforce the law. Generally, we understand that the courts interpret law meaning that they fill in the blanks if a law is not clear. But exactly what are courts and where did they originate? What authority do they really have?

The Birth of Courts

Courts were created thousands of years ago when the first civilizations needed an enlightened method to resolve disputes. Physical fighting and retribution just did not work very well in an organized society. The early civilizations created tribunals that decided disputes based on the rules of the society or its leader. The ruling person or body, the prevailing religion, and/or the tribunals themselves generally set the rules. The early courts enforced their decisions much as we do today - by ultimately bringing the power of the state to force compliance. Today, law enforcement personnel, such as police, in the end enforce court orders. In the beginning, the same approach proved very successful at making court decisions meaningful.

Courts in the U.S. are uniquely divided into two very separate systems. We have court systems in every state, as well as a federal court system. The state court systems act independently from the federal system with their own rules and authority. The only connection between the state and federal systems is the appeal from state supreme courts to the federal Supreme Court when an issue decided in the state system is alleged to conflict with the federal Constitution, or a federal law or regulation.

State constitutions and laws typically create the state court systems. All of the states have constitutions, as do some U.S. territories. Territories without constitutions create courts under authorizing legislation passed by the U.S. Congress. Constitutions may provide great detail for the organization, authority, and structure of the state courts, but sometimes provide simple authority for the legislative branch of the state government to create courts through statute. But all state courts are established under the laws of the states.

Federal courts are created under the authority of the U.S. Constitution. The Constitution establishes the U.S. Supreme Court and gives the Congress the power to create any other federal courts it deems necessary. In fact, all federal courts except the Supreme Court are created and given their authority by the Congress. And Congress by a simple majority vote can eliminate these courts or change their authority.

Power of the Courts

The authority of a court to act is called its jurisdiction. Jurisdiction is not all encompassing. Courts can only rule on issues for which they have the authority to act. This power is set by either the Constitution that created the court, or by the legislative branch of the state in which the court sits, or by the Congress for federal courts.

Jurisdiction is limited to particular subject matter and location as defined by the legal authority that creates the court. For example, the U.S. Court of Claims can only hear claims against the U.S. A U.S. District Court can generally hear any case under common law or U.S. statutes and regulations. But, common law cases in the U.S. District Court are limited to disputes between parties residing in different states and to only those disputes that exceed $75,000 in claimed damages.

State courts are generally limited to only hearing cases that involve at least one party residing within the state. Specific dollar amounts for civil cases or types of crimes may also limit state court jurisdiction. Most states, for example, have "small claims" courts that have their authority limited to relatively small amounts of money in dispute. State courts are generally limited in authority to those issues that arise under state law, but they may have also have jurisdiction to rule on some federal statutes or regulations. They cannot make any ruling contrary to the U.S. Constitution.

Court Structure

Courts are structured to provide safeguards against improper or incorrect rulings. A system of court appeals is available for almost every court decision. The federal courts and the states' court systems all have multi-level systems in which court decisions are reviewed and sometimes reversed or changed.

While court systems may have different elements and different layers in their structures, depending on the various state and federal designs, the models are all similar at a basic level:

Trial courts determine whether a legal dispute or a crime exists and they find the facts. The trial court, after deciding what the facts are, applies the law to those facts and makes a finding. In a criminal case, the finding is whether the defendant is guilty, and in a civil case the finding is whether one of the parties caused the other party to suffer damages and what those damages are.

Appellate courts provide a losing party at the trial level with the opportunity to challenge the application of the law at the trial court. While facts found at the trial level are usually not questioned at the appellate level, in some circumstances appellate courts can review them. The primary role of the appellate level court is to make sure that the trial court correctly determined the law applied to the facts. If an appellate court finds that the law was incorrectly applied, it can overturn the ruling of the trial court or order a new trial based on the correct application of the law. In a criminal trial, however, an appellate court can only overturn a conviction; the Constitution allows only one trial for a crime.

Reviews by **supreme courts** can be requested if a losing party at the appellate level thinks the appellate court erred in its determination of the law. A state supreme court determines the law of the state and all other courts in the state are required to follow its decisions. The U.S. Supreme Court determines the law of the U.S. and all state courts and federal courts must follow its decisions.

While the above description provides an overview of how court systems function, a more detailed view of the federal court system is shown below. Within each state court system, there are similar but different levels of trial and appellate courts. Note that the federal system contains a number of "specialty" courts such as the Tax Court, Bankruptcy Court, and Court of International Trade that have their jurisdiction limited to specific areas of the law. Many state systems also contain specialty courts.

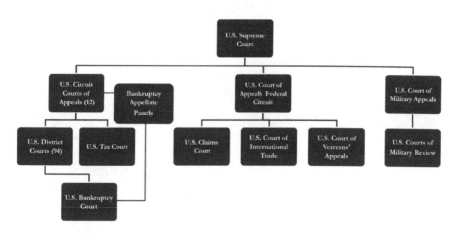

A brief discussion of the various federal courts will help clarify how our court systems work.

Trial level courts in the federal system include all courts below courts of appeals level. These include the U.S. District Courts, the U.S. Tax Court, the U.S. Court of Claims, the U.S. Court of International Trade, the U.S. Court of Veterans Appeals, the U.S Court of Military Review (commonly called Court Martials), and the U.S. Bankruptcy Court.

The U.S. District Court is the only court of general jurisdiction. This means that district courts have the authority to hear many different types of cases. District courts conduct all federal criminal cases (nonmilitary), are generally available for any action involving civil matters with the U.S. as a party and for civil cases arising under U.S. statutes and regulations. They are also available for disputes such as torts and contracts arising under the common law so long as the jurisdictional limitations that require more than $75,000 is in dispute, and that the parties reside in different states, are met.

Specialty trial courts have limited jurisdiction. That means that they can only hear the types of cases for which they are granted authority. The Tax Court, for example, can hear only certain kinds of federal tax cases, including income tax, before the taxes are assessed as legally due. Like the Tax Court, the names of other specialty courts often describe their limited jurisdiction.

Interestingly, persons bringing a suit often have choices about the court they use. The concept of having court options is more complex when both state and federal courts are available for an issue. While federal issues, such as bankruptcy determinations cannot be brought in state courts, many common law matters may be tried in either the federal or the state court.

For example, an automobile accident that involves people from two different states may result in a suit that can be brought in either the state court where the accident occurred or in the U.S. District Court if more than $75,000 is in dispute. Both courts have jurisdiction to hear the case, and the person bringing the suit must choose in which court to file his action. Note that only one court can hear the case; there is not an opportunity to file in two courts either at once or over time.

Appellate courts in the federal system involve three different courts with jurisdiction limited to only specific trial courts. The U.S. Courts of Appeals for the Circuits hear appeals from only the courts that are appealable to them and only within the geographic areas in which they have authority. The graph below shows the geographic division of the 12 U.S. Courts of Appeals. There are 11 circuit courts and the federal circuit that sits in Washington, DC. The final appeals court is the U.S. Court of Military Appeals.

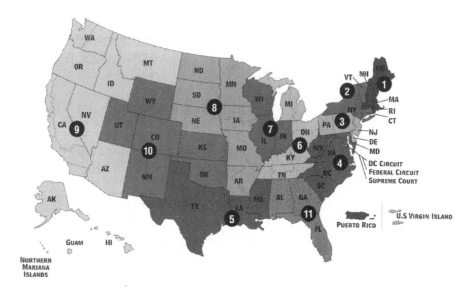

Appellate courts typically review the law, not the facts. Trial courts find the facts and appeals courts usually do not change the facts found. Appellate courts exist to assure that trial courts are correctly and uniformly applying the law. When an appeals court determines that the trial court made an error in the application of the law, it will reverse the decision and direct the trial court to decide the case based on the correct law as stated by the appellate court.

Supreme courts make final determinations of the law. In both the state and federal systems, the supreme courts have discretionary jurisdiction, meaning they do not have to hear an appeal. They choose the cases they want to review.

Of the thousands of cases appealed each year to the U.S. Supreme Court only a few hundred are accepted. If the Supreme Court refuses to review a U.S. Court of Appeals case, the ruling of the appeals court stands. In practice, the Supreme Court typically only hears cases that raise U.S. Constitutional issues or those that involve differing rulings from the appeals courts on the same issue.

The Supreme Court's decisions decide the law and the application of the law. All other courts must follow a Supreme Court's determination. Failure to do so would result in reversal of the lower court's decision upon appeal.

Common Law Precedent

As a final matter regarding our courts, we must discuss the practice of precedent. This practice arose under the old English common law and continues today with full force and effect. Under precedent, once a court decides an issue of law, other courts adopt and follow that decision.

Precedent plays out most effectively in our multi-layered court systems. Once a trial court decides a new area of law, other trial courts will normally follow it. However, if two trial courts disagree, an appellate court will find the law and all trial courts under its jurisdiction will be bound to follow this decision. And if two appellate courts disagree, the Supreme Court will decide the issue, and all courts in the U.S. must then follow this determination.

In Conclusion

Courts are a powerful and influential force in our legal system. Under common law precepts, courts can and do make law. That is a part of our legal system adopted in the Constitution. However, the legislative branch of government has the ultimate authority to make law, and once the legislative branch enacts a statute, the courts are required to follow the law as stated in the statute.

Courts only have the power to make law when statutes do not provide legal direction. Courts can, however, review statutes to assure that they do not violate any of the provisions of the Constitution. If a court finds a

Constitutional contradiction, it has the authority to find a statute invalid and without effect. When a court nullifies a statute, we say that it finds the statute unconstitutional. The courts can be overruled by an amendment to the Constitution.

A Story from the Real

In the U.S., there are multiple trial courts. In many circumstances, a plaintiff has a choice of tribunals. For example, if an automobile accident takes place in New York, but one of the parties lives in New Jersey and the other lives in New York, there may be at least two courts available to hear the action for damages. The U.S. District Court in New York could hear the case if damages claimed are over $75,000, or the state trial court in New York also has jurisdiction to hear the case. The plaintiff must make a decision about where to file.

An interesting example of this dilemma is the availability of trial courts to hear federal income tax disputes. For a person who wants to fight the IRS over an audit, there are four different courts available. The U.S. Tax Court is available before the tax is even assessed and made final. The U.S. District Court has jurisdiction if the tax is paid first. The U.S. Court of Federal Claims also has jurisdiction after payment of the tax. And finally, the U.S. Bankruptcy Court may have jurisdiction to resolve the issue(s). How can this be?

The U.S. Tax Court is a special court of limited jurisdiction. It was created by Congress to hear income and certain other kinds of tax disputes before they are assessed. This provides an opportunity for a court hearing before any additional amounts are due. The tax court is recognized as a court with tax technical expertise, meaning that the judges of this court probably know and understand tax law as well as is possible. In tax court cases, the government is represented by IRS attorneys. The tax court judges "circuit ride," meaning they hold trials across the country to afford convenient forums for trials. If a person wants a court hearing before assessment and believes he is correct in his technical position, this is the court for him. But there is no right to a jury in this court.

The U.S. District Court has general jurisdiction meaning it can hear most tax cases. Department of Justice lawyers represent the government in this court; these attorneys (and the district court itself) may deal with many different kinds of cases and not just tax cases. In the district court, there is a right to trial by jury. If your issue is perhaps technically confusing, and it has good facts to obtain the compassion of the jurors, this may be your court. But remember that the tax must first be assessed and paid, and the government must reject your claim for refund before there is a right to go to this court. And, it will take longer.

The U.S. Court of Federal Claims is a court of limited jurisdiction that can only hear claims against the federal government. It fact, the court was created to give citizens a place to seek justice from the government. It refers to itself as "the people's court." The court's location is in Washington D.C., and there is no jury option. As in the district court, the tax must be assessed and paid, and a claim for refund disallowed by the IRS before this court can hear your case. Because the court hears many types of claims issues, it is not a court with particular tax expertise. A reason to go to this court might be because any appeals from this court would go to the U.S. Court of Appeals for D.C. (often called the Federal Circuit). Appeals from the tax court and the district court must be made to the appeals court for the location where the trial was held. Different appeals courts may differ in their interpretations of tax law, at least until the Supreme Court has made a clarifying ruling.

Then there is the bankruptcy court. It hears a surprising number of tax cases. When an individual (including a corporation) files bankruptcy, and the bankrupt person owes federal taxes, the government is a creditor that must file a claim like any other creditor. The bankruptcy trustee can contest all claims filed in the bankruptcy court. There are many instances where a trustee disputes a tax assessment as not being proper. In particular, if the bankrupt person was under audit at the time of filing, the IRS has a procedure to simply assess tax it thinks may be due. There are deadlines for filing claims, and if the IRS cannot complete the audit in time, it will just assess some "reasonable" amount of additional tax and file its proof of claim with the court. Of course, the bankruptcy trustee will challenge the validity of this claim, and hence, the bankruptcy court must decide the issue(s) and the amount of tax really due. Or maybe, the proposed tax will bankrupt the person under audit. He can immediately file bankruptcy to both resolve the amount of tax due, and obtain a discharge of his other debts. It should be noted that most taxes cannot be discharged in bankruptcy.

So, like in our first example of the car accident in New York, how does a person decide which court to use? For most situations, including our tax example, there are many factors to consider:

- Do I feel good about the technical correctness of my issue and is there good law and facts to support my position?

- How has the court held on this type of issue before?

- Do I have facts that will cause a jury to empathize with my situation?

- Do I have the funds available to pay the tax due, so that I can file a claim for refund?

- How has the court of appeals for the court I am considering ruled on similar issues? Remember that the courts that are appealable to a particular court of appeals are bound by precedent to follow the prior decisions in the circuit.

- Do I have time frames for ending the dispute?

- Will the amount of tax at issue cause bankruptcy?

- What about the judge or judges in the court I am considering? Are they known to be "genial" to those "confronted" by the IRS? Judges, like all of us, have reputations!

So how do I make this decision? A lot of research can help, but it is probably best if you're this far into a dispute with IRS to talk with an attorney who practices in this area!

Chapter 4
Practice and Procedure

(Survival in the Courts)

Practice and procedure knowledge is the essence of the realm of trial lawyers. The rules of the court and the process for taking a case through a trial are vital to obtaining justice. A mistake in handling the paperwork or the trial process can cut off the opportunity for a court hearing.

The rules of practice and procedure are different for criminal and civil cases; in some ways, very different. In addition, every court has its own unique set of practice and procedure rules. To pursue an action in any court requires a complete understanding of these rules. Attorneys that don't know the rules or do not follow them better have malpractice insurance. Cases can be dismissed if the rules are not followed.

For federal courts, the rules of procedure are prepared by committees under the direction of the U.S. Supreme Court. Similarly, state supreme courts oversee the rules for the various state courts. At the federal level, the rules are submitted to Congress for review and approval. The Federal Rules of Civil Procedure are 170 pages long; the Federal Rules of Criminal Procedure are 88 pages long. The Federal Rules of Evidence that are also part of the court process add another 28 pages of directions. Local courts can and do supplement the rules with their own additions. The rules can be as detailed as the size of paper and the type of font that the court will accept.

The rules of civil procedure and the rules of criminal procedure are different for several reasons. The cases are initiated in different ways, the rules of evidence and the standards of proof are different, and most importantly, the criminal rules protect the rights of the accused.

With the foreboding introduction above, we will explore the rules in a general way to show how cases are filed and how they proceed through trial. The discussion will not focus on specific rules of any court because there are hundreds of variations among the various courts in the U.S., but we will look at a typical progression through the court process. We will use a civil case as our example.

The Beginning

Every lawsuit begins with a dispute. The conflict can arise from an accident, breach of contract, or some other event.

Consult with an attorney – If the parties cannot resolve their dispute, the injured party consults with an attorney and retains him. Before any court action is initiated, the attorney will conduct an informal investigation to better understand the facts. He may then send the opposing party a "demand letter" advising of the damages suffered, the liability of the party, and making a demand for payment.

File a Complaint in court – If the dispute is not resolved, the person seeking damages (plaintiff) will file a complaint in the appropriate court (the proper court in which to file is itself an important part of procedure). The complaint must state facts and law that support the claim and the damages suffered. The complaint must be served on the defendant with a summons. Service can be waived; sometimes it can be served by mail, other times personal service on the defendant is required.

The Answer – The defendant must answer within a prescribed time (times vary by court, but usually between two weeks to 45 days). The answer must respond to the claims of the plaintiff by admitting or denying each one and must assert any defenses or counterclaims. The answer must be carefully drafted to assure that all claims of the plaintiff are addressed.

Default – If the defendant does not answer the complaint, the plaintiff may seek a default judgment in which the court will award the plaintiff the amount of damages sought in the complaint. In most situations, however, before a court will issue a default judgment, the court will require the plaintiff to prove actual service. Many courts also require that the plaintiff proves the damages before issuing a default judgment.

In most U.S. courts, the rules for setting aside a default judgment are often difficult to meet; the defendant must show a "good cause" for not appearing in court.

Pre-trial Motions

Before a trial takes place, there is a series of steps and motions that precede it.

A motion is a request to the court to make a determination about the case and issue an order. The procedural rules of the court determine when and how they are made, but the format and timing below are typical of most courts.

Venue – When filing the pleadings (Complaint and Answer), the defendant may make a **Motion to Change the Venue** (location) of the lawsuit to a more convenient location. This motion is normally made with the filing of the Answer and must be supported by good reason (e.g., the distance of the court is too far away, the subject of the lawsuit is in a different location).

Dismiss – The defendant can file a **Motion to Dismiss** if the complaint does not state a proper cause of action, the facts stated in the complaint do not support the claim, or if the plaintiff failed to follow proper procedure in filing the complaint. This motion must usually be filed before or with the answer.

Judgment on the Pleadings – Either party can make a **Motion for Judgment on the Pleadings**. This motion requests that the Court makes a ruling based on the facts in the complaint and answer. It can only be granted if there are no facts in dispute. This could arise, for example, if the defendant does not dispute any of the facts in the answer.

Summary Judgment – A **Motion for Summary Judgment** can be requested by either party based on the pleadings and/or the facts found in discovery. Most often, this motion is made after discovery when all of the facts are known. Again, the court will only grant this motion if no important facts are in dispute.

Discovery – Discovery is a procedural process intended to uncover and make all facts available to both sides. Both parties can make requests for discovery from the other party. Discovery has several different forms. Interrogatories are questions presented to the other side that he must answer in writing and under oath. A Request for Admission is a set of questions provided to the other side that he must answer simply "admit" or "deny." A Request for Production asks the opposing party to produce and/or explain documents relative to the dispute. Depositions require the parties and/or witnesses to give oral testimony under oath. Depositions are recorded.

If a party fails to comply with discovery requests, the party not receiving the response can make a **Motion to Compel** that will cause the judge to review and order the request. If requested information is not provided the party may be considered to admit to any questions not answered. He may also be subject to contempt findings by the court.

Discovery is intended to speed up the trial process by having all of the facts and evidence exposed before the trial begins. Recent procedural changes in some courts impose mandatory disclosure of relevant facts to the other side even if not requested by through discovery.

Pretrial Conference – After all pretrial motions and discovery are completed, it is common for a pretrial conference to be called by the judge. The purposes of the conference include simplifying the issues and eliminating invalid claims, clarifying the facts, scheduling, and exploring settlement options. The judge may issue an order after the conference that sets the future course of the action.

The Trial

After the pretrial conference, the judge and the clerk of the court will schedule the trial.

A trial finds the facts and applies the law to the facts. Most of a trial is devoted to proving the actual facts of the situation.

Jury – A trial can be with or without a jury. In a civil trial, either party can request a jury. A trial without a jury is called a "bench trial." In a bench trial, the judge both determines the facts based on the evidence from the trial and decides how the law applies to those facts. In a jury trial, the jury decides all of the questions of fact and the judge instructs the jury about the law and how to apply the law to the facts they find. The jury is selected from a pool of candidates usually drawn from property, voting and/or drivers' licenses, or other public lists in the locale.

Jury selection involves *voir dire*, a series of questions presented to the jurors that they each must answer under oath. The judge and both parties may question the jurors, and they all participate in selecting the final jury members. Each side has several "peremptory challenges" that allow the dismissal of a potential juror without any reason. Each side can also ask to remove any potential juror "for cause." For cause removal requires the requesting party to show why the juror could not serve without prejudice or bias. A jury of six or 12 members depending on the jurisdiction is selected. Alternate jurors may be chosen to participate in case one of the original jurors cannot finish the trial (e.g., due to illness).

The trial process – After the jury is seated, the trial begins. It proceeds through several phases generally in the order below. In all of the steps of the trial, the plaintiff usually goes first.

Opening Statements – Both the plaintiff and defense give opening statements. The opening statement is a summary of the party's position and the evidence and arguments that will be presented to support it.

Witnesses and Testimony – Witnesses are called and examined. The plaintiff has the burden of proof and therefore must provide overriding evidence of the facts supporting his position. Evidence may include the examination of witnesses to produce testimony, the introduction and explanation of documents and other physical evidence, and the presentation of "expert testimony" relative to complex or scientific matters.

The defendant may counter the plaintiff's facts with evidence and testimony of its own. The defense, however, only needs to raise questions about the plaintiff's presentation to show that it did not meet the burden of proof (preponderance of the evidence in a civil case).

Cross-examination – Cross allows each side to question the witnesses of the other side. This is done to bring out contradictions, uncertainties, and differences from other testimony or evidence. Redirect and re-cross-examination are allowed to clarify any issues raised in the cross-examination.

Damages – Although proving the legal action is the primary purpose of testimony and other evidence, it is essential in a civil action for the plaintiff to prove his damages. This means presenting evidence about the amount of damages suffered in monetary terms. In some cases, the plaintiff can also ask for a court order to carry out a contract (specific performance) or to stop some action of the defendant (injunction). A request for the defendant to do or not do something must also be supported by evidence that money is not sufficient to compensate the plaintiff or that continuing harm is being caused. The defendant can refute the claimed damages with evidence of his own. The amount of the damages is a factual matter determined by the jury.

Evidence – The role of evidence in a lawsuit is critical, and as previously mentioned the rules of evidence are long and complicated. The parties are not permitted to introduce just any information into a trial. Evidence must be "relevant," meaning that it bears directly on the matters disputed and is likely to prove or disprove an element of the case.

Some evidence will be barred from the trial even if it is relevant if it is so biased as to mislead the jury. For example, the plaintiff's settlement discussions and offers to resolve the dispute before trial may be relevant, but may prejudice his position with the jury. Likewise, "hearsay" evidence is generally not admissible in a trial. Hearsay evidence is testimony about a statement made by somebody else. Normally, the court requires the testimony of the person who actually made the statement.

Closing Arguments – After both sides present their cases, testimony, and other evidence, each side makes its closing arguments. This gives them the opportunity to summarize their cases and show how the evidence supports their positions.

Jury Instructions – After the closing arguments, the judge gives instructions to the jury. These instructions explain the applicable law for the case; the judge tells the jury the law. The jury is told the issues they need to decide and to use this law to determine those issues based on the facts presented in the trial. The parties participate in the instructions and have the right to propose jury directions or to object to explanations they believe are incorrect.

Directed Verdict – Before the case goes to the jury for consideration, either party can make a **Motion for a Directed Verdict**. This motion asks the judge to take the case out of the jury's hands because the other side did not prove its position with the evidence. The moving party is basically saying that there are no facts that dispute its position, so there is nothing for the jury to consider.

Jury Deliberations – The jury is sent to the jury room to deliberate and determine a verdict.

The jurors select a jury foreman to lead the discussions and take the votes. During deliberations, the jury discusses the facts and the jurors express individual opinions. The discussion can often bring out contradictions in the evidence, and lead to discussions of different interpretations. If there is questionable evidence, and some of the jurors are not convinced that the plaintiff has met his burden, they have the opportunity in deliberations to review the evidence again, ask the court questions, and fully explore each part of the record and testimony to resolve the doubts.

The jurors' duty is to make a decision for or against the plaintiff based on a preponderance of the evidence that was proved to them.

Votes are taken to determine the verdict. In the federal system, jury votes must always be unanimous, but in many state courts, civil verdicts may only require a majority vote. If a unanimous verdict is required and the jurors cannot reach an undivided vote, the result is a "hung jury." If there is a hung jury, the dispute is not resolved, and another trial can take place. Note that a conviction in a criminal trial always requires a unanimous vote.

Motions after the Verdict Is Delivered

After the jury delivers its verdict to the court, the parties have the opportunity to request the court not to enter it.

Notwithstanding the Verdict – After the jury presents its verdict to the court, the losing party can make a **Motion for a Judgment Notwithstanding the Verdict**. This motion asks the court to vacate the verdict and issue a verdict for the moving party because the facts proved in the trial did not support the verdict reached by the jury.

New Trial – A losing party can also make a **Motion for a New Trial** requesting that the verdict be set aside, and a new trial conducted because of a serious miscarriage of justice in the trial. This could include substantial error by the judge, newly discovered evidence, prejudice of a juror, attorney misconduct, or other serious reason that caused a profoundly unfair result.

Judgment

If the judge denies any motions filed after the verdict, the trial is completed. The judge will enter a judgment. A judgment is a final decision that ends the case. It typically includes the decision of the court as well as the damages to be paid by the losing party.

After the court renders a judgment, the losing party may have the opportunity to appeal. Another set of procedural rules applies to the appeals process.

Also after a judgment is issued, the action between the parties may not end. Unless the losing party voluntarily comes forward to pay the damages, additional steps must be taken to collect the amount awarded. These include court hearings to force a defendant to disclose his assets, obtaining a writ of execution from the court, and obtaining the assistance of a law enforcement officer to enforce seizure of assets. When wages or any funds held by a third party (e.g., bank accounts) are sought to satisfy a judgment, a new separate court action must be initiated.

Finally, the court process outlined above is based on a typical civil action. As stated at the beginning of this chapter, the rules of the various courts define this process in much greater detail that provide time frames, formats, sequence, and other requirements for almost every step of the process. A criminal case process has similarities, but is different in many aspects and has much more restrictive rules of evidence to protect the rights of the accused.

In Conclusion

The rules of procedure for the conduct of a legal action in the courts are detailed, varied by the court, and challenging for a layperson or non-trial attorney to comprehend. In many small claims courts and other courts where a lay person is encouraged to proceed on his own, the clerk of court's office will provide guidance, forms, and helpful advice for moving through the system. In higher courts, such as the federal district courts, an attempt to try one's own case would most likely fail because of the procedural rules alone. In these courts, it is not likely that assistance will be available.

A Story from the Real

Sometimes the actions of a party to a case and those of his attorney are amusing because of the total irresponsibility they demonstrate. They are amusing perhaps to we observers, but probably not to the party. Consider the case of the homeowner (and his attorney) who apparently didn't understand civil procedure.

A builder was hired to do some home remodeling. A dispute arose, and the builder sued the homeowner for breach of contract. The builder requested discovery, and when a Request for Admissions was sent to the homeowner, he simply ignored it. When the time for answering the discovery passed, the builder made a proper motion to consider all of the answers to be admissions. The court granted his motion.

The homeowner tried to file two Motions for Reconsideration of the discovery order. The clerk of the court rejected the first for improper form. The homeowner took the second one off the hearing calendar because he was not prepared for the hearing.

Nothing happened for almost a year. The builder then made a Motion for a Summary Judgment based on the admissions from the ignored discovery requests. The court scheduled a hearing on the motion, but the homeowner failed to respond with a written opposition. He did, however, on the day before the hearing personally apply for a continuance (a delay in the hearing), alleging attorney error for not having timely filed the opposition. The court denied his continuance application.

At the summary judgment hearing, the homeowner did not appear. The judgment was granted after the builder proved his damages.

This is bad, but it doesn't end here.

The homeowner filed a Motion for a New Trial, and then a few days later filed an appeal. The builder promptly filed a Motion in Opposition to the New Trial under the rule that once an appeal is filed, the trial court no longer has jurisdiction. So, our homeowner dropped the appeal.

The homeowner based his Motion for a New Trial on attorney error for mixing up the scheduled date of the Summary Judgment hearing. Under the rules of procedure for this court, attorney error mandates relief, meaning that if an attorney makes a serious error, his client is entitled to a new hearing. The court did not find error and denied the homeowner's motion. After the trial court denied his Motion for a New Trial, the homeowner then filed an appeal alleging an error in not granting it.

The builder filed a Motion to Dismiss the appeal because the homeowner had used the wrong language in his motion in the trial court. The appeals court gave the homeowner the benefit of the doubt and denied the Motion to Dismiss. The homeowner's first win!

But things did not get better. The rules of procedure required mandatory relief from a "default judgment" which is defined as a judgment entered when the defendant does not answer the complaint filed starting the action. But this case involved a "summary judgment," something based on the evidence before the court and totally different from a default judgment. The appeals court found that the homeowner had errored. Mandatory relief was not available under the rules.

There was still discretionary relief available under the procedural rules, meaning that the court could grant a new trial if good cause was shown. Attorney error may be the basis for good cause.

The appeals court discussed the procedures for requesting a new trial based on attorney error. It found that the homeowner did not provide the required information and documentation. For relief to be granted the rules required that the party seeking it must not only show a satisfactory excuse but must also show that he acted with diligence. The appeals court agreed with the trial court that the homeowner did not show an adequate excuse, nor did he act with care. The court found that the long delay in filing the Motion for a New Trial (over three months) showed a lack of diligence. And, his explanation of the attorney error showed neither diligence nor good excuse.

To support a claim of attorney error as a basis for not acting timely, the rules required the submission of several different supporting documents explaining the error. One of these was an affidavit from the attorney stating his reasons for failing to act. The homeowner submitted only the attorney affidavit, and it did not provide a good reason. It generally stated that the lawyer was busy, had too much work, and didn't have a secretary.

The appeals court found that the facts submitted did not support good excuse or diligence. The trial court in its refusal to grant the Motion for a New Trial had determined that the homeowner did not act diligently in seeking relief. The appeals court found that determination was amply supported in fact and law. The homeowner lost his appeal, and the judgment stood.

How many procedural mistakes were made in this case? Lots were made.

As a result of those errors, the homeowner ended up with a judgment against him that may or may not be justified by the real facts of the dispute. He is now liable to the builder. He has no other appeal. He didn't follow the procedural rules.

The attorney probably also has liability. It appears the homeowner can sue him for malpractice. The damages awarded against him could include both the judgment amount against the homeowner and the costs of all of these actions. The attorney may also lose his law license if his client files a complaint with the State Bar Association. He didn't follow the procedural rules!

And so much time and money were wasted. This leads us nicely to the next chapter...

Chapter 5
Alternative Dispute Resolution

(A Better Way to Fix Legal Problems?)

The two chapters above describe the U.S. court systems and the practice rules for trying cases in them. We commented on the complexity of the systems and rules. It is also an unfortunate fact that resolving issues in court takes a very long time (sometimes many years). In addition, court resolutions are expensive and uncertain for both parties. Finally, court actions are part of the public record, meaning that the "dirty laundry" that may be part of the issues involved in the cases is open for review and discussion by the public, including the news media. Oh, if only there was another way!

And there is another way to resolve legal disputes. We call it alternative dispute resolution (ADR). ADR uses methods other than trials to work out legal discords. There are some compelling reasons to use ADR, foremost being the usually lower costs and faster resolution times of the processes. ADR generally includes three separate methods, with several other methods being variations of them. The three primary methods are negotiation, mediation, and arbitration.

Negotiation

Negotiation is nothing more than the two disputing parties working together to find a solution. In life and in business, this is by far the most common way of settling disputes. The two sides discuss their disagreement and find an agreement. Negotiation can be very formal involving lawyers and expert witnesses, or it can be very informal involving a phone call or lunch meeting. Everything in between is possible. Most negotiation is informal.

Negotiation tends to follow one of two different paths to resolution. The first is positional based negotiation in which each party starts from a stated position and makes its case by giving reasons why the position is the correct one. After that, the parties tend to make concessions to each other and finally reach a compromise. Such a compromise will always take into account the costs and effort of proceeding with the fight. A more humanistic approach to negotiation considers the continuing relationship of the parties, the real interests of each side and in general finds a resolution that will keep everybody happy and friendly (e.g., the parties maintain business relationships). In real life, most negotiations probably draw on both approaches.

Mediation

Mediation resolves disputes by bringing in a third party who is independent of both disputing parties. Mediation is required by statute or court rules in many judicial actions before a trial can take place. For example, many states require mediation of property settlement and child custody issues in divorce cases. Even when not required, many judges will encourage the parties to try mediation.

Mediators can be drawn from lists maintained by organizations such the American Arbitration Association or can be former judges, experts in the field of the dispute, or in reality anybody that the two parties agree to use. A mediator's job is to bring the parties to an agreement. Although he can suggest solutions, he does not impose an agreement. He cannot force the parties to settle. Mediators commonly use one or both of two approaches to steer the parties to an agreement.

The first approach is by leading a discussion of the strengths and weaknesses of each position and the likelihood of prevailing if the dispute goes to a trail. An experienced mediator can help the parties understand how a court and jury will see their individual facts and how the law will be applied to them. In most situations, both sides have strengths in their positions and weaknesses. A skilled mediator can cause compromise and agreement by showing the parties that they each have substantial risks in court.

The other common method used by mediators is to discover and satisfy the interests of both parties in the disputed matter. Sometimes, disagreements are not about only money but may involve pride, reputation, preservation of a standard or practice, or satisfaction of others (e.g., bosses, stockholders). In this approach to reaching an agreement, the mediator will try to learn the underlying concerns and issues of the parties and find a solution that meets the interests of both.

Mediation is a very successful route to the settlement of disputes. Most analyses of mediation find that about 85 percent of mediation efforts are successful in reaching an agreement.

Arbitration

Arbitration is the third type of ADR. It has grown so common that almost all of us are parties to arbitration agreements, even though we may not be aware of it. Most credit card contracts, automobile and household goods purchases, warranties, lease agreements, and even many insurance contracts require arbitration. We do not have the right to go to court to fight with the banks, car dealers, manufacturers, landlords, or insurance companies because we have agreed to arbitration clauses in these contracts. The courts favor arbitration, and the Federal Arbitration Act requires enforcement of mandatory arbitration clauses in contracts. The right to trial in a court is ceded by these clauses. Because the Federal Arbitration Act is a federal statute, state law cannot supersede it.

So, what is arbitration? Let's call it "trial by contract" because, in an arbitration agreement, the parties agree that a third-party arbitrator will determine the outcome. The arbitration agreement contains the rules that will be followed, how the arbitrator will be selected, and the kinds of determinations he can make. The American Arbitration Association provides model agreements that are commonly used and provides lists of available arbitrators. In many arbitrations, especially those in consumer contracts and provided by government agencies, the process is somewhat informal. The parties agree on an arbitrator, each side presents its position and evidence, and the arbitrator makes a decision that is binding on the parties. There is no right to appeal to the courts.

The parties, however, can make the arbitration processes as complex as necessary to fairly present their cases. Formal legal briefs can be filed, hearings held, witnesses called, and the arbitrator can be limited in his resolutions (e.g., he may be able to make a decision with a range of results, or he can be limited to an absolute winner/loser determination). The important aspect of arbitration is that it is an agreement between the parties about how they want to resolve their legal dispute. Their agreement can contain any rules and provisions they want it to include.

While contract arbitration that is "hidden" in the small print of consumer contracts may seem offensive and unfair, the history of arbitration does not show abusive results. As a general rule, it works in providing fair resolutions. The benefits of arbitration are claimed to outweigh the occasional unfair result.

These benefits include reducing the burden of the courts, lowering the cost and speeding resolutions of disputes, giving the parties the opportunity to "pick their judge," keeping disputes confidential, and bringing finality to the dispute resolution process. However, the costs of arbitration are not always less than a trial. In a formal arbitration, the fees for filing, the expense of the arbitrator(s), and the costs of the presentation can be significant.

Variations

There are many variations of the three primary types of ADR. For example, mock trials are a method in which lawyers conduct pretend trials for the parties giving them insights into how their disputes will play out in a courtroom. Mini-trials are shortened trials presented to a "judge," who may be another lawyer or a specialist in the subject matter, who renders a decision giving the parties insights into the strengths or weaknesses of their cases. Similarly, a summary jury trial allows both sides to present their positions to a "mock jury" that provides its evaluation of the issues to the parties. And conciliation is a process that brings in a neutral third party to lead and moderate settlement discussions without imposing or suggesting a resolution. All of these methods are primarily tools in negotiating as they help the parties better understand the issues.

The parties can also agree to "nonbinding arbitration" in which they conduct a full arbitration process, but either party can elect to reject the decision of the arbitrator. This process may be expensive and time-consuming without reaching a resolution, but it maintains the rights of both parties to file a court action.

In Conclusion

ADR plays a critical role in resolving legal disputes. Our courts and legal system favor it, it speeds a very time consuming process, and it works.

A Story from the Real

Matt and Patricia were married 15 long years. Finally, Matt found refuge with a friend (a girlfriend), and the mêlée began. A divorce action was filed by Patricia, and while neither wanted the marriage to continue, there was the usual animosity over separating their "stuff."

They were not people of wealth, but they did have a few dollars saved, the typical household belongings, and Matt had a red 1969 Chevrolet Corvette he bought the year after they were married. He actually liked the Corvette more than he did Patricia. Patricia thought that, and Matt knew it.

Meetings between the attorneys could not resolve their property division. Patricia insisted that she should get the Corvette and would not back down. Matt, of course, thought the Corvette was his and refused to even talk about giving it up. The Corvette was valued at $40,000 and made up about half of the value of the property the couple owned.

Why did Patricia want the Corvette? It was pretty obvious that she had no real interest in the Corvette itself, but she did see the value in "punishing" Matt for his bad behavior. She knew that taking the Corvette from him was probably the most despicable thing she could do. And she wanted to be really spiteful. So, she demanded the Corvette. Matt thought that losing the Corvette was akin to losing his right arm. It could not happen.

What could be done? In a normal divorce proceeding, if the parties can't agree on a property settlement, they have a hearing before the judge, and he decides who gets what. Fortunately for Matt and Patricia, their state had a mandatory mediation provision in its laws. Divorcing parties are required to meet with a mediator to try to find a resolution of their property disputes. So the mediation was scheduled.

Again, fortunately for Matt and Patricia, they had a good mediator. He knew how to bring parties to an agreement, even when they didn't want to agree on anything. He used two mediation methods.

First, he explained the process, their legal rights, and how it could go if they went before the judge. He told Patricia that her objective was pretty clear and the judge would see it. He told her the judge might very well give the Corvette to Matt and give her a majority of the other "stuff" with a real value less than the Corvette. She could lose her play to punish, and lose money. He explained to Matt that the judge might sympathize with Patricia because of his dalliance with the "friend." He could easily be blamed for the divorce. The judge would probably not give the Corvette outright to Patricia, but he might require it to be sold and the money divided along with the rest of their property. They would both get equal money, but the Corvette would be history. This explanation, of course, did not make Matt and Patricia feel very comfortable about going before the judge. One or both of them could lose.

The mediator then explained that he wanted them to both be satisfied with the outcome. He also explained this might make both of them not be winners. The first part they liked; the second sounded ominous. But they agreed to consider his thoughts.

The mediator asked Matt if he could borrow the value of the Corvette. Matt said that he could not. He would not qualify for a loan of that size, and if he used the Corvette for collateral, he would only get part of its value. Any loan like that would cripple him financially anyway. The mediator asked about relatives. He knew from the introductory discussions that Matt had a widowed mother.

The mediator asked if Matt could borrow the money from his mother. Matt had the proverbial conniption fit. While his relationship with his mother was friendly, she too blamed him for the divorce, and she did not approve of his current lifestyle. She had been critical of his work, his marriage, and basically everything about his life in recent years. It would be a cold day in Hades before he would ask her for money. He did admit, however, that she probably had it.

Patricia knew about Matt's mom. The lady didn't like her much, and she knew very well that Matt very much resented his mother's interference in and disapproval of his life. She also knew that Matt would do almost anything to avoid ever going to his mother for help. Almost is the key word. Patricia was excited. She saw an opportunity to humiliate Matt and obtain her revenge.

So here is the mediator's proposal. A trial was not a good idea. Either could lose wholly or they both could lose partially. No happiness was likely. Therefore, Matt should swallow his pride and ask his mother for a loan of $40,000. The $40,000 and half of the savings account would go to Patricia, along with her personal items and jewelry. She would also get two rooms of furniture that she chose. Matt would keep the Corvette; get half of the savings, his own personal property and the rest of the furniture. They also resolved some addition details about minor contested property.

Matt was not happy about approaching his mother, but he loved winning on the Corvette. Patricia was very happy with the indignity suffered by Matt and she was pretty excited about walking away with a good size amount of cash; she was not happy with him winning on the Corvette.

As it turned out, Matt went to his mother and was able to borrow the money from her. Mom demanded interest and a lien on the Corvette, so he suffered the intended disgrace a little more than anybody expected. But he kept the Corvette, enough of their cash to keep his finances in some kind of order, and enough other property to find and furnish a new place. He was not completely happy, but he was satisfied.

Patricia got a large amount of cash and enough other property to start out on her own in very good shape. She also succeeded in wounding Matt's pride and ego. She didn't get to take the Corvette away from him, but overall, she was very satisfied with the result.

Did our mediator do his job? Did he make this work so one of the parties did not have to lose everything? Did he find and satisfy the real interests of both parties? The answer to each of these questions appears to be yes. Mediation works.

Chapter 6
Criminal Law

(The Bad Guys' Remorse)

This is the stuff of television, from *Perry Mason* to *Law and Order*, and many more before, between and after. We love to follow the pursuit of criminals by the police and in the courts.

But what is criminal law in the real world? Simply stated, a crime is a violation of a criminal statute passed by the legislative branch of the federal, state, or local government. It has its roots in the desire of society to prohibit certain actions and punish those who do them. A crime is, therefore, a wrong against society. When a crime is committed, it is society as a whole, through its government, that apprehends the criminal and punishes him.

We must, however, differentiate a "tort." A tort is one person committing a wrong against another person. While this sounds similar to a crime, there are very important differences. A tort is a civil wrong that must be addressed by the injured person. The wronged person must sue the person who committed the wrong for money damages that compensate him for his loss caused by the other person's behavior. In such a contest, the person seeking damages must file the action himself, hire his attorney and prove the wrong and the damages he claims by a preponderance of the evidence. The other party must defend himself with his own attorney. If the wronged person wins, he receives money damages.

A crime instead involves the violation of a criminal statute. The state must arrest the offending party, and a government prosecutor must prosecute him. The prosecutor must prove beyond a reasonable doubt that the person committed the crime; this means that the state must show very convincing evidence. In a tort trial, a preponderance of the evidence simply means the evidence shows that the defendant more like than not committed the act. In a criminal trial, the evidence must be overwhelming to convict. And, the state must provide a person accused of a crime a lawyer at the state's expense if he cannot afford one himself. If convicted of the crime, the consequences might be fines, prison, or even death.

Perhaps the greatest difference in a criminal action is the many Constitutional rights that protect an accused person. The Bill of Rights provides the source for these rights. The rights include protections from unreasonable searches and seizures, no arrests without probable cause, rights to due process of law, a speedy trial, an attorney, and trial by jury. Also, a person cannot be required to testify against himself and bail must be reasonable. The Bill of Rights also forbids cruel and unusual punishments.

Before police can talk to a person charged with a crime, they must advise him of his rights, including his right to an attorney provided by the state. Also, criminal trials follow strict rules of evidence and procedure, and evidence obtained in violation of one of the constitutionally protected rights cannot be used in the trial. These protections reflect society's desire to protect us all from the overwhelming power of government. We believe that it is better to let a guilty person go free than to imprison an innocent one.

A crime cannot take place unless:

- There is a criminal statute prohibiting the act;
- There is intent to commit and mental understanding of the act;
- And the act is attempted or completed.

There are many thousands of criminal acts described in statutes passed by Congress, the various state legislatures, and the many counties, cities, and townships in the U.S. We are obligated to know all of them, even if that is not practical. Ignorance of the law will not provide safety from a criminal conviction.

Intent to commit a crime is defined very broadly. Generally, intent means that malice or ill-will is involved in the act. Conduct and even negligent or reckless behavior can show or infer intent. For example, if I rob a store and my handgun discharges accidentally killing a person, my conduct alone shows intent to murder.

Thinking about committing a crime is not a crime, but doing something to make it happen, even if the act is not completed, may be enough for a crime. The crime is committed once an overt action takes place to initiate the criminal act.

Categories of Crime

We all have a pretty good idea of behavior that is criminal; but it is worth discussing the different types of crimes.

Crimes against persons – These are violent crimes that can cause injury to a person. Murder, assault and battery, rape, and robbery are examples of crimes against persons.

Property crimes – These are acts intended to take or damage the property of others. These include theft, arson, malicious destruction of property, burglary, and forgery.

Morals and public safety crimes – These are activities that are dangerous to either public health or safety. They include prostitution, alcohol and drug misuse, and gambling crimes, as well as laws that cover air and water protection, food and drug controls, and product and workplace safety.

Cybercrimes – These are acts that interfere with the use of the internet and electronic communications and transactions. They include the use of computers to steal information, misdirect funds, alter data, or harass, blackmail or spam individuals or businesses.

White collar crimes – This is a broad category of acts carried out inside a business enterprise. These acts can include insider trading, securities and accounting fraud, embezzlement, tax evasion, employment and labor law violations, and bribery.

As the above listing shows, some crimes can fit into one or more of the various categories, and some do not precisely fit within any of them. Frequently, people that commit crimes are charged with multiple criminal acts. For example, the cybercrime of unlawfully entering a computer system may also result in a charge of theft, a property crime and embezzlement, a white collar crime.

Crime Classifications

Crimes also fall into two classifications by the degree of severity.

Felonies – These are more serious crimes that can result in a sentence of one or more years in prison.

Misdemeanors – These are lesser crimes that impose sentences of less than one year. And some crimes, such as most traffic violations, and in some states marijuana possession, are treated as noncriminal civil offenses with only fines for violations.

Criminal Defenses

How does a criminal defend himself? First, of course, he can contest the facts (e.g., he was not at the scene and did not commit the crime). The prosecutor must prove the facts beyond a reasonable doubt. He can also find defenses from the requirements for a crime. He can challenge the statute, and he can attempt to show a lack of intent. And, the various rights provided by the Constitution, as described above, provide many opportunities to attack the case built by the prosecutor.

Mental incompetency – Some people are unable to form the required criminal intent. Without criminal intent, there can be no crime. Underage, mental illness, and mental incapacity due to drugs or alcohol may all indicate the inability to consider or understand the criminal nature of the conduct.

The insanity defense, while rarely successful in the real world, is often depicted in movies and television. The Model Penal Code requires a defendant claiming insanity to prove that he lacks the mental capacity due to mental defect or illness to understand the wrongfulness of his conduct or to conform his conduct to the requirements of the law. This is a tough standard and goes beyond the concept of knowing the difference between right and wrong.

Alcohol and drug use is also a difficult defense to criminal conduct. While accidental or unknown intoxication may show an inability to have criminal intent, the voluntary consumption of intoxicating substances will not succeed because the person consuming them acted recklessly, and like any other careless conduct, will infer an understanding of any criminal outcomes.

Constitutional protections – The Constitution's foremost protection is the requirement that the government must prove beyond a reasonable doubt that the crime was committed. The defendant does not have to prove anything or even say a word at his trial. He does not have to prove his innocence.

Our law prohibits the government from abusing its power and taking advantage of uninformed defendants. The courts rigorously apply the various rights described in the Constitution. Our system requires that statutes define crimes in ways that are clear and understandable. And trials for criminal violations must be public, fair, and with a jury if the defendant so requests. Strict rules of procedure, including the admissibility of evidence that is only legally obtained, are enforced (and are the bases for many successful appeals).

But despite these safeguards, we all know that even in our well protected system, convictions of innocent people still sometimes occur.

In Conclusion

Criminal law is society's avenue for restricting bad behavior and stopping it from occurring. Criminal statutes provide society's guidelines for acceptable behavior and the consequences for not complying with them.

The idea is that punishment will prevent criminal conduct, or at least take the criminals out of society. We have also attempted to reform criminals while they are in jail by providing education and work skills.

We can debate the effectiveness of punishment and our attempts to restore criminals to society, but the fact is that the U.S. has the highest percentage of its people in jail of any country in the world. Are we a society of criminals or a society of unrealistic rules? Or do we simply make a greater effort to remove criminals from our midst?

A Story from the Real

A man was murdered in his home. There was no sign of a break in, and the only missing item was a Bible. There was blood at the scene, bloody footprints, and hair samples. There was also DNA found that was not from the victim.

A man and his two teenage children became suspects. The police interviewed them. They were neighbors, had interacted with the man, and he was a janitor at the children's high school. The crime scene evidence did not implicate them in any way. Footprints and the hair samples found at the scene did not match. DNA analysis failed to connect any of them to the crime scene as well. During his interview with police, the father commented that he must be the prime suspect.

The police used bloodhounds and scent to attempt a match. Using six empty paint cans, they put the scent of the father and five other men into separate cans. They then used the victim's clothing to give the scent to the dogs. Three trained bloodhounds were allowed to sniff the victim's scent on his clothing first. After the clothing, the dogs sniffed each of the cans. All of the bloodhounds identified the victim's scent in the can containing the father's scent.

Based on his statement that he must be the prime suspect, and the dog's connecting his scent to the victim, the police arrested the man.

While in jail, he made some comments about the crime to his cellmate. All of the statements started with "I heard." The police were aware of some the information in the statements although they had not released the information to the public. Some of the information in the statements was new to them. After a police investigation, some of the information in the statements turned out true, and some of it was not.

Based on the above evidence the man was tried and convicted of murder by a jury. The appeals court affirmed the conviction. The man then appealed to the state supreme court.

The supreme court found that for a conviction to be legal, the evidence supporting the crime must be sufficient enough that in the most favorable light any rational trier of fact could have found the essential elements of the crime beyond a reasonable doubt.

The court then reviewed the evidence. The statement made during his interview with police was not a confession nor did it in any way suggest he did the crime. It was a mere statement of his feelings while being interviewed. It was not sufficient to convict. The statements to his cellmate were likewise not admissions that he personally knew anything about the crime. The conversations took place several years after the crime. They were just "talk" about what he may have heard in the community about the crime. Some of the information was not even correct. The dog scent was the strongest proof and based on jury questions was the evidence that they most relied on to convict.

The court accepted that dogs can and do identify people and other things by smell. The scent they identify is from skin cells that humans constantly shed from their bodies. It is well established that dogs can track based on this and that they can identify people and objects that pick up those skin cells by transfer from another. Moreover, the scent of one person can pass to another through mutual contact with an intermediary object. For example, if a man wears a coat one day and a different man wears it the next, the first man's scent will transfer to the second man, even if they never met each other. So, the mere fact that scent was present on a person does not mean there was direct contact.

After analyzing the evidence, the court found that the evidence, viewed even in the most favorable light, raised only suspicion. It could not prove guilt beyond a reasonable doubt. The man was acquitted.

Note: The man's two children were also identified by the dog scent, and both were tried for murder as well. One was acquitted at trial; the other was found guilty but was acquitted on appeal. The best case was against the eldest of the children, a 17-year-old girl. But even for her case, the strongest evidence was the dog scent. In her case too, the supreme court found as a matter of law that the evidence was not sufficient to sustain a conviction beyond a reasonable doubt.

Chapter 7
Family Law

(The Law in Our Homes)

Family law sets society's rules for building a family and for breaking one down. It provides for marriage, divorce, child welfare, and adoption. We can divide family law into two straightforward sections: building families and taking them apart.

Building Families

Marriage – Under U.S. law, it is a marriage that creates a legal union we usually refer to as a family. Marriage is both a religious ceremony and a legal license that entails legal obligations and commitments. A religious ceremony creates a union in the eyes of God as accepted by the parties. A legal marriage, however, creates rights and duties that are enforced by the government.

A marriage under the law grants literally thousands of specific legal rights. These include tax benefits, government entitlements such as Social Security and disability income rights, and contract benefits such as medical coverage and being the beneficiary of life insurance. State laws also give married persons property rights and status that confer indivisible rights to the property they own and a right to claim the property of a deceased spouse contrary to a will. Marriage even provides a right to not testify in a trial regarding information that a spouse knows about the other spouse's illegal activities.

Legal obligations that arise in marriage include spousal support, support and custody of children of the marriage, taking over the affairs of a spouse who may lose his mental capacity, and a fiduciary duty to act fairly and in good faith in transactions between the spouses.

The rights and duties of marriage may vary by state law because the states create marriage relationships. Marriages made only in heaven do not create legal rights and duties. A few states still recognize common law marriages. By living together for a stated period in these states, a couple becomes legally married. This type of union receives a lot of attention, but only eight states currently recognize common law marriage, and some for only specific purposes such as inheritance.

Although some states still have laws that prohibit the marriages of same-sex persons, the U.S. Supreme Court ruled in *Obergefell v. Hodges* on June 26, 2015, that state laws prohibiting same-sex marriage are unconstitutional. Same-sex marriage is now legal.

State laws generally provide that a state official must issue a marriage license after the couple meets state defined criteria. The qualifications typically include age restrictions, identification verifications, limitations on related parties, and perhaps premarital preparation courses, blood tests, and citizenship requirements. After the state issues a license, a person authorized by the statute must solemnize the marriage. The authorized persons typically include ministers, priests, rabbis, and other religious clergies, as well as public officials such as judges, clerks of court, and notaries. Many states have processes for others to obtain authority to perform marriages.

Let's consider a few areas related to marriage and building families.

Common law marriage – Traditionally, when a man and woman lived together for a period of time in a way that exhibited married behavior to the world, the law recognized a marriage. The law acknowledged that in the less formal world of the past, many people tended to marry without formality. Common law marriage bestowed the privileges of marriage on these couples. In most states, living together for seven years was deemed common law marriage. Almost all of the states no longer recognize common law marriage. Hence, living together no longer carries with it the many privileges of being married, such as Social Security benefits, property interests, and tax benefits.

Prenuptial agreements – Prenuptial Agreements are legally enforceable contracts between two persons contemplating marriage.

"Prenups" typically describe the division of assets and the amounts of alimony required if divorce occurs. They may also address issues regarding behavior, child rearing, and even social media content, although many states will not enforce these provisions. Significantly, most states will not enforce child custody or child support prearrangements either.

Adoption – Adoption laws are intended to protect the child, the birth parents, and the adoptive parents in adoption proceedings. An adoption changes the future of the child because it places him or her in a new family permanently. It forever dissolves ties with birth parents and relatives and takes away the birth parents' rights and their legal duties to the child. The new parents assume legal responsibility to provide for the care and nurturing of the child. An adopted child has the same legal rights and privileges regarding the new parents as a naturally born child.

Although usually any minor can be adopted, the states each have adoption laws that may vary substantially. Generally, there must be a court hearing and formal order issued by a judge approving an adoption. The court will consider detailed information about the child, the future parents, and the living environment intended for the child. Either a state agency or an approved private individual or organization must investigate the ability of the adoptive parents to care for and support the child.

Birth parent consent must be obtained, including that of a biological father even if the mother is not married. Absent birth parents must be sought out through efforts defined in the statutes. Many states also require notification of grandparents. State laws provide safeguards to make sure that birth parents understand their decisions and most states provide revocation rights for some period. State laws may also require that a child actually lives in the home of the adoptive parents before the adoption is approved.

Family legal responsibilities – Federal and state laws provide for many legal duties in the family relationship. These duties include:

- The obligation to care for and support a spouse.
- The obligation to support children until they reach majority, or for life if they are disabled.

- The obligation to share property under state marital property, inheritance, and divorce laws.

- The obligation to make decisions regarding health and finances if a spouse becomes incapacitated.

- The obligation to provide confidentiality, comfort, sexual relations and love. Although these are often difficult for the courts to address, they provide bases for legal action in many of the states.

- A fiduciary obligation to a spouse. A fiduciary duty requires loyalty to the other in all interests and a good faith protection of the rights and financial interests of the other.

Taking Families Apart

The law also provides for the dissolution of the family unit. Families break down from separation, divorce, abuse, and death.

Separation – A legal separation results when a court order is issued establishing that the parties can live apart and have separate lives without divorce. They cannot remarry.

Legal separation is not available in all states and is mandatory before divorcing in others. The most important aspects of a legal separation are that it protects certain marital benefits such as being the beneficiary of medical and life insurance policies, and it separates often contentious factors such as further debt by either of the parties.

Many states require that a legal separation addresses property, child custody issues, and support. Other states, even those that may not permit legal separation, will recognize and enforce the provisions of a separation agreement. A separation agreement is a contract between the parties that provides for these matters. It is enforceable in the courts.

Divorce – A divorce dissolves a marriage and places the parties into a new status of single. Divorce in the past required fault by one of the spouses, but today all states allow divorce without placement of blame. In many states this is known as "no-fault" divorce.

Like so many areas of our law, states' laws control divorces, and each has its own statutes regulating the termination of marriages.

Divorce requires the filing of a petition with the family court in the state where at least one of the spouses resides. The other spouse must be notified and can either contest the divorce or agree to it (an uncontested divorce). Courts will hold hearings in contested divorces to determine whether to grant the divorce and to resolve property and child custody disputes. In a noncontested divorce, the parties will meet and agree not only to divorce but also to the division of property and the custody of any children.

Many states require waiting periods before a divorce. This is intended to allow time for the parties to resolve their differences and reconcile. In a few states, this waiting period can be a year, or longer if a court so orders. Many states also require the parties to participate in counseling to see if they can salvage the relationship.

Most divorces today are granted based on "irreconcilable differences" or similar terminology and a showing of misconduct by one of the parties is not required. Most states do not require fault by one of the spouses to grant a divorce, but if one of the parties contests the divorce, the court may examine the circumstances and has full authority to deny it. The evidence placed in the record during such an examination of the facts may also influence the court's determination of property and child custody matters.

Property settlements in divorce are determined in two ways depending on state law. In community property states (Arizona, California, Idaho, Louisiana, Nevada, New Mexico, Texas, Washington, and Wisconsin), all property obtained during the marriage is community property equally owned by both parties regardless of its source. Equal distribution of assets is the rule in community property states. But property that was owned by individual spouses before the marriage will continue to be individual property in the property settlement. This same rule also generally applies to gifts and inheritances received during the marriage.

In the other states, the property is divided by "equitable distribution." In these states, the source (such as earnings) of the property is reviewed, as well as the needs and financial positions of each of the parties to determine how property is divided. The property is not necessarily divided equally, but rather based on the efforts of each party to create it and the relative needs of each. Fault may also enter into this determination. Again, property that was owned by individual spouses before the marriage will continue to be individual property in the property settlement, as will gifts and inheritances received during the marriage. These items remain separate property not subject to division in a divorce.

Child custody is perhaps the most difficult part of a divorce. If there are minor children involved, the courts will take their interests into account in property division to assure their future care and support.

In determining child custody, the parents often are encouraged to and do in fact frequently reach an agreement. Joint custody that allows both parents to look after and provide for the children, and in many cases share time with the children, is the dominant resolution today. But even with that said, women take primary custody in about 90 percent of all U.S. divorces.

When parents cannot reach an agreement, the courts hold hearings to determine custody. Courts consider the children's welfare and examine all factors that will affect the health and safety of them.

The courts seek evidence of each parent's ability to provide for the physical, emotional, developmental, educational and extraordinary needs of the children. The courts consider the financial and mental stability of each parent. Considerations take into the account the relationship of the children with each parent including affection and attachment. The courts also look at the parents' willingness to allow the children to spend time with the other parent. The preferences of the children are important considerations, and in some states, the children are permitted to choose if they are old enough (typically 14 years old). Courts may also review the children's relationship with each other, their current school, friends, and social lives. Courts also scrutinize a parent's drug or alcohol abuse, any evidence of physical abuse, work record, and criminal activities. Most states will refuse custody to a parent that was abusive in the family.

Child support is a separate issue from the custody of the children. BOTH parents are required by the law to support their children. That concept often surprises a spouse who believes that surrendering custody will also relieve him of support. It also may be a surprise that after a divorce, the custodial parent cannot just "stay home with the kids."

Federal law provides that states must have statutory guidelines for determining the amount of support required for the number of children involved. State law then establishes and allocates the child support to the parents based on their individual earnings. If one parent voluntarily does not work, his income potential determines his ability to pay child support. The court can order child support as though he is earning the imputed income. The rules for determining income, both earned and imputed, are complex and vary depending on state law. In determining modifications from statute based amounts, the courts may consider other factors including the age of the children, schooling, medical circumstances and standard of living. State child support guidelines typically require 20 - 25 percent of income for one child, and more for each additional child.

Alimony is support for a spouse paid by the other spouse after divorce. When one of the spouses was financially dependent on the other and is unable to permanently or temporarily support himself, the court can award alimony. The award may apply to either spouse. The amount of alimony depends on state law, and most states consider the length of the marriage, the relative incomes of each party and the earning ability of the spouse seeking alimony. Standard of living is a common consideration in the amount of alimony, particularly when one of the spouses has much larger earnings. Many states consider fault in the award of alimony and may reduce or even eliminate it if the party seeking the alimony caused the breakup of the marriage.

Abuse – Abuse is a significant cause of marriage failure. While it may ultimately lead to divorce, it has a much more draconian impact on the family relationship. Abuse can take many forms, from physical abuse to drug abuse, verbal abuse, sexual abuse, and psychological abuse that may include intimidation, degradation, control, and criticism. While family units deteriorate and suffer untold mental and physical damage, divorce frequently does not follow.

The law provides protections for abused spouses and children. The federal government and all of the states have statutes that punish domestic abuse. At the federal level, laws provide for interstate cooperation and information sharing as well as funding for state and local law enforcement in domestic abuse matters. State laws make spouse and child abuse criminal and contain provisions for protecting victims.

As in most legal matters, domestic abuse laws differ from state to state. Some states, for example, do not recognize nonphysical abuse. States also have varying requirements for mandatory reporting of abuse. Most states require that medical professionals and police report domestic violence and some give the police authority to issue immediate protective orders keeping the violator away. Many states also require the police to arrest one of both of the parties in spousal abuse situations to protect victims.

State laws also provide for protection in the form of court issued restraining orders that keep the violators away from the victims. Special criminal charges, as well as traditional assault and battery charges, are also provided, often raising domestic violence in any form to the felony level.

Additionally, tort law provides that civil suits can be filed to recover damages for pain and suffering, medical expenses, and attorney fees from abusers. Many states also provide for other penalties such as loss of driving privileges and child custody and visitation rights. The legal system treats domestic violence as a grave matter, but the law is frequently the last resort for protection.

Annulment – An annulment determines that a marriage is null and void. It is different from a divorce in that an annulment means that a marriage never existed. While a divorce occurs when the divorce is granted by a court, an annulment relates back to the date of the marriage.

There are generally two types of annulment actions. One seeks to nullify the marriage because it was not legally formed. Examples of this type of an annulment might include underage spouses, bigamy, and incest in violation of state statute.

The other type of annulment seeks to void a marriage that was legal, but was formed under invalid conditions. Examples include a forced marriage, where one or the other of the parties is unable to consummate the marriage, or where there was fraud.

An annulment is court determined, and the party seeking the annulment must file a petition outlining the reasons. The other party can contest the petition and a trial can result.

In Conclusion

In the U.S., there are over 50 sets of rules regarding marriage and divorce. Each state, the District of Columbia and all of the U.S. territories have different laws and rules. While the information in this chapter provides a general overview, it is important to understand the law of your particular state to evaluate individual circumstances.

The status of the family was once considered a foundation of the American legal system. The law provided a legal framework for its establishment and for its termination. Over the years, the ability to break the family unit down, or to live without ever forming the traditional family, has slowly but surely been more reflected in the law. Today, many households exist without marriage, but they may not all have the traditional safeguards the law provided.

A Story from the Real

Some states still recognize common law marriage. But in these states, state law sets the criteria for determining whether a valid common law marriage exists. This caused a widow somber consequences.

Our couple was married two months before the husband died. Before that, they had apparently lived together for six years. The husband was a veteran who had served in Viet Nam. His death was the result of a service related illness. Surviving spouses of veterans like this are entitled to benefits from the Veterans Administration (VA).

The widow applied for surviving spouse benefits. Her claim was denied by the VA because the statute authorizing the benefits required at least one year of marriage before death. The widow filed an appeal and provided evidence of common law marriage. She presented evidence that included her own statements, copies of documents that showed Mr. and Mrs. on them, and a written statement from a friend stating they had been living as husband and wife for six years. The VA rejected her appeal.

The widow pursued her claim through the administrative appeal process of the VA; all levels of appeal denied her benefits. She appealed to the U.S. Court of Appeals for Veterans Claims, and again the court denied her claim. She finally appealed to the U.S. Court of Appeals for the Federal Circuit.

The claims were denied at all levels because she failed to meet the requirements of the state statute for establishing a common law marriage. The statute required "(1) capacity, meaning that both parties must be at least fourteen years old and mentally competent; (2) a present agreement or mutual consent to enter into the marriage relationship; (3) a public recognition of the existence of the marriage; and (4) cohabitation or mutual assumption of marital duties and obligations." To our widow's ruin, the state statute required "clear and convincing proof" of each element to prove common law marriage.

The widow argued to the appeals court that the state standard was not applicable to veterans' cases because VA rules guide veterans' actions, not state rules. The VA regulations require a "benefit of the doubt" approach meant to give a liberal opportunity for veterans and their survivors to make claims for benefits.

Unfortunately, the appeals court agreed with all of the other hearings and appeals and ruled that in determining common law marriage, the VA must follow state law. Therefore the clear and convincing proof rule had to be followed because it was part of the state's law.

When reviewing the evidence, the Court of Appeals found particular problems with the proof of statute requirement number 2 - an agreement by both parties that they were married. The evidence showed that the deceased veteran had on several occasions, sometimes in official records, denied he was married or stated that he was single. He listed his nearest relative in VA records as his brother. The court found that there was no evidence that the deceased had ever agreed that he was married. The court, therefore, affirmed the VA findings.

Chapter 8
Tax Law

(Paying the Price of Civilization)

Most of us think that tax law is both mysterious and unfair. More than any other area of law, the average person is intimidated by tax law and actually afraid of it. Even though the IRS writes its instructions at the eighth-grade level, few people prepare their own returns.

Perhaps there is a feeling that the law is not understandable and therefore difficult to follow leading all of us to certain violation. There is also a deep-seated disdain for paying taxes that adds to the general dislike of everything to do with them.

This chapter will look at taxation in its various forms and provide the societal bases for them. We will also review the general rules for complying with tax law. We discuss the following existing taxes:

- Income taxes at the federal, state, and local levels.
- Employment taxes.
- Social Security and Medicare taxes.
- Unemployment taxes.
- Workers' Compensation.
- Sales taxes.
- Property taxes.
- Estate and Inheritance taxes.
- Excise taxes.

Because of the media attention to several tax proposals, we will also discuss these structures:

- ◘   "Fair Tax" (national sales tax).
- ◘   Value Added Tax (VAT).
- ◘   Flat tax.

We will discuss tax administration and enforcement as well.

Tax Authority and Policy

Taxes are a necessity of human society and community. Since the beginning of human civilization, taxes have been levied to provide for the common good. From the beginning, members of the community were expected to pay for its security and its infrastructure and public services. Without taxes, there could be no generally available water supply, roads, sewers, parks, or education. Individual defense of property and protection from the selfish and violent actions of both other community members and foreign invaders is simply not possible. Hence humans created taxes to pay for all of these things, and as time evolved many more things as well.

The legal foundation of the government provides its ability to tax. The Constitution of the U.S. and the constitutions of all of the states provide the authority to tax citizens. This authority is exercised through statutes passed by the Congress and by the various legislative bodies in state and local governments. The Constitution authorizes every tax in place today and statutes properly exercise this authority through tax law and tax administration. The courts long ago approved of every tax we have in place. There is no Constitutional argument to avoid current U.S. taxation.

Statutes levy taxes and our elected representatives craft and put these statutes into place. Through taxing laws, Congress not only raises money for government operations but also effects political policy. For example, taxing some people at higher rates than others is a policy decision that is intended to make taxes fair. Allowing home interest to be deducted from taxable income is a policy decision to encourage home ownership. Exempting food from sales tax is a policy decision recognizing that some expenditures are so basic and necessary that hindering them with taxation is unjust. The tax law is explicitly filled with policy determinations in every sentence of the statutes that created it. Our representatives determine what aspects of our society they want to encourage or discourage and tax laws provide the vehicles to accomplish that influence. We must recognize that this is inherent in our tax law and respect that our law generally reflects what a majority of us wants, even if we individually may not agree.

Income Tax

Federal, state and local governments levy income taxes. The federal system is the most familiar to all of us, but many states also have similar and separate systems. In addition, many cities also tax the incomes of their residents.

The Internal Revenue Code (IRC), and the regulations written by the Treasury Department to apply the law in the IRC, contain the compilation of federal income taxation law. It is a very comprehensive and detailed set of laws that optimistically levies the tax in a way that is clear and that is not subject to manipulation. We know how that works out in the real world. Modern business and financial transactions are so complex and varied that it is essentially impossible for the law to address every set of facts that may arise.

But income tax in and of itself is not complicated intellectually. The law imposes the tax on taxable income, which is essentially all income from all sources, minus the "policy determinations" that we call deductions. Deductions reduce taxable income. There are many deductions available to individuals including exemptions for each person and dependent, house interest, medical expenses, state taxes paid, charitable donations and so on.

The costs necessary to generate business income reduce taxable income as well. These costs include the expenses of a business and the costs of purchasing assets and services needed to conduct the business.

Tax rates are applied after taxable income is determined. At the federal level and in many state systems, we have "graduated" rates meaning that the more income a person has, the higher the rate that he pays. Income earned on the sale of property, including stocks, is called capital gains and it is taxed at a lower rate than earned income.

More policy determinations allow "credits" or subtractions from the tax after it is determined. There are many credits available. Some examples include taxes paid to foreign governments on the same income, amounts expended on research and development of new technologies, credits for each child in a family, and several special credits that give tax reductions to lower income families.

Businesses pay income taxes as well as individuals. Businesses that are not corporations include the income on the owners' returns. Corporations file and pay income tax based on substantially the same rules on their own separate returns. The rate structure for corporations is different from individuals, but it is similarly graduated. Corporations and other businesses must use accounting rules to properly reflect income; and often income is based on accrued income and expenses rather than funds actually received during the year.

Income tax itself is simple. Income determines the amount of tax paid. A business determines income by subtracting the costs to produce it. This is not complex. It is the huge number of policy determinations that politicians include to influence society that make the income tax complicated and difficult to comprehend. The decisions made by politicians are not always bad; they just make the system more perplexing.

Collecting income taxes presents problems, but during World War II Congress exhibited a stroke of pure genius. It created withholding. Today, over 70 percent of personal income taxes are withheld by employers. While collecting this money from employers is not always an easy task, it is far easier than collecting from a 100 million wage earners individually. And IRS examinations indicate that those subject to withholding are nearly 95 percent compliant. Those who are not, such as independent business people, are much less compliant according to IRS audit analyses.

The IRS has substantial authority to collect taxes of all kinds. Its enforcement officers and systems are empowered to levy wages and bank accounts and seize property of delinquent taxpayers without court action. Its audit and assessment programs are mostly automated and summarily assess additional tax if it finds unreported income or unallowable deductions. The IRS estimates that it collects about 85 percent of the taxes that are legally due. Compared to other nations, this is a very substantial percentage.

Employment Taxes

The term "employment tax" is a general term used to describe all of the taxes imposed on employers. It is not a separate tax, but rather the combination of Social Security tax, Medicare tax, unemployment tax, workers' compensation tax, and the income tax that employers are required to withhold from employees. As such, only part of "employment tax" is a direct tax on employers. The majority of employment tax is the amounts withheld from employee salaries and paid over by the employer to the government.

We describe each of the employment taxes individually below. But first, let's understand that these taxes are costly to business. Employment taxes create a direct expense to employers in terms of the Social Security, Medicare, unemployment, and workers' compensation taxes that employers pay. They also generate a significant expense for employers in collecting income taxes and Social Security taxes that are withheld from employee salaries, and timely paying them over to sometimes several government entities.

Social Security and Medicare Taxes

Although we discuss Social Security and Medicare taxes together, they are actually two separate taxes for two different purposes. Social Security taxes support the Social Security retirement and disability and survivorship system and Medicare taxes fund the Medicare health system.

Both the employer and the employee pay Social Security taxes. Each pays 6.2 percent of salary. The salary subject to Social Security tax is limited to an amount determined each year based on inflation adjustments. For 2017, the base subject to tax was $127,200. The employee's share is withheld from his pay, and together with the employer's share, the employer remits the taxes to the government on quarterly returns.

Social Security determines retirement benefits based on the number of years that the employee paid taxes and the amount of income earned. At normal retirement age, benefits in 2017 can reach $2,685 per month. Social Security also provides survivorship benefits for the minor children of persons that die and disability benefits for those that cannot work due to physical or mental illness.

Medicare taxes are paid much like Social Security taxes. The tax rate is 1.45 percent of salary for both the employee and the employer. There is not a maximum amount of salary that is subject to this tax. And, higher income employees pay an addition 0.9 percent for all income in excess of $250,000 to supplement the government costs of The Affordable Care Act (Obamacare). Like Social Security, the employer withholds the taxes from the employees' wages and reports and pays the employer and employee shares on the quarterly employment tax returns.

Medicare provides medical insurance for those over the age of 65, and to those disabled under the Social Security system criteria.

Self-employed persons also pay both Social Security taxes and Medicare taxes. The rates and taxable income amounts are the same, but there is a small adjustment made to the total tax due. Unlike employees, however, where the employer pays half of the tax, the self-employed person must pay the entire 15.3 percent (6.2 X 2 percent for Social Security and 1.45 X 2 percent for Medicare).

Unemployment Taxes

Unemployment taxes support unemployment payments to those that are out of work. Both the state and federal governments have this tax. Employers pay the entire amount.

State law provides for unemployment compensation for out-of-work persons. The state taxes its employers to support the system. The amount of tax paid varies depending on the state and on the employee retention record of the employer. This means that if an employer has a history of laying off employees, it will pay a higher unemployment rate.

The rate of unemployment tax varies widely by state; it ranges from 2.5 to 7.5 percent of wages. But the wages subject to the tax are limited, and this too varies by state. The amount of individual employee wages subject to the tax varies from $7,000 to $45,000 in 2017.

The federal unemployment tax system supports the state systems. It does not pay benefits directly to unemployed persons. The federal tax rate is 6.0 percent of the first $7,000 of wages paid to each employee, but if the employer paid state unemployment taxes as required, this amount is reduced by 5.4 percent. The effective rate, therefore, is .6 percent of the wage base.

The federal system supports the state systems by providing loans if the state system runs out of funds and by encouraging employers to pay the state tax by allowing substantial credits on the federal returns.

Workers' Compensation

Workers' compensation laws provide for medical care, wage replacement, dependent support and disability payments when a worker is injured or becomes ill due to his employment.

In a few states, workers' compensation is similar to a tax that is levied by the state on employers; the state pays benefits and administers both the taxing system and the claims. But in most states, workers' compensation is mandatory insurance required by state law that employers must carry. In the insurance states, there are state oversight and backup funding systems in place.

The injury experience of the employer, and the industry in which the employer operates, determine workers' compensation rates in both tax states and insurance states. In other words, a company in the construction industry will likely pay more than a company in a professional services business, and a construction company that has experienced many injuries will have higher rates than a construction company with no injuries.

Workers' compensation rates vary substantially among the states and industries. Employers pay between one and five percent of payroll, although some industries (e.g., tree trimming) may be much higher.

Most states also have programs for self-insurance that allow large businesses to establish their own programs to meet the workers' compensation law. Under these programs, the employer essentially pays the medical and other costs itself based on state guidelines.

An important aspect of workers' compensation laws is that they not only provide benefits for injured employees, but they also remove liability for injuries from the employers. Under common law concepts, an injured employee could sue the employer and recover damages for his injury or illness from the employer, including damages for pain and suffering. With workers' compensation laws, injured employees simply file claims and receive payment under the standards set by the laws; and these standards do not allow compensation for pain and suffering. Although there are exceptions, a worker cannot usually sue an employer that participates in the workers' compensation program.

Sales Tax

State and local governments levy sales taxes at the retail level. It is a tax on the sale of goods, and it is the responsibility of the seller to collect it and remit it to the government authority. A few states have no sales tax, while others range from four percent to seven and one-half percent. In addition to state level sales taxes, many counties and cities have local sales taxes that can add up to two percent to the total sales tax bill. When local and state sales taxes are considered, everyplace in the U.S. has some sales tax in place.

State and local governments use sales taxes to fund operations, everything from road maintenance and public salaries to welfare and education. In many states, sales taxes are a significant source of total state tax receipts. Sales taxes often fund specific liabilities or services of the government. For example, a ten-year additional sales tax might fund a highway project or pay off an outstanding state pension liability. These special project sales taxes are usually time limited to a period necessary to pay for the initiative.

The products and services subject to sales tax vary depending on the state and locality. In some states, all products and services sold to retail customers are subject to the tax. In others, only the sale of goods carries sales tax. In many states, the tax is not applied to specific products or services that are considered essential. These items might include drugs, food, and/or rent, for example.

Retailers collect sales tax as part of the sale. Prices of products or services typically do not include the sales tax; it is added to the purchase price when the sale occurs. The seller is then responsible for paying the collected sales tax to the state or local taxing authority. Most states require monthly or quarterly filing, and they may require deposits of the collected tax as often a daily or weekly.

From a consumer perspective, the tax is easy to collect. We cannot buy a product or service unless we pay the tax. Tax authorities, however, find that collecting sales tax from vendors who have collected, or should have collected it, to be one of the most difficult challenges of tax administration.

There are many sellers of products and services, and many do not register with the state to collect the tax. Others collect the tax but do not pay it over. Even if a seller does not collect the tax, he is still responsible for it. Finding and collecting this tax from millions of sellers is a very challenging task because of the large numbers of vendors and the frequent use of the collected funds to continue the business operations of the sellers.

An interesting and mostly unknown companion of the sales tax is the "use tax." Every state with a sales tax also has a use tax in place. In simple terms, a use tax requires the purchaser of a product that was not subject to the state sales tax (perhaps because it was purchased in another state) to pay the sales tax rate on the product.

States actively pursue the use tax in a number of different ways; a common method is to examine the bills of lading of freight trucks entering the state and identifying the buyers of untaxed goods. The states follow up with a use tax bill to the purchaser. Some relief from the use tax is provided, however, by intrastate agreements that provide that the purchaser of goods that pays the sales tax in one state will not be required to pay the use tax in another.

Property Taxes

Property taxes take several forms and both state and local governments commonly levy them. The most usual and well known property tax is real estate taxes levied on the value of real property. But there are many others including property taxes on the value of stocks, bonds, contracts, royalties, automobiles and boats, and business equipment and inventory.

Property taxes are the largest source of state and local revenue in most states. Local governments such as counties and cities rely heavily on property tax revenues. The collected funds are used to finance all aspects of local government including education, infrastructure and medical assistance and support costs. Property tax rates vary considerably by state and location. They range from less than one percent of value to over five percent of value depending on the locale and the types of property subject to tax.

Property taxes often cause government conflict with the citizens impacted by them because the value of the property determines the amount of the tax. The government typically determines value by using appraisers or some type of appraisal methodology created by statute or regulation. (In some states, business owners must file personal property "rendition" returns in which they self-determine values.) There is typically an appeal process available to property owners to challenge the government valuation. Because valuation is an art and not a science subject to 100 percent verification, the contests between property owners and government are sometimes contentious.

Although the establishment of value and the amount of tax due can be combative, collection and enforcement of the tax are relatively easy for the government. Under most property tax laws, the government automatically obtains a lien on property subject to property tax. If the property owner does not pay the tax, the government enforces its lien through property seizure and sale.

Estate, Gift, and Inheritance Taxes

So called death taxes seem to be a uniformly disliked form of taxation even though most citizens are not subject to it. The government imposes estate taxes on the value of the property of a deceased person at the time of his death. Inheritance taxes are levied on the value of property received by an heir of the deceased person. The federal "death tax" is an estate tax. Some states have either an estate tax or an inheritance tax. One state has both.

At the federal level, estates with a taxable value greater than $5.5 million are subject to the estate tax; this amount increases each year to reflect inflation. The tax, therefore, impacts a relatively small number of people. The tax rate, however, is substantial at 40 percent of the amount of the value of the estate over the $5.5 million exemption amount.

Estate tax law is complex because it must value all of the property and property rights of a decedent. In large estates, this can become a momentous task as property rights might not always be apparent. For example, a right to appoint the ultimate recipient of a property that is not even owned by the decedent might be something included in the value of his estate. The tax code is very broad to include all property and rights to property so that careful planning to exclude interests owned at death may not avoid the tax. The basic premise of the estate tax law is that all "value" owned or controlled by a person at the time of his death is subject to the tax.

The law permits various deductions from the value of the estate before the taxable value is determined. These include the costs of administration, debts of the decedent, bequests to charity, and bequests to a surviving spouse. The idea behind allowing a deduction for value passing to a spouse is that the tax will be subsequently collected from the spouse's estate. Deductions are often planned to remove or reduce the estate tax. For example, if a person dies with property interests worth $10 million, and leaves $4.5 million to a charity, his taxable estate would be $5.5 million. Applying the estate tax exemption of $5.5 million to this would reduce the amount taxable to zero, and there would be no estate tax due.

Federal gift taxes compliment the estate tax. It makes sense that the tax law could not allow a person to simply give away his property to his heirs before he dies to avoid the estate tax. Therefore, Congress created the gift tax to levy basically the same tax on transfers during life.

The law excludes "smaller gifts," those under $14,000 per year, from the gift tax scheme. In other words, a person can gift up to $14,000 per person per year without any reporting. Once gifts exceed $14,000 per person, however, the person making the gift must file a gift tax return. No gift tax is due, however, until the total taxable gifts during a lifetime exceed $5.5 million, which is the same amount as the estate tax exclusion.

At death, the estate tax return includes not only the property owned by the decedent at the date of his death but also all of the property gifted during his lifetime. In this final return of all transfers, the estate tax exclusion is applied to determine if there is a taxable amount.

For example, if a person makes $3 million of gifts during his lifetime (and this would require the payment of no gift tax because it is less than the $5.5 million amount), and dies with $5 million of property remaining, his taxable estate subject to the estate tax will be $2.5 million. We determine this by adding the lifetime gifts of $3 million to the $5 million of property still owned at death, and subtracting the estate tax exclusion amount of $5.5 million. Gift tax and estate tax are therefore a combined system of taxing wealth.

There are less than 10,000 estate tax returns filed each year, and after deductions, less than half of them require the payment of tax. Estate and gift tax laws impact only the very wealthiest citizens. Out of roughly 2.5 million deaths each year, only 5,000 pay federal estate tax. That is just 0.2 percent of the population.

The purpose of estate and gift taxation is not just to raise funds for the government. It also serves as a social tool to redistribute wealth. If properly enforced, the estate tax would "redistribute" 40 percent of all wealth over $5.5 million every generation. That could have a substantial impact on reducing the wealth of the most affluent.

But taxation is never quite that simple. Most wealthy people are not sitting on just piles of cash or large bank accounts that can easily be divided and paid to the government. Most of the wealth is in the form of businesses and other investments that might not be cash liquid (farms, for example). The estate tax law provides avenues for family-held businesses and farms to escape large estate tax bills, primarily through provisions that allow for special valuations far below market values and/or extended payments of the tax due.

Please also note that wealthy families can and do employ the best tax planners and tools. This allows for many holdings to pass through the estate tax net without taxation. Often, just the correct valuation of a wealthy person's holdings is a difficult if not impossible task to accomplish with any accuracy, and experts hired by the wealthy estates can often persuade IRS examiners, or if necessary the courts, that a value is far smaller than it actually might be. As a wealth redistribution methodology, the estate tax has mostly failed because of the complexity of modern wealth and the many legal alternatives for controlling it.

About a dozen states still levy estate or inheritance taxes. The estate tax laws of these states are somewhat similar to the federal estate laws, but have much lower rates and may have much lower exclusion amounts. There are still a few states that levy estate tax on estates with values of $1 million or less.

Six states still collect inheritance taxes. This tax applies a tax rate (usually in the five to 15 percent range) on the value of property inherited. Some states have exclusion amounts of $25,000 to $50,000 that are not subject to the tax, and often rates are lower for sons and daughters of the decedent. Like the federal system, most state estate and inheritance laws do not tax amounts passing to a surviving spouse. New Jersey levies both an estate tax and an inheritance tax.

Excise Taxes

Excise taxes are an indirect tax levied on the sale or production of specific goods. It is a hidden tax that we all pay without truly realizing we are paying it. Both states and the federal government have excise taxes in place. Perhaps the most well-known excise tax is the gasoline tax. Currently, the Federal excise tax is 18.4 cents per gallon. State gasoline taxes range from 26 cents to 69 cents per gallon. Some excise taxes, like that on gasoline, can be very costly for consumers.

The federal government collects excise taxes on the manufacture or sale of 55 products and services, including various fuels, chemicals, and sporting goods, as well as telephone usage, airline tickets, and insurance policies. Excise taxes also apply to truck tires, vaccines, and even indoor tanning services. Of course, we are all familiar with the "gas guzzler tax" that is an excise tax on automobiles that do not meet government mileage standards. Excise taxes range from relatively low rates to substantial amounts. The consumer of the taxed products (that's you), of course, ultimately pays the tax because the manufacturers just pass it on through pricing.

The manufacturer or producer of the taxed item remits an excise tax return and pays the tax four times per year. The avoidance of excise taxes was a significant problem when some of the taxes were levied at the retail sale level (e.g., diesel fuel tax), but now most are collected directly from the manufacturer. Companies file almost one million excise tax returns each year, and the taxes generate over $75 billion of revenue for the federal government.

States also levy various excise taxes, most notably the fuel taxes mentioned above. States also tend to apply excise taxes to various "sin" or "luxury" products like tobacco, alcoholic beverages and various transportation and communication services.

Excise taxes are meant not only to raise revenue but also to influence the cost and therefore the purchase of the products taxed. Many of the products require government regulation and monitoring that is expensive in terms of rulemaking, inspections, and enforcement. The excise taxes offset the costs of regulating these products, many of which are considered hazardous or even dangerous.

Other Taxes

In addition to those described above, there are many other taxes imposed by both the federal and state governments. These include a highway use tax paid by large trucks and trailers, customs taxes on many imported products, recording taxes for deeds and mortgages, and occupancy and amusement taxes on vacation sites and hotel rooms. Anything a politician sees as a likely source of revenue may be subject to tax, and probably is.

Proposed Taxes

The last sentence in the previous section leads perfectly to this discussion. Many in our society, both the taxers and the taxed, are looking for more "fair and equitable" ways to raise the funds needed to pay for government activity and programs. The income tax is constantly under attack for being unfair and regressive, and for being too full of "loopholes" allowing many to escape its reaches. Several proposals are on the national stage for consideration. Some have been advocated by politicians or by political parties. They may have merit, but none of them are easy to administer, and none of them will eliminate loopholes.

"Fair Tax" (national sales tax) – The Fair Tax is a national sales tax. We know that most states have sales taxes in place that impose a four to seven percent tax on the sale of goods and services. The federal proposal is for a much higher tax rate. Although proponents commonly suggest 22 - 23 percent, that rate is misunderstood and misleading. Advocates say that with the tax in place the price of goods and services will be increased by 23 percent, and that is true, but the tax itself would be 30 percent. Consider that a good that sells for $100 would have a $30 tax added to it when purchased. This makes the price $130 instead of $100. The advocates say that the tax impact or percentage of the new cost is $30 / $130 or 23 percent. Aren't politicians wonderful!

Many advocate that the Fair Tax would be simpler to collect and that we could abolish the IRS. They propose that the states, which already have sales tax operations in place, could collect the tax along with the state sales tax and then forward the federal part to the federal government. This sounds very simple, but there are a couple of caveats.

The states do not have enforcement people or systems in place to handle the volume of taxes they would be collecting. With the federal government depending on this revenue to operate, fund social programs, and our military, would it really be wise to turn this over to the states? If we could succeed in eliminating the IRS, the states would have to hire many more people than the IRS now employs because the collection system would be scattered to at least 50 different centers.

The fair tax proposal would collect a staggering amount of money from U.S. businesses. It would require every seller of goods and services in the country to collect and pay over up to 37 percent of its sales to the government when we include the state sales taxes with the federal tax. These huge amounts of money might strain small business operations, and the temptation to use these funds to prop up the businesses would be tremendous. Also, sellers might sell goods without the sales tax applied because of the huge reduction in price that would result. Who would police the many sellers without an IRS?

And what would be taxable? Every transaction? Would the law exclude some things like food and medicine? Who would define what is a food product (flour may count, but how about chewing gum?) No matter what the law excludes or does not exclude, the exclusions would not match the exclusions that are now allowed by the various states. And the proponents think that the state governments would sort this out.

Finally, the black market would blossom. Goods smuggled in from other countries, or products sold under the table would proliferate because of the huge savings. A product bought in Canada, for example, would cost 30 percent more if purchased in the U.S. Planning a trip yet?

The fair tax may also not be fair at all. The poor spend more of their money on goods and services than rich people do and the same tax rate would apply to both. The tax burden would fall much more on the poor and middle class. Proponents have a rather unique way to deal with this issue. They suggest that the government give each person in the country a check each month equal to the sales tax on necessary expenditures. That would essentially eliminate the tax for poor families. But who is going to manage and run this check-a-month program? There is no IRS anymore. A good thought, but in practice, it sounds difficult to implement and maintain.

Value added tax (VAT) – Europe and many other places have used value-added taxes for years. It is similar to a sales tax, but it compounds at each level of production. The idea is that the value added at each stage of production is taxed. So, a bicycle might have many levels of this tax added as it is produced. Value is added, and thus a tax, when the metal is extracted from the ground and processed; there is value added when the bicycle parts are stamped at the factory; and there is value added when the bicycle is assembled by the manufacturer. And finally, both the wholesaler and retailer of the finished bike might add value by bringing it to market. At each increase in value, a tax is added.

Value added taxes work and raise large sums of money, but like sales taxes, they are regressive impacting the poor more than the wealthy. They are also very difficult to administer because, at multiple steps in the product cycle, someone must determine and verify "value."

Flat tax – The concept of a flat tax is attractive to many people because in its pure form it is simple. The concept is that everybody pays a single rate of tax on their income without any deductions allowed. This is simple, and it is the method of income taxation used by many cities that have an "earnings tax." The cities apply a flat percentage to all earnings. There are no deductions. Workers do not file returns; the tax is just withheld by the employer on the gross wages and remitted to the government entity.

Problems arise, however, when this tax applies to businesses. Do we tax gross income with no business expenses allowed? Or, do we allow business deductions, such as the costs of doing business, wages paid to employees (that were already taxed), and costs of goods that the business resells to customers? Some propose the gross income tax that would tax business receipts without deductions, at a much lower rate for example.

But, cities that have an earnings tax allow all business deductions, and business entities are required to file returns showing income and expenses. But now the simplicity is gone. The IRS spends most of its resources auditing businesses. The IRS must determine if businesses are reporting income correctly and taking only allowable deductions. In a flat tax environment, this would not change a bit.

It is also true that a flat tax, like a sales tax, tends to be regressive taxing lower income people at the same rate as the very high income people. A 10 percent flat tax might cripple a low income family, but it might not have as much impact on the wealthy.

In Conclusion

Now that we know the real story of taxation, it is evident that governmental bodies at many levels of government take a substantial part of the income and wealth of the country. Estimates place the amount of national income taken and spent by the government to be as high as 35 percent. That means of every dollar of income produced in the U.S., the government spends 35 cents of it.

How our government entities spend this money is often questioned, and for years the federal government has spent far more than it collects each year. This forces it to borrow money on which it must pay interest. The interest on the national debt today equals a substantial part of total federal expenditures. Is this a wise way to spend our money? What solutions do we have?

A Story from the Real

A U.S. company saw opportunity in Afghanistan. When the U.S. expelled the Taliban government from Kabul in 2001, many thought that the years of war and mayhem in the country were finally at an end. These optimists saw reconstruction, and the development of a more progressive and modern society coming. And they saw a society that was lacking almost every skill needed to create this new culture.

With the encouragement of the U.S. government, the company spent $3 million building a school to teach diesel mechanics. They completed the school outside of Kandahar in 2003. It operated just 13 months before the renewed fighting and a resurgence of the Taliban and other groups simply made doing business impossible. Unable to find anyone interested in buying the facility, the company abandoned the property in 2004. It was not even able to remove the equipment it had installed or its vehicles.

The IRC allows a deduction for any losses incurred from the abandonment of business property. The owner must terminate all rights to the property, without any opportunity to recover them, to qualify for an abandonment loss. According to the language of the law, the abandonment must be "evidenced by closed and completed transactions, fixed by identifiable events, and actually sustained during the taxable year." The company met these standards. Rebels and residents plundered the property as soon as security withdrew.

On its 2004 Corporate Income Tax Return, the company showed a profit from its other operations of $2.5 million before this loss. The actual loss allowed after adjustments for prior depreciation claimed on the property was $2.6 million. For the 2004 tax year, therefore, the company showed a $100,000 loss and paid no tax after deducting the loss. It could carry back the $100,000 loss to the prior year, and by doing this, received a refund of $35,000 of taxes paid for that year.

Is this a tax shelter? The company had $2.5 million of profit for the year, yet it paid no taxes. In fact, it obtained a refund of $35,000. Or, is this a "loophole" that allows a profitable company to avoid paying taxes? It is, of course, neither. The company spent $3 million that it lost. The income tax law permits a business to deduct its costs of doing business.

Normally, if a company spends $3 million to build a plant, it expects to make money on the operations there for many years. Under depreciation rules, it is required to write off (deduct) the $3 million cost a little each year as the plant produces income. Under any business plan, the company would expect to earn over the years far more than the $3 million invested. The difference between the two is the taxable profit.

Here the cost was $3 million, but there was no income. When the company abandoned the property, there was no opportunity for ever making any money from the investment. Rationally, the law allows the invested money to be deducted in full when there is no longer any chance to earn a profit from it.

With a few exceptions that Congress put into tax law to encourage economic or social behavior, no tax deductions are available unless money is spent. That means there are no loopholes that simply allow individuals or businesses to simply take deductions. Every deduction requires the expenditure of money. And they cannot recover some of the expenditures for many years. Depreciation, for example, is taken over the life of the property. If I buy a machine for my business today that costs

$1 million, I cannot take a $1 million deduction this year. I must spread that deduction over seven years, taking part of it each year. That almost sounds like a money hole instead of a loophole!

Sometimes Congress allows deductions for money spent even before a company produces any income. This is more like a tax shelter, but it is legal. For example, because oil and gas discovery is so expensive, and because many drilling efforts fail, it is a high risk, high return type of business. Congress encourages investment in this risky business by providing deductions for the exploration costs before any income is generated. It allows the deduction of costs before there is even a chance of profits. Investors can offset these deductions against income from other investments that are producing income - "sheltering" that income from tax. But in any event, the amount deducted this way cannot exceed the amount of the investment. And when the investment does produce income, it is taxed.

Finally, there are illegal tax shelters that manipulate the law to produce deductions or decrease income. For example, let's say a company buys wine in Italy for $2 per bottle and sells it in the U.S. for $10 per bottle. That would produce an $8 difference that would be taxable income after other costs, such as shipping, are subtracted. But we have a different plan. We create a company in Bermuda. Our Bermuda company buys the wine in Italy for $2 per bottle and then sells it to our U.S. company for $9. Now when we sell in the U.S. for $10, we have only $1 of profit to be taxed. Of course, the Bermuda company has a profit of $7 per bottle ($9 - $2). But Bermuda does not have an income tax! This is a pretty good tax shelter, right? We saved a lot of tax.

Unfortunately, the tax law allows these transactions, but will not recognize the pricing used. The law requires that all such "related transactions" must be conducted at fair market values. And the markup between Bermuda and the U.S. is excessive and would not be allowed.

There are legal ways to reduce income tax, but with a few exceptions they require the expenditure of money equal to the deduction that is allowed. And remember that tax rates are not 100 percent.

If we use our Afghanistan company as an example, it spent $3 million. Through depreciation and the abandonment loss, it was able to deduct $3 million. This lowered its taxable income by $3 million. But how much tax did this deduction save? The highest corporate tax rate is 35 percent, so it saved just a little over $1 million of tax. In 2004, its taxable income without the loss was $2.5 million; that would have generated $875,000 of tax. It received a $35,000 refund from the prior year, and in the prior couple of years, it had already deducted the balance of $400,000 saving $140,000 of tax in those years. The total tax saved was, therefore, a little over $1 million. This is not a good return for any business. They didn't pay tax, but they are in the hole almost $2 million on this failed adventure.

Media and other accounts we see often mislead us by talking about tax shelters and major companies that pay no tax. The truth is that many businesses do not pay tax because they have current year deductions for money they spent in the past. Or, some do not pay U.S. taxes because their profits are earned in foreign countries. They may or may not have to pay taxes in those countries. Some companies have credits, which are direct offsets against income that are allowed by law. These credits, like those allowed for research and development expenditures, are encouraged by Congress to promote new discoveries.

Our Afghan company was not avoiding tax, nor was it employing a tax shelter. It simply made a bad investment. The law encourages investment by allowing businesses to deduct the costs of their efforts to grow. The fact that it paid no taxes in 2004 only reveals a failed effort, not something nefarious.

There are many legal reasons that companies may not pay U.S. income taxes. All of them were designed by Congress to promote business growth and success, or to advocate a particular political goal. They are not necessarily bad. Moreover, some view these business tax savings as opportunities for the businesses to spend the money they keep instead of sending it to the government for it to spend.

Chapter 9
Regulatory Law

(The Scourge and Beauty of the Bureaucrats)

Regulatory law is the body of rulemaking and regulation issued and enforced by administrative agencies of the federal and state governments. The term "administrative agencies" means all of the boards, bureaus, offices, commissions, departments, agencies, and organizations created by the legislative branch to oversee and supervise business and social activities. The legislative branch in effect delegates law-making authority to these agencies.

Federal agencies typically operate under the Executive Branch, and the President directs and oversees them. He also appoints the heads of the agencies as political appointments. There are, however, some "independent" agencies. They operate outside of the Executive Branch. In total, there are over 600 federal agencies or agency like organizations. There are thousands more at the state and local levels of government.

Foundation of Regulatory Authority

Although the U.S. Constitution does not mention regulatory power or federal agencies, it is the source of authority for federal regulatory law.

Article I states that "legislative Powers herein granted shall be vested in a Congress of the United States," and the "necessary-and-proper" clause, in the same article, states that Congress shall have power "to make all Laws which shall be necessary and proper for carrying into Execution the foregoing Powers, and all other Powers … in any Department or Officer thereof." Finally, the Commerce Clause in Article 1 gives Congress the power "To regulate Commerce with foreign Nations, and among the several States…" The courts have accepted these grants of power as authority for Congress to create federal agencies.

But regulatory authority and law are far more revolutionary than mere clever Constitutional construction. Just 150 years ago, there was very little regulatory law or even much of a concept of such a legal brute! But the economy of the U.S. changed from one based on simple agricultural and home based businesses to one made up of vast enterprises like railroads, large factories, and nationwide markets.

In this new environment, Congress found itself lacking the expertise to protect the welfare of the country and its citizens. When the specialization of modern society outgrew the routine knowledge of legislators, they chose to create federal agencies that would be the subject matter and industry experts to oversee these new economic conditions.

The Supreme Court ruled that because Congress had the authority under the Constitution to regulate commerce, it also had the power to delegate that authority to the agencies it created. Thus, the myriad of federal agencies was born and ordained! And the regulatory beast grew and continues to grow ever larger with the increase in complexity and the technical industrialization of our society.

Regulatory Authority, the Separation of Powers, and the Regulatory Process

A fundamental feature of the U.S. Constitution is that it separates powers between the legislative, executive, and judicial branches of government. The common understanding is it provides a "checks and balances" approach to prevent excessive power in any governmental function.

But regulatory law is especially unique and daunting because it has become an unholy combination of law making (legislation), enforcement (executive function), and adjudication (traditionally a court function) all vested in one government body. The Constitutional separation of powers is dramatically muddied and missing.

Congress creates regulatory agencies by statutes. Agencies are normally given specific areas or industries to oversee, monitor and control. They usually have the power to create law through regulation writing and publication. They have authority to investigate and enforce compliance with those regulations through inspectors, agents, and enforcement officers. They rule on disputes and enforce their actions through administrative law judges, hearing officers, or appeal boards. While appeals to the federal court system are ultimately available, the courts seldom interfere with agency determinations.

Legislative power – When agencies make rules, usually called regulations, they exercise legislative power. The regulations they issue have the force and effect of laws. They have the same level of authority as statutes passed by Congress. Only two criteria limit the rules made by agencies. An agency cannot write rules that exceed the scope of the statute that created the agency, and it cannot write rules that violate any provision of the Constitution. Agency authority is limited typically to particular defined areas of responsibility, such as workplace safety, the environment, or securities trading. Congress must set standards for the agencies that give them direction and scope.

Agencies have to follow rules when they write regulations. They must abide by the procedural requirements imposed by The Administrative Procedure Act. These rules provide that agencies must publish all proposed regulations before they are issued. They have to invite public comment. Interested persons can comment in writing and at public hearings. Agencies must respond to any responses received by either modifying the rules or explaining why no changes were made.

A regulation becomes final when it is published in the Federal Register. It is later included the Code of Federal Regulations. In addition to regulations, agencies issue a tremendous volume of rules, opinions, and guidelines that supplement them.

Enforcement – Agencies have the authority to police the regulations they issue. In general, this means they have the legal authority to verify compliance with the rules they set and enforce them when they find violations. Agents, officers, and inspectors of the agencies themselves conduct the enforcement actions. They can be armed, and they have the right to audit, test, inspect, issue subpoenas and obtain search warrants. In some situations, they can make arrests. Some health and safety inspections do not even require warrants. Enforcement can result in fines, seizures of property, and the closures of businesses.

An administrative agency itself cannot imprison a violator, but it can develop a criminal case and refer the offender to the Department of Justice for criminal prosecution in the federal courts.

Adjudication – When an agency finds violations of its regulations, the most common resolution is a negotiated settlement between the agency and the violator. These settlements usually involve agreements to change behavior and pay fines. Most violators settle to avoid a formal complaint (that is public record) and to avoid a costly process to adjudicate the case.

The judicial authority of agencies is separate from the judicial branch of the government. The administrative law judges, hearing officers, or other judicial mechanisms they contain are usually part of the agency itself. There are a few exceptions where the judicial function is at least organizationally removed from the agency, but all agency judicial processes lack some of the elements guaranteed by the Constitution and the federal judiciary. Some of these lost rights include the prohibition of warrantless searches and seizures, the rules of evidence, and the right to trials by jury. Agency hearings typically review the record and the facts, listen to the testimony of witnesses, and review the applicable law. Whether the enforcement officers of the agencies do terrific jobs, or there is some bias in the hearings, the record shows that the agencies uphold their own findings in the vast majority of cases!

A violator has an appeal right to an agency board or commission that governs the agency. Once the agency appeals are exhausted, the administrative law judge's decision is the final order.

Most agency decisions are subject to judicial review. While it may sound like some degree of fair treatment is finally evident in the system, judicial reviews are very limited. A person contesting an agency finding cannot obtain court review until all administrative remedies are exhausted. This means full adjudication in the agency system and review by the agency board or commission. Even then, courts are limited in their reviews.

The courts accept the facts found by the agency; there are no further hearings on what happened or why. The courts only review two aspects of the agency process: did the agency exceed its authority, or did the agency violate some provision of the Constitution? This is a very narrow analysis of the cases. And courts seldom overrule agency decisions.

An agency might exceed its authority if through regulations or actions it attempts to control, limit, or prohibit something outside of the subject area of the statute granting authority to the agency. For example, if the EPA issues regulations that restrict the number of vacation days for all U.S. workers, the agency may be outside of its authority.

An agency might violate a Constitutional provision if it issues rules that restrict a right. An OSHA regulation prohibiting workers from owning guns probably violates the Second Amendment of the Constitution.

Outside of these two specific areas, courts only review the case record of the agency. The agency must provide bases for its decisions and obvious errors in facts can be challenged, but beyond agency procedural errors like these, the courts will not overrule the regulatory process.

In Conclusion

Regulatory law did not exist 150 years ago. It is a phenomenon of modern times. Did the writers of the Constitution foresee the need for agencies and their authority? It is doubtful that they saw such a need in the rural America in which they lived. But the Constitution has an attribute of flexibility that has allowed it to "grow" with the passage of time and changes in circumstances.

A bureaucratic mass of agencies that write new laws at an ever increasing pace now rules us. There are currently over 170,000 pages of federal regulations alone. And still, they increase. Everybody is expected to know the law, but that has become impossible due to sheer volume. When politicians attempt to rein in agency and regulation growth, it is typically we the people that object because some good they provide to us personally may disappear.

There is much discussion about the role of regulatory agencies in our government. Many view agencies as contrary to the three branches of government and the controlling forces they bring to each other. They see agencies as costly, limiting business growth, and intruding into every aspect of modern life. Others see them as avenues to a more responsive government that reacts to problems with oversight and guidance. They are saviors in a complex world that out of control business operations and greed could bring to its knees. Both sides are probably right in some ways. But without major changes in our government, we have them and must live with them.

A Story from the Real

The Secretary of the Interior and its Fish and Wildlife Service (FWS) are well known federal agencies. The FWS administers the Endangered Species Act (ESA). It has carried out its mission to protect endangered species with vigor and great success. Many endangered animals, including the American bald eagle and the Florida alligator, have recovered and are no longer endangered because of the exercise of the FWS's authority granted by Congress.

But their activities have not pleased everybody. In the Northwest, the FWS issued an order restricting lumber cutting in a wide area inhabited by the red-cockaded woodpecker and the northern spotted owl. The woodpecker was endangered, and the owl was a "threatened" species.

As might be expected, this order impacted the livelihoods of loggers, sawmill operators, timber and land owners, and others economically dependent on the forest products industry. They organized and filed an action in the U.S. District Court seeking a declaratory judgment that the FWS had exceeded the authority granted to it with the order.

The ESA makes it unlawful for any person to "take" endangered or threatened species, and defines "take" to mean to "harass, harm, pursue, wound, or kill."

In regulations written by the FWS, the word "harm" was further defined to include "significant habitat modification or degradation where it actually kills or injures wildlife by significantly impairing essential behavioral patterns, including breeding, feeding, or sheltering."

The wood products group argued that the statute passed by Congress uses the word harm and defines it. They argued that the agency exceeded its authority when it further defined the word in its regulations to mean habitat degradation.

What do you think? What does the word harm mean?

The district court agreed with our injured woodsmen and issued an injunction (an order stopping the government's enforcement of the regulation). The FWS appealed, and the U.S. Court of Appeals upheld the injunction. The FWS then appealed to the U.S. Supreme Court, and the Court accepted the appeal. The Supreme Court was called upon to define the word "harm!"

As discussed in this chapter, the courts almost always support agency decisions. Congress made the agencies the "experts" and granted them full authority to administer the law and decide the best ways to do that through the regulatory process. The courts will normally not interfere with what they see as an act of the legislative branch. The Supreme Court followed this established rule and overturned the injunction. The FWS was allowed to define harm anyway it thought appropriate to carry out its mission to protect endangered animals.

The Supreme Court explained its decision in that way. After lengthy discussions of the definition of the word "harm," the statute, and the statute's definition of the word, the Court found that the agency's further definition was not only reasonable but even necessary to protect the animals. The Court said that "The plain intent of Congress in enacting this statute…was to halt and reverse the trend toward species extinction, whatever the cost." But the real crux of the decision boiled down to these simple words:

> "The latitude the ESA gives the Secretary in enforcing the statute, together with the degree of regulatory expertise necessary to its enforcement, establishes that we owe some degree of deference to the Secretary's reasonable interpretation.... The proper interpretation of a term such as "harm" involves a complex policy choice. When Congress has entrusted the Secretary with broad discretion, we are especially reluctant to substitute our views of wise policy for his."

So as in most challenges of a federal agency, the folks in Oregon lost the decision, interestingly "no matter what the cost." This situation demonstrates the very extensive power given to federal agencies by the Congress, and the recognition of this power by the courts. Because the Supreme Court had to spend considerable time defining the word "harm," we can see that regulatory actions are frequently questionable and sometimes challenged. We also see that those challenges are very difficult to win.

Chapter 10
Torts

(The Law of Righting Wrongs)

What is tort law? Tort literally means "wrong," and tort law sets the rules for righting wrongs. It provides a set of guidelines for determining when a person (including a business) is held liable for the "wrongs" he, she or it commits or causes.

Our society, and most others, long ago decided that the responsible person must pay for the damages done if he causes an injury. This seems like a simple and just rule, and it is. The complexity comes in determining the circumstances under which a person "causes" an injury that allows for compensation.

Almost all of us in our lives are victims of torts, and probably most of us commit torts. We all want a person that injures us to pay for the injury or loss he caused, and we should all expect to pay for the injuries we cause to others.

Crimes versus Torts

Both crimes and torts involve wrongs, and the two are sometimes related to the same event. Simply stated, a crime is a wrong against society, and a tort is a wrong against an individual.

A crime:

- Violates a criminal statute passed by a federal, state or local government to make reprehensible actions "criminal."

- Is prosecuted by the state - for example, by a prosecutor employed by a state or the federal government.

- Requires a high level of proof - beyond a reasonable doubt.

- Results in loss of life, liberty (aka jail), and/or property (fines) when a conviction results.

A tort in contrast:

- Is a common law principle that permits an injured person to recover damages from the person who caused the injury.

- Is brought personally by the injured party against the party who allegedly caused the injury.

- Requires only a preponderance of the evidence to prevail (51 percent).

- Results in an award of money damages to compensate the injured party and punish the person causing the harm, or in some situations an injunction ordering the defendant to stop the offensive behavior.

Torts Divide into General Groupings:

There are four general categories of torts:

- Intentional torts
- Negligence
- Strict liability
- Negligence *per se* and statutory negligence

Another type of tort, properly categorized as an intentional tort, but often discussed separately, is intellectual property infringement. This category has both property law and tort aspects, and we will look at it in Chapter 11.

Intentional Torts

These are wrongs done with at least an implied intent to harm. For example, if I swing a bat at you, my intent to cause injury is understood. If I miss, I have assaulted you, perhaps causing "injury" in the fear I provoked. If I make contact, my battery on you is complete, and the injury is obvious. There are many intentional torts that the law recognizes. They have common aspects of intent to cause injury, and actually doing so.

If an employee confides in his boss that he has contracted a disease, he may be seeking accommodation, or just some consideration and empathy. The employee undoubtedly expects that the information will be kept confidential. If the boss reveals this information to the employee's co-workers, is an injury caused? Can intent be found?

The law provides tort rules to cover this situation. Invasion of privacy is merely revealing to others information that we would reasonably expect to be confidential. The revelation is an intentional tort. Our employee above could probably recover his damages.

The law similarly provides tort rules to cover the disclosure of false information that injures another. For example, the tort of defamation of character would result if a boss, or even a co-worker, tells others that an employee has a disease when in fact he does not. Spreading an office rumor might very well be a tort!

Intentional torts cover a broad range of deliberate actions. They include all of the following:

Assault – This is the threat of physical harm that causes injury to another. For example, a person walks into a room swinging a chain and states he wants to hurt another. The intended victim falls over furniture trying to escape and is injured. The person with the chain is liable for the injuries under the intentional tort of assault even though he never touched the victim.

Battery – This tort is actual physical contact that causes injury to another. For example, in our incident above, the man with the chain strikes and injures the victim. This is battery, and the chain swinger is liable for the injuries caused.

Invasion of privacy – This is putting information intended as confidential into the public. For example, acquiring medical records and publishing them on the internet.

Defamation – Defamation is stating or writing something about another person that is false. Oral defamation is slander; written is libel. Truth is always a defense. If accused of defamation, the person making the statement must prove it is true. Defamation is the only tort where the injured party may not have to prove damages; if the defamation is in writing and obviously false, the victim can use the courts to clear his name by requesting "assumed damages."

Conversion – This is taking another's property. Damages include not only the value of the property taken, but also any profits made with its use.

Trespass – This tort is entering or using someone else's property. Sometimes damages are hard to prove.

Misrepresentation and fraud – These refer to intentional false statements and deceptions that result in financial losses to another.

False imprisonment – This tort is the placing of another into a confinement from which they cannot escape.

Intentional infliction of emotional distress – This is not what many of us think! This is not an injury such as pain and suffering that is part of damages; it is an extreme action by one person to cause monstrous anxiety and mental damage to another. For example, an employee tells his boss that on the way to work, he saw the boss's child hit by a car when in fact the child was not hit.

The events that lead to intentional torts also often (but not always) result in crimes. O.J. Simpson's situation is perhaps the best case of all time to illustrate this. Someone murdered O.J.'s wife and another person. The police charged O.J. with the crime under a criminal statute. State prosecutors (remember Marsha and Chris?) prosecuted him under state law. The jury had reasonable doubts based on the evidence presented at the trial. The jury acquitted O.J. of the crime.

The victims' families then sued O.J. for an intentional tort - perhaps the extreme version of battery - to recover damages they suffered by the loss of their family members. The families hired their own attorneys. The burden of proof was now just a preponderance of the evidence or just 51 percent. This jury found that O.J. committed the tort and awarded damages of $33 million. O.J. is required to pay the damages to the family - at least to the extent he has the financial ability to do so.

The difference in requirements and results of the two trials is evident. Can you understand how one jury could acquit for murder because they had some reasonable doubt O.J. did it, but that another could still have doubts but find that 51 percent of the evidence showed he did it?

Negligence

The tort of negligence provides an opportunity for recovery of damages when another person is careless. Negligence law provides a set of rules for determining when society will hold a person responsible for carelessness. The rules require:

◻   A duty to the other person.

◻   A breach of that duty.

◻   Injury suffered by the other person.

◻   That the breach caused the injury.

Duty – Society requires all of us to avoid injuring others by our actions - we have a duty to be careful. This includes when we drive, when we interact with others, when we construct buildings, and when we manufacture products. To how many people do we owe this duty? We owe everybody a duty to act carefully in everything we do. But, with a few exceptions, we do not have a duty to take a positive action to help others or prevent their harm by something we do not control.

Businesses have an even higher duty to exercise care. When a business invites people onto its premises to purchase products or services, and when a business sells products or services, our society not only requires a duty to be careful, but a higher duty to actively watch out for customers. A business owes a duty to everyone to be careful; it owes a special duty to look out for its customers! Defining the duty is just the first of the four necessary steps described above.

Breach of duty – How is duty breached? By doing something that may cause injury or by acting in an unreasonable or careless manner. If a business does not take affirmative steps to avoid danger and injury to customers, a breach may occur.

Injury – Before there is negligence, there must be an injury. The mere fact that a duty exists and there is a breach of that duty is not enough. If I am driving recklessly down the street, I have breached my duty to others. If I am lucky and don't hit anything, no injury results, and there is no negligence action possible. Injury may be physical harm or death to a person, or it may be property damage.

Cause – Finally, even if there is a duty, the duty is breached, and there is injury, the cause of the injury must be the breach. If I prepare your tax return, I have assumed a duty to do so carefully. If I charge you for the preparation, I owe a duty to look out for you, and I need to ask questions and explore your financial situation. You may be penalized by the IRS because there are mistakes on your return. If you can show that I did not ask about the money you kept in the mattress, I may have breached my duty to do the correct job. But if the IRS penalized you for not reporting income and you deceived me when I asked about any money you may have at home, I did not cause your injury even if the return I prepared was incorrect. I am not liable, and the damages (the amount of penalties) are not my legal responsibility.

There is also a requirement called **"proximate cause"** that means the injury must have been foreseeable by the negligent party. In other words, even though careless conduct caused the injury, if the resulting injury could not have reasonably been anticipated, there is no liability under negligence law. As an example of this consider a speeding motorist who strikes a deer crossing the road. The deer's head separates and is thrown into a passing car severely injuring the occupant. At least one court has recently ruled that "proximate cause" did not exist because the driver of the speeding car could not reasonably foresee that his speeding would cause such an event and injury. Therefore, there was no negligence.

Many states have comparative negligence laws that require the court to apportion the "cause" among the parties by percentage. For example, in the tax return situation above, if you sue me for the penalties, the court (or jury) could decide that I was 40 percent responsible and you were 60 percent responsible and divide the liability for the damages between us in the same percentages.

Strict Liability/Product Liability

Strict liability used to be a relatively minor area of tort law, relegated to unusual circumstances. That has changed!

In the past, society placed "strict liability" for injuries caused by dangerous acts. The duty of care was absolute. If a person was engaged in an inherently dangerous activity, such as using explosives or keeping wild animals, it did not matter how much care he exercised. The breach was automatic. If an injury to another resulted, the person conducting the activity was liable. This basic rule still applies.

But strict liability has broadened its scope. It is applied now to product liability. If a product is made and sold and it is defective and causes injury, the manufacturer and seller are liable for the damages caused. It does not matter how carefully the manufacturer designed the product, how well it managed the manufacturing process, or how tightly the quality control function operated. If a defective product causes injury, "we were careful and met our duty" is not a defense.

Strict liability has serious ramifications for business operation. Consider a company that manufactures and sells medical equipment. It has the brightest engineers, a very modern facility, and a redundant quality review process. But if one of the company's machines injures a patient, chances are a design flaw will be found that caused a malfunction. The company is liable automatically because it sold a defective product. Liability can be extreme in dollar amounts.

Negligence Per Se/Statutory Liability

The final torts we will discuss arise from liability under statutes. Under negligence *per se*, the law considers any injury caused by violation of a statute to be automatic negligence. For example, if I am speeding and I cause an accident, I am negligent and liable because I was violating the speed limit law. The injured party must still prove his damages, but the burden shifts to me to prove that I did not breach my duty of care, rather than the normal requirement that the injured party must prove that I did.

Many statutes give us rights to sue those who are in violation of them. For example, several statutes create a legal right for individual citizens to sue polluters. Some of these statutes also provide for "statutory damages," which are stated award amounts if the citizen prevails. Proving damages may not be necessary under these statutes.

Dram Shop laws carry an odd name derived from old liquor store practices that sold alcohol by the dram (⅛ of an ounce). Under these laws, which have been adopted by all of our states, if a bar or restaurant sells liquor to a person that has had too much, the store is liable for any damages the customer may cause. This does not forgive the intoxicated person from liability, but it makes the seller also liable. These laws create a high degree of risk for establishments that sell alcoholic beverages. Laws today have been expanded to include in the liability envelope many others including bartenders, businesses and homeowners that serve alcohol at parties, and even amusement parks and sporting events. The great office parties of the past are now almost unknown because of extensions of the Dram Shop laws!

Defending Tort Claims

We began our discussion of torts with a statement that almost all of us occasionally commit torts. After reading the descriptions of the various kinds of torts, it may appear that we are all targets of legal actions to recover damages, even as we go about our daily routines. Even intentional torts can occur. Have you ever repeated a rumor about somebody? Did you verify that it was true?

So is our liability absolute in these cases? The answer is no. There are defenses to tort allegations.

Defense of intentional torts – Certainly, self-defense is a major one. The law permits us to use as much force as is necessary to protect our life or the lives of others. But we are not allowed to injure another person to defend property - ever! Our society places the value of human life above that of property. Even criminal lives are worth more than our property. We do not have the right to injure trespassers or those taking or vandalizing our property unless there is also a real threat to human life. If there is no threat to life, a battery allegation could result in the bad guy receiving a damage award.

As we discussed earlier, we can defend defamation of character by proving the statement was true. But this is dangerous territory, because there may be other torts involved. Maybe a statement was true, but how was the information acquired? Was there an invasion of privacy or a trespass involved?

We can defend against other intentional torts by showing no intent to harm or by showing no damages were caused. For example, if you told me I could borrow your lawn mower, I did not convert it when I used it. If I walk across your lawn, I may trespass, but what are the damages? All torts, except some types of defamation, require the aggrieved party to prove damages. If there are no damages, there is no tort.

Defenses of negligence – First, there is contributory negligence. If the injured party was also negligent, the common law did not allow him to recover. For example, I am negligent if I am speeding. But if I hit a car that ran a stop sign, he was also negligent. The common law would say that neither of us can recover from the other because we were both contributorily negligent.

Only one or two states still recognize absolute contributory negligence. Most states now use comparative negligence that allows the court to determine the degree of negligence and apportion liability based on it. In my car example above, if I was driving just 10 miles over the speed limit, the court may determine that I was only 10 percent responsible and the stop sign runner was 90 percent liable. If I was driving 100 miles per hour, the court might find I was 90 percent liable. Damages would then be allocated based on the percentages found.

Another negligence defense is the assumption of risk. This means that sometimes we know there is a risk of injury in an activity and we agree to that risk when we do it. If I go to a baseball game, I know I could be hit by a foul ball. I assumed the risk, and I cannot recover from the baseball team (or the player) for the careless hit. If I decide to take a dispute "outside" and I am injured in the ensuing "resolution," I cannot sue my opponent for the injuries I receive - whether they were intentionally or negligently caused.

In any negligence claim, the alleged negligent party can escape liability by showing that he met his duty of care, or that his actions were not the cause of the injury. Even under the Dram Shop laws, a person may be able to avoid liability by showing he did his best to stop an intoxicated person from driving.

Insurance – Finally, we protect against tort liability by buying insurance. Given that accidents happen and that sometimes we cause them, insurance provides a safety net for our careless mistakes.

Damages

Any discussion of torts must include at least a brief discussion of damages. Reality requires a view from four perspectives.

First, if there are no damages, a tort usually does not exist. By definition, there must be an injury to meet the legal requirements for a tort to exist. There is the exception for defamation - a person has the right to use the public forum of the court to clear his name if he was obviously libeled, even if there were no actual money damages suffered; he can request assumed damages that may be less than $1!

Second, damages fall into several categories.

Compensatory damages – Compensate for actual losses suffered. They cover lost income, medical expenses, incidental costs, and damage to property. Other compensatory damages cover special injuries such as pain and suffering (that must be proved by convincing medical evidence).

Punitive damages – Punish extreme conduct and hopefully change future conduct. There is usually a requirement that the defendant's behavior was grossly reckless.

Injunctive relief – The court can order the person committing a tort to stop his activities. This form of damages is available when ongoing behavior is causing harm to others, and it can be ordered in temporary form before the case itself is heard in court. A polluter, for example, may be ordered by the court to stop discharging a hazardous substance from its factory immediately.

Compensatory damages for monetary losses are the most common damages; injunctive relief and punitive damages arise in only some special circumstances.

Third, damages must be proved. To say injury occurred without the ability to show it in dollar terms will cause the dismissal of most tort actions. There must be an injury that can be made right through payment of money damages or stopped by an injunction. The injured party must provide evidence that proves the amount of the damages.

Fourth, a valid tort action may exist, but bringing it may be pointless if the defendant has no financial resources. It is an expensive effort to obtain a judgment. And, nothing will be collected if the defendant has no money or assets that can satisfy the judgment. Our society does not have debtor prisons. Therefore, we do not generally sue the indigent. Thankfully, some defendants have insurance!

In Conclusion

Tort law protects us from the bad behavior of others, whether that behavior is intentional or not. If an injury occurs because of another person's intentional or careless conduct, we have the legal right to pursue the damages we suffered because of the person's conduct in the courts.

While tort law often is criticized for its seemingly reckless application that results in huge verdicts for minor injuries, the truth is contrary to that. Judgments almost always reflect the actual monetary loss suffered and proven. In cases of extreme behavior, punitive damages may also result to punish bad behavior and hopefully prevent it in the future. Of course, what businesses and insurance companies choose to do outside of the courtroom in making settlements does not reflect the law; it often reflects a need to get rid of the matter and move on.

A Story from the Real

No discussion of torts could be complete without the infamous story of the older lady burned by McDonald's coffee. Her name was Stella Liebeck, and supposedly she got millions from a crazy tort system for her carelessness while driving a car with hot coffee. The real story is a little bit different from the tale that we hear.

Mrs. Liebeck and her nephew stopped at a McDonald's drive-through for coffee. The nephew was driving. They received their coffee order and then pulled into a parking space so that Mrs. Liebeck could add the creamer and sugar. As she struggled to remove the plastic lid from the Styrofoam cup, the contents spilled on her lap. My guess is that a similar incident has happened to many readers.

Unfortunately for Mrs. Liebeck, the coffee was 185° Fahrenheit. She spent eight days in the hospital. She had third-degree burns on her thighs and groin area and required surgery to remove dead tissue and graft skin. Let's just say that it was a nasty and painful result from a cup of coffee.

The coffee we make in a drip coffee maker at home is about 135°. Some coffee shops serve coffee at 150°. Coffee at the temperature Mrs. Liebeck purchased is a dangerous liquid, and McDonald's was selling it at a drive-in window where they knew people would open, drink, and sometimes spill the coffee. In fact, over 700 people had reported burns before Mrs. Liebeck was injured.

At trial, McDonald's testified that they served the coffee that hot because people bought it to take to work and the high temperature kept it hot until they got there. However, other testimony stated that the coffee was made so hot because cheaper beans could be used as hot water extracts more flavor, and the hot coffee cut down on refills inside the restaurant! I don't know about you, but I buy coffee at the drive-through so that I can drink it on the way to work. And so do a lot of others, and McDonald's knew that.

While McDonald's was trying to justify the super-hot coffee, Mrs. Liebeck's attorney had a different kind of testimony. Doctors and other experts testified about the dangers of 185° liquids, and to make the point, they cooked a chicken in 185° water in the courtroom. And, they showed the court and the jury pictures of Mrs. Liebeck's severe burns. Finally, testimony established that coffee at 150° would not cause third-degree burns, or probably anything more than a loud scream.

The jury awarded Mrs. Liebeck compensatory damages of $200,000, which were reduced to $160,000 because they found her to be 20 percent liable (comparative negligence) for spilling the coffee. The jury also awarded $2,700,000 in punitive damages because they found McDonald's behavior to be reckless. After the jury award, however, the judge lowered the punitive damages to $480,000. Judges are permitted to lower jury awards when they determine them to be excessive. Many states have rules that do not permit punitive damages to be greater than some multiple of actual damages. So, Mrs. Liebeck's trial resulted in a total award of $640,000. But this was not the end.

McDonald's appealed the ruling. Mrs. Liebeck and McDonald's subsequently settled the case for an undisclosed amount, almost certainly less than $640,000.

What is the real story in this case? First, it was not the outrageous situation described by the media. Second, Mrs. Liebeck did not recover "millions" of dollars. Third, the law was correctly applied, and the damages were proper.

McDonald's as a business owed its customers a duty of care. A higher level of care than we owe each other in our day-to-day interactions because McDonald's invites customers to buy its products. The duty of care was to provide reasonable safety on the premises, good and safe products and services, and to look for potential dangers and promptly fix them as soon as possible.

Did McDonald's meet this duty of care? The jury said no. The 185° coffee breached the duty of care. Not hot coffee, but coffee so hot that it was known (remember 700 prior burns) to cause injury. Did McDonald's do anything to look out for its customers? Was this product safe, especially being served at a drive-through window? McDonald's breached every element of the duty of care here. The finding of the jury and the court was unquestionably correct under U.S. tort law.

What about the damages? Before trial, Mrs. Liebeck had requested only $20,000 from McDonald's. This may have been the amount of her insurance deductible. Her actual damages, considering eight days in the hospital, surgery, and a lot of follow-up care were no doubt much more. And this does not even consider pain and suffering from the horrific experience. The actual damages were proper.

Under comparable negligence, which is the law in many states, a jury is permitted to find that both parties shared fault. Here, the jury found that Mrs. Liebeck's actions to remove the lid were partially at fault for her burns; in fact, they determined that she was 20 percent responsible. So her damages were reduced.

The punitive damages are the real message sent to McDonald's in this action. Punitive damages are appropriate when a person acts recklessly without regard for the welfare of others. McDonald's did not intend to hurt its customers, but its behavior in selling such ridiculously hot coffee was found by the jury to be reckless.

Punitive damages serve two purposes. They punish, and they prevent. By awarding punitive damages, the jury let McDonald's know that they could not continue to serve coffee at this temperature. And the following week, the coffee at the same location was reportedly being served at 150°!

By bringing this action, Mrs. Liebeck subjected herself to humiliation that exists to this day, but she also probably prevented hundreds if not thousands of other people from being burned. That is the impact of punitive damages in this case and many others where they are awarded.

There are other issues in this case. What about the cup? Serving 185° coffee in a Styrofoam cup is asking for trouble. The cups get soft at that temperature and tend to either split or cause the lids to pop off, as it did here. Reportedly, the cup manufacturer settled with Mrs. Liebeck.

What about product liability? Remember under this tort, if a product is defective, the seller is liable for any damages it causes. This theory was used in the Liebeck case and in fact the court based its ruling on this cause of action.

What about warranty (see Chapter 15)? Did McDonald's breach the implied warranty of merchantability, or one of the other UCC warranties for food service? Mrs. Liebeck's attorneys also raised this issue, and the court found that McDonald's breached the warranty.

Chapter 11
Intellectual Property

(Protecting Our Creativity)

As might be supposed, intellectual property is created by the human intellect. When the human mind puts ideas into a design, invention, written work, music or art, it makes something of value, and the law attributes this value to the creator and makes him the owner of it. The laws are intended to encourage creativity as well as to protect it. The U.S. Constitution established this property right by granting authors and inventors the exclusive right to their creations (Article 1, section 8). Subsequent statutes have expanded this right and provided mechanisms for acquiring and protecting it.

The Constitution specifically describes patents and copyrights, but the law protects a wider range of intellectual property. The law extends property rights to trade and service marks and trade secrets. In the past 40 years, protections were expanded to protect computer and internet designs as well as the intellectual materials stored within them. In the world economy that exists today, intellectual property rights are protected globally through several treaties.

Intellectual property rights typically belong to the creator, but an inventor, author or artist can sell his rights outright, or license the use of the rights in exchange for royalty payments. And, any material created while in the employment of another, belongs to the employer.

Copyrights

The creators of art, literature, music, choreography, movies, and sound recordings receive copyrights. The author must set the protected property in a permanent means, such as a printed document, art canvas, tape or computer storage medium, film, or sculpture. The material must be original and must be more than mere ideas or concepts. The Computer Software Copyright Act of 1980 extended copyright protection to software.

A work produced in a "tangible medium of expression" creates a copyright automatically under the law. There is no need to register a copyright. It rises automatically under the law. Registration only becomes necessary if there is an infringement. Before an action can be filed in the courts to seek damages for infringement, the copyright must be registered. This requirement gives the U.S. Copyright Office the duty to determine who first published the work. The court will only deal with the infringement, not with the identity of the first source.

Copyright infringement can result in actual damages plus all of the infringer's profits, or statutory damages up to $100,000 as determined by the court. Willful infringement can even result in fines and prison.

The reproduction of copyrighted material does not always result in infringement. The law permits duplication under the fair use doctrine. This doctrine allows use for educational purposes, commentary, news stories, research, and parody. While fair use is permitted, the person using it must be careful. For example, the use of copyrighted material in a "for-profit" school may not qualify for the fair use education exception.

Copyrights last for the life of the author plus 70 years for individual creators. For copyrights granted to a corporation (i.e., the employer of the creator), the life is 95 years from first publication or 120 years from creation, whichever is shorter.

Patents

Patents grant inventors of "genuine, novel, useful, and not obvious" designs, processes, or inventions legal ownership of their innovations. A patent gives the holder the exclusive right to the invention for a period of time.

Patents require application and approval through the U.S. Patent and Trademark Office. A patent application ordinarily contains a description of the invention together with detailed drawings to illustrate and explain the invention or design. After application, there are searches of patent files to assure that the new invention is unique and not similar to something else that already has a patent. Because of the large number of patents and patent applications, this process can take substantial time. If an inventor places the invention in the market before the Patent Office grants the patent, the term "patent pending" notifies others of the patent process and the patent filing date. Patent pending protects the invention and the creator's rights to it.

A short form process called "provisional patent" is also available to establish a filing date. The provisional patent protects the invention for one year until the inventor files a full application. A provisional patent allows testing of the marketability of an invention and provides time for further development and locating financial backing before beginning the full application process.

Patents come in two different flavors. A design patent protects the ornamental features of a manufactured item; it covers shapes and decoration. Some examples include jewelry designs, furniture, beverage containers, computer icons, and fonts. Utility patents protect processes, machines, devices, manufactured items, or chemical compounds that are new and useful. Examples include new motors, appliances, or drugs. Utility patents cover the operation and use of a product, and design patents cover the looks of a product.

Patents have much shorter lives than copyrights. Under current law, a patent for a design is granted for 15 years and a utility patent for an invention for 20 years from the date of filing. There are a few extension opportunities available, the most significant being the extension granted for a new drug equal to the time required for FDA approval of the drug.

Like copyright infringement, the theft and use of a patent creates a legal cause of action for damages. Infringement occurs when there is a "literal use" of the patented design, meaning it is copied. "Equivalent infringement" occurs when a product may have differences, but achieves the same performance in the same way as the protected invention. Equivalent infringement is much harder to show.

Damages for patent infringement are generally determined by the amount of royalties lost to the owner, or by the profits earned by the infringer. The court may also order an injunction to stop any further use or sale of the copied product.

Trade and Service Marks

A trademark is a distinctive symbol or logo that a producer attaches to his products that identify them as belonging to the producer. Trademarks are badges of known quality and allow easy identification of products in the marketplace. A service mark is a distinctive symbol or logo of a service provider. There are many that we know and love. For example, the Coca-Cola logo is a well-known trademark, while the Delta Airlines red triangle and the NBC peacock are familiar service marks. Marks must be unique and cannot be common words or objects.

Trademarks do not have to be registered; simple use will provide protection. But registering the mark provides the owner with a clear date of ownership and use. An owner can register a trademark after the mark is already in use, or when its use will begin within six months. After the owner submits an application, the U.S. Patent and Trademark Office Federal registers the trademark, giving it national protection. Registration can also be made at the state level, but only state protection results. Federal registration lasts ten years, with indefinite renewals available every ten years. After the first registration, the owner must file an affidavit of use between the fifth and sixth year to certify usage and preserve the registration.

Trade mark infringement results when a mark is directly copied, or when a similar mark causes confusion about the supplier of products or services. Damages can be awarded for actual damages proved, and perhaps more commonly, injunctions can be obtained ordering the offender to stop using the mark.

Trade Secrets

Trade secrets are any business information that gives a company an advantage in the marketplace that is not known to the public and that the owner reasonably tries to protect. Examples include customer lists, pricing studies, developmental and marketing plans, and production methods and systems.

Trade secret protection historically relied on tort law, particularly conversion, appropriation, and invasion of privacy to provide protection and damages when trade secrets were violated.

But today most states provide statutory protection through the adoption of the Uniform Trade Secrets Act. This law provides standard definitions of trade secrets, defines violations, and provides for both monetary damages and injunctions to stop the use and spread of the confidential business information. The federal government also recently enacted the Defend Trade Secrets Act of 2016 which provides similar definitions and protections. The federal statute also gives the U.S. District Court the jurisdiction to hear cases brought under the act.

Trade secrets today are protected in most employer and client relationships. Businesses may use formal contracts commonly called nondisclosure agreements (NDA). Companies can seek damages from current or former employees that disclose trade secrets.

Intellectual Property and Electronic Storage and Communication

All forms of intellectual property are protected online and in electronic communications. Today there are widespread efforts to "hack" computer systems to steal or expose computer stored information, but common law, intellectual property law, and cyberlaw protect owners.

Most are aware of the music industry's long and ultimately successful battle to protect its copyrights of recorded music. Massive web transfers of music without compensation to the authors and owners of music were pervasive, and it took years of litigation to stop it. Ultimately the persons originating the music availability, the persons receiving the music and the persons facilitating its transfer (e.g., Napster) were found to be infringing the copyrights, and music owners effectively stopped the massive transfers.

International Factors

With world commerce reaching every country and the internet available almost everyplace, national protection of intellectual property would be almost pointless. Any infringer could simply locate to another country and copy at will. The international community took a series of steps over the years to provide worldwide protections.

The Berne Convention is an international treaty first signed in 1886. It provided for the recognition of intellectual property rights granted by one country in all countries that were signatories. Originally only a few European countries were parties, but over time amendments and additional signatures made the treaty a global agreement.

The World Trade Organization's Agreement on Trade-Related Aspects of Intellectual Property Rights (TRIPS), adopted in 1994, established the current standards for international intellectual property rights and recognition. The international standards are similar to U.S. law because all countries, including the U.S., had to modify their laws to comply with the treaty standards. The global community including 172 countries has now adopted the international standards and rights. In 1996, the World Intellectual Property Organization Copyright Treaty provided for protections of computer software and internet databases.

In Conclusion

Intellectual property is critical in modern industry. Research and development, with the intention of producing new and better products and services, requires huge investments of money. The results of this research, as well as the processes of the research itself, must be protected to encourage the expenditures required for technical and industrial as well as artistic advancement. Intellectual property law protects the creator and the owner of new and useful products, services, art, and aesthetics.

A Story from the Real

If you want to take a break from reading this book, now is a good time. Fire up your computer and find a couple of old songs - one older than the other. In 1964 Roy Orbison, a legendary rock musician wrote and recorded a song called Oh, Pretty Woman. In 1989, the rap group 2 Live Crew recorded a song it wrote called Pretty Woman. 2 Live Crew's version is an obvious copy of the music and some of the words of the Orbison original.

2 Live Crew, as might be expected, changed the lyrics to a crass rendering of the original. While Orbison's lyrics talk of a beautiful woman and a man admiring her, 2 Live Crew's words describe a hairy woman and her bald friend and their perhaps unsavory activities.

Although 2 Live Crew sought permission from the owner of the copyright to use the song, the owner denied it. 2 Live Crew released the song anyway on an album in 1989; the album sold at least 250,000 copies.

The copyright owner sued for copyright infringement in federal court. The U.S. District Court ruled for 2 Live Crew, but the U.S Court of Appeals reversed the ruling. Amazingly, this case was accepted by the U.S. Supreme Court for review!

The Supreme Court found for 2 Live Crew. The Court analyzed the fair use doctrine in the copyright law and found that the 2 Live Crew version was a parody and that parody is a "fair use." Parody copies the style and substance of a work for comic and critical effect. The Court found that humor alone may not qualify as parody; there must be an element of critique or ridicule.

The Justices determined that the 2 Live Crew version of the song was such a comic ridicule. While not condoning the content of 2 Live Crew's song, they found it to be critical of the banal approach to women found in the original song, and a comment on a simpler time and perspective. The Court found that commercial profit was not a prohibiting factor and that the parody version probably had no substantial impact on the market value of the original anyway.

This decision is considered a landmark in copyright law. The Supreme Court had not addressed parody before this case. The copyright statute itself is unclear; it does not use the word parody in defining fair use.

So, if you have a comment about a copyrighted work, and you can present that comment as a comical representation of the original, the fair use rule allows you to plagiarize freely.

Chapter 12
Cyberlaw

(Law of the Cloud)

Cyberlaw provides both civil and criminal laws for regulating activities involving the internet, email, electronic data storage, and electronic privacy. Cybercrime is committed using computers, email, the internet, or other electronic means, including cells phones. E-commerce refers to business conducted via the internet.

The internet grew without any preset legal constraints or rules. It was and still is a unique phenomenon in the modern world. Without the intent to create an entirely new communication and data storage and sharing platform, the creators of the internet brought us a totally new mode of living and working. No one imagined the opportunities it possessed for bad behavior.

"Cyberspace," as the new electronic environment became known, rapidly turned into the premier method of communication, business, and information. Developments in the law to deal with cyberspace issues started slowly and with hesitation. But now, we have a whole new discipline referred to as cyberlaw.

Court Actions

The law began to slowly adapt with the creation of computers in the 1960s. It started with court rulings that applied traditional common law concepts of torts, contracts, privacy, and theft. Later, it grew with a variety of statutes at both the federal and state levels. The internet is international. Its use and its abuse are worldwide and have no real "place" of occurrence. This unfortunately complicated the application of U.S. or any other national standards.

Most of us have some familiarity with the criminal aspects of cyberlaw. Bank account tampering, and copyright and other intellectual property theft, are good examples. But there are other issues. The law had to revise many areas of contract and tort law. For example, if an enforceable contract must be in writing and signed, how is this accomplished in cyberspace? If defamation occurs on the internet, how do we address it?

Many of the first cases dealt with privacy issues because of the large amounts of data that were stored and shared through electronic means. Courts quickly applied right to privacy concepts to such data. They held those storing the information liable for its unauthorized transfer.

The courts resolved contract questions in the 1980s by determining that a cyberspace contract met the definition of "writing" and that pushing the "accept" or "order" button was a legally proper signature.

The courts also quickly provided common law intellectual property rights to software designs. And intellectual property theft was firmly addressed by the courts in *A&M Records, Inc. v. Napster, Inc.*, which effectively led to the demise of widespread online file sharing. But the court resolutions were too slow, and often too specific to one set of facts, to adequately address the myriad of issues coming from rapid internet expansion.

Statutory Protections

Congress began to take notice of electronic data issues as early as 1974, and over the next 35 years passed a multitude of new laws to deal with internet and electronic storage issues. Many of these deal with privacy, illegal access, intellectual property rights, and child protection in cyberspace. State legislatures similarly passed many laws to take care of the issues brought to them by their constituents.

Some of the leading federal statutes include the following:

The Privacy Act of 1974 – This was perhaps the first major statute dealing with the new electronic medium. It made rules about the collection, maintenance, use, and distribution of personal information collected in record systems by federal agencies.

Computer program copyrights – In 1980, Congress added the definition of "computer program" to U.S. copyright law.

The Counterfeit Access Device and Computer Fraud and Abuse Act (CFAA) – This act, passed in 1984, made it a crime to use a computer to obtain (1) restricted U.S. government information, (2) financial records of banks and other financial institutions, or (3) credit reports of consumer reporting agencies. It criminalized the use of counterfeit or stolen access methods, such as cards or pin numbers to access accounts or transfer funds. It also made it a crime to sell devices capable of making unauthorized access. This act has also been applied to employee theft of computer data.

The Electronic Communications Privacy Act of 1986 (ECPA) – This law, which includes the **Stored Communications Act (SCA)**, included transmissions of electronic data via the internet in the prohibitions on wiretaps that previously applied only to telephone calls. Title 2 of this statute, the SCA, prohibited accessing electronic communication systems without authorization.

The Information Infrastructure Protection Act (IIP Act) of 1996 – This act made it a crime to intentionally retrieve information from a protected computer without permission.

The Child Pornography Prevention Act of 1996 (CPPA) – This law attempted to prohibit a broad range of computer transmissions and posts that included children in sexual situations. This law was declared unconstitutional by the Supreme Court in 2002 because it infringed too broadly on the 1st Amendment rights to free speech. Congress followed up with **The PROTECT Act of 2003** which criminalized any illustrations showing child pornography. The Supreme Court subsequently upheld this revision.

The Digital Millennium Copyright Act (DMCA) – This act put two 1996 treaties of the World Intellectual Property Organization (WIPO) into effect. It criminalized the access of copyrighted materials on computer systems and any technology meant to hack into computer systems to get into copyrighted materials.

The Identity Theft and Assumption Deterrence Act of 1998 – This statute criminalized the use of another's identity for any unlawful or unauthorized activity as defined by federal, state or local laws.

The Electronic Signatures in Global and National Commerce Act – In 2000, Congress finally enacted a statute that recognized electronic contracts and electronic signatures on contracts. Although the courts had established this rule of law in the 1980s, this statute codified the rule and gave it universal effect.

The Unlawful Internet Gambling Enforcement Act of 2006 (UIGEA) – This act outlawed the acceptance of payments for bets or wagers that involve the use of the internet and that are prohibited by any federal or state law.

And every state also passed and implemented numerous statutes to protect electronic information and provide for both criminal and civil consequences for violations. Many states protect cyberdata more stringently than the federal laws described above.

In Conclusion

We can expect that cyberlaw will continue to grow. The internet and its usage are expanding rapidly. Like many other aspects of modern civilization, the variety of ways people can use it for both good and bad are nearly unlimited. As the internet matures, the law will adjust.

A Story from the Real

Sometimes, despite the best efforts of the legislative branch of government to pass laws that protect society, its efforts are not successful. Cyberlaw is a new area of law, and although almost 50 years have passed since computers arrived in our lives, the ability of government to regulate the use of this technology is still a work in process. Consider an issue that did not arise until 2012 that impacts just about every computer user.

In 2012 a student researcher discovered that Google was installing "cookies" on computers that tracked and reported a user's web browsing.

Google used this information to sell advertising on its websites. By tracking the web browsing of its users, Google was able to develop a database of "interests" of the users. This information was used to direct advertisers to persons potentially interested in their products. What made Google's actions particularly bothersome, however, was that the cookies they were inserting bypassed the settings made by users.

Many of us do not really understand the workings of our computers or the options we have in using them. But, we have an option to deny cookie placement on our machines. It is a simple check the box option in the settings. Of course, computers, when purchased, do not have this option checked. But even for those that understood and elected the option, Google secretly bypassed the option and allowed the placement of tracking cookies.

All of us have experienced a sort of *deja vu* when we do a search. The next day we receive multiple advertisements for the product we were researching or for related products. Sometimes it's unsettling, sometimes just bothersome, and sometimes it's helpful. But it does seem to be an invasion of our privacy, especially when we checked the option to block the tracking of our browsing.

After the discovery of Google's bypass cookies, numerous lawsuits were filed across the country. The parties agreed, and the courts ordered, that the cases be consolidated in the U.S. District Court in Northern California (Google's location) for one trial as a class action.

The plaintiffs alleged multiple violations of federal and state cyberlaw statutes and common law actions based on fraud and tort. The district court ruled for Google on all of the actions; the plaintiffs appealed to the U.S. Court of Appeals.

The court of appeals sustained the district court's ruling except for one cause of action.

The court of appeals found that because Google was a party to intercepted browsing, there could be no violation of the Wiretap Act. The Wiretap Act does not prohibit the interception or recording of a non-governmental call when one of the parties agrees to the intercept.

Google by its very actions of conducting and using the browser information was one of the parties. Therefore, Google did not violate the Wiretap Act.

Under the Stored Communications Act, the intrusion must be to a "facility" that stores communications. After a lengthy discussion of the Congressional statutory history and intent, the court found that a personal computing device was not a "facility" as intended by the statute.

And under the Computer Fraud and Abuse Act, the court found that the plaintiffs had failed to show they suffered any monetary losses as required by the statute.

So much for Congressional action to protect us!

The court of appeals similarly ruled on the state statutes that were invoked by the plaintiffs. Like the federal statutes, the court found that none of them covered this kind of computer invasion. The state legislatures did no better than the Congress in shielding residents in their use of computers.

The court did find for the plaintiffs, however, under the California Constitution and California common law tort. (The court applied California law because federal courts apply the law of the state where the action is located, which here was in California). The court found that under California law, the right to privacy has the following requirements:

> "First, the plaintiff must possess a legally protected privacy interest. Second, the plaintiff's expectations of privacy must be reasonable. Third, the plaintiff must show that the intrusion is so serious in nature, scope, and actual or potential impact as to constitute an egregious breach of the social norms."

The court ruled that Google's wily actions (to go around the plaintiffs' choices about cookies) could reasonably lead to a finding that there was an invasion of privacy under these requirements of California law.

So the case was sent back to the trial courts for determination under state law. In the end, Google settled, agreeing to stop going around cookie blockers and paying $5 million to several public consumer privacy advocacy groups.

It is interesting to note that the various federal and state statutes failed to provide protections, even though Congress and the various state legislatures passed scores of cyberlaw protection statutes. Under the facts of this case, the court was required to use its common law authority to apply the law that was "on the books" for hundreds of years already.

Chapter 13
The Uniform Commercial Code (UCC)

(Trying to Make Legal Issues Lucid)

Each state has its own laws, and while state laws are similarly based on common law principles, there are individual differences and unique statutes in each. Today, business and many personal activities cross state lines as a matter of course. Variations in the law affecting business transactions and personal relationships create too many obstacles to the smooth conduct of legal proceedings and commerce. There was a need to standardize the laws across state borders.

The National Conference of Commissioners on Uniform State Laws (NCCUSL) and the American Law Institute (ALI), work with legal scholars to create standardized laws. These organizations do not create law, but they write and present Uniform Acts to the states for consideration. They have developed and presented over 100 uniform laws to the states. Some of those that were widely adopted include The Uniform Partnership Act, Uniform Probate Code, Uniform Transfers To Minors Act, and of course, the UCC.

All 50 of the states and all U.S. territories adopted the UCC. It is an important statute because it makes the law of sales contracts and other business transactions uniform among all of the states. The UCC provides rules of law for sale and lease contracts, negotiable instruments, bank and funds deposits and transfers, bailments, and credit security involving personal property. It is a critical part of business law in the U.S. today.

Perhaps the UCC itself provides the best statement of purpose:

"The Uniform Commercial Code must be liberally construed and applied to promote its underlying purposes and policies, which are: (1) to simplify, clarify, and modernize the law governing commercial transactions; (2) to permit the continued expansion of commercial practices through custom, usage, and agreement of the parties; and (3) to make uniform the law among the various jurisdictions."

UCC Articles

We briefly discuss each of the areas covered by the UCC below.

UCC - Article 1 - General Provisions – Article 1 is an introductory chapter that provides a statement of purpose and defines the various terms used in the statute.

UCC - Article 2 - Sales – Article 2 deals with commercial sales of goods. It applies only to sales of goods, not to sales of services or real estate. It does not cover sales to consumers. Article 2 does not change the basic rules of contract law as explained in the next chapter, but it does allow businesses flexibility in making contracts and changing them.

UCC - Article 2A - Leases – Article 2A applies many of the rules of contracts to leases.

UCC - Article 3 - Negotiable Instruments – Article 3 standardizes the rules for negotiable instruments such as loan notes, checks and other promises to pay. See Chapter 16.

UCC - Article 4 - Bank Deposits and Collections and UCC - Article 4A - Funds Transfers –Articles 4 and 4A create standardized rules for the processing of checks, bank deposits and electronic transfers of funds. See Chapter 16.

UCC - Article 5 - Letters of Credit – Article 5 provides rules for the issuance and use of letters of credit. A letter of credit is used to guarantee payment, typically for the delivery of goods. International commerce relies on them. A letter of credit is a notice from a bank that a customer has been granted credit in the amount designated. The letter also states that an amount up to the line of credit is payable to a third party upon presentation of required documentation. When the documentation is provided, the bank must issue the funds to the designated payee.

Letters of credit are common in international trade. Because international law does not have an effective enforcement element, parties to contracts that are in different countries must protect their rights to payment for goods delivered. The letter of credit process guarantees payment by a large bank to the provider of the goods when the provider shows delivery of goods.

A typical arrangement might involve a manufacturer in Asia and a buyer in the U.S. The buyer contracts for the purchase of goods with the Asian producer and provides a letter of credit from an international bank. The bank is bound by the terms of the letter to pay the Asian producer the amount stated when the producer provides a bill of lading (a document provided by a shipper when it takes delivery of goods that assigns the title to the purchaser) or other stated evidence of delivery or acceptance.

UCC - Article 6 - Bulk Sales – Article 6 provides protections to creditors of businesses with inventories that are financed by the creditors. Article 6 requires that single buyers of bulk amounts of inventory (outside the ordinary course of business) must provide notice to any creditors having an interest in the inventory. The seller is required to provide a listing of all creditors claiming an interest and the buyer must notify them of the sale. The buyer must also retain records of purchases for six months. If the buyer and seller do not follow the provisions of Article 6, the creditors can seek damages from the buyers or void the sale. The rules of Article 6 also apply to auctioneers selling bulk amounts of inventory.

Article 6 protects creditors from the unscrupulous acts of businesses that may try to sell off large amounts of inventory without sending the proceeds to the creditors as may be required under financing agreements.

UCC - Article 7 - Documents of Title – Article 7 provides rules for the storage and shipment of goods for commercial purposes. The rules apply to warehousing of goods and the shipment of goods by carriers. The necessity for such rules has existed for hundreds of years and was well established in the common law rule of bailments. Under bailment, legal rights and duties are imposed by the law when parties agree to a bailment.

A bailee (one who holds, but does not own the goods) has rights to temporary control and possession, perhaps use of the goods as stated in the agreement between the parties, compensation, and reimbursement for expenses. A bailee has the duties to care for the property and to surrender possession and control according to the terms of the agreement.

A bailor (the owner of the property) has a duty to deliver the goods without hidden defects that could injure the bailee, and has the right to receive the property back in the same condition as he gave it to the bailee.

Violation of any of the duties or rights by the other party is a tort creating a right to recover damages.

Article 7 recognizes and reinforces all of these duties and rights and provides for various documents to establish title to goods and to transfer title to goods in storage or transit. The two most common documents involved in bailments include:

A **warehouse receipt** – A warehouse receipt is a document that provides proof of ownership of stored goods in a warehouse or other place for safekeeping.

A **bill of lading** – This is a document issued by a carrier that itemizes a shipment of goods and assigns the title of the shipment to a named party.

The UCC provides that the parties can make warehouse receipts and bills of lading negotiable. This means that the rights to the goods they represent can be transferred to others for value. If the transfer takes place in the normal course of business, and there are no known claims or defects involving the goods, the transferee takes the goods free from any claims of others regarding the goods that may come up later.

Article 7 also provides rules for electronic evidence of title. While warehouse receipts and bills of lading are written documents, modern commerce relies on electronic means of ownership and transfer of title. Because most bailment documents are negotiable, electronic maintenance requires special protections and rules to assure that ownership is properly known and recorded. Article 7 provides rules for establishing electronic records and transfers that protect the parties and their creditors.

UCC - Article 8 - Investment Securities – Article 8 provides rules for the handling of securities by companies issuing them and by brokers. See Chapter 16.

UCC - Article 9 - Secured Transactions – Article 9 provides uniform rules for the creation and recording of security agreements that protect a creditor's interest in collateral for a loan. See Chapter 17.

In Conclusion

Uniform laws have enabled businesses and individuals to deal with multi-state legal matters more easily. Standardized rules and the UCC's emphasis on liberal interpretation and fair dealing allow businesses to operate and function more efficiently and with fewer legal disputes.

A Story from the Real

A woman moved to the west coast and hired a moving company to transfer her household goods. Upon arrival, she placed the goods in temporary and then permanent storage. The moving company issued a warehouse receipt.

Two years later the woman went to the storage location to retrieve some of her property. She found her goods to be in disarray, with some pieces missing and others damaged or broken. She filed a claim with the moving company, and they refused to pay. She sued.

The mover argued that the woman did not prove negligence and he, therefore, had no liability for damages. The court found that under the state's bailment law (which was UCC Article 7), there was no requirement to prove the elements of negligence. The mover was a warehouseman under the statute, even if he did not realize it, and as such he was required to exercise ordinary care over the goods in his possession. If he returned the goods in a damaged state, or if they were missing, he did not meet his duty. The duty and the breach of duty did not require proof because the statute established them.

The court found not only that the woman did not have to prove negligence, but that once the goods were discovered to be damaged, the warehouseman had the burden of proving that he exercised ordinary care. He offered no evidence to support his level of care.

This situation shows how a bailee, one who takes property and agrees to hold it for another, is held to high standard of care. If the bailee returns property damaged, or loses it, he must prove that he was not careless. Sometimes the law requires that we prove a negative!

Chapter 14
Contracts

(The Law of Promises That Must Be Kept)

Society expects its members to keep promises. What an incredible concept this is! And it's a concept we must have.

Contract law is nothing more than society's rules for enforcing promises. Every day it impacts us, our employers, our businesses, and everybody else with whom we interact. Did you enter any contracts today? Almost surely you did. When you went to work this morning, you formed a contract. When you ordered that sandwich at lunch, you made a contract. When you bought this book, you entered a contract. Every day, we follow the rules for keeping promises, often without any thought of what we are doing. The law of contracts is firmly ingrained in all of us.

Of course, not all promises are enforced. We make many promises that the law will not enforce. Courts will only compel contract promises that meet a detailed set of rules. This set of rules, mostly developed over hundreds of years in common law, is what we call contract law.

Contract Law Rules

For a promise to be enforced by the legal system, it must meet a set of requirements. These rules are summarized as follows:

- There must be an agreement.
- There must be consideration.
- There must be mental competency.
- There must be a legal purpose.
- There must be mutual assent to the terms of the agreement.
- There must be proper "form."

Agreement

Agreement refers to the exchange of promises that occurs when a contract is formed. It arises when one party makes an offer to perform in exchange for another party's performance or promise to perform, and the offer is accepted. Performance can be doing something, paying money, or not doing something. The offer and acceptance must be certain, timely, and apparent.

If a lawyer meets with a prospective client and they discuss the client's problem and the lawyer tells the client what he might do to help him, there is no agreement. There were no promises made. However, if the lawyer states that for a given amount of money he will represent the client and work with him to solve his problem, the lawyer has made an offer. He discussed what he would do, and the efforts he would make. If the client accepts the offer, we will have a contract. The lawyer promised to do certain stated work to resolve the problem, and the client promised to pay for the work performed.

Consideration

Consideration means that value has to be exchanged by the parties. Both have to provide value to the promises. Value means "legal value," which includes money value, and/or the value of granting or giving something up. For example, a promise to not work in a particular area in exchange for money (this is commonly called a "Covenant Not to Compete" or a "Non-compete Agreement") is consideration. Such agreements are often part of employment contracts. A non-compete agreement is basically being paid not to work; one party to the agreement promises to do nothing! But he is giving up a right to do something he has a legal right to do, and that has legal value.

In the potential contract above between lawyer and client, the value provided by the lawyer is his personal services and expertise. The value the client provides is money. We have consideration.

But what if a person agrees not to work because he is just trying to help a new competitor? Is this a contract? No, because the new competitor has promised nothing of legal value. He cannot force the other party to keep his promise to not work because there is no consideration on his part.

Legality

Contracts must have "legal purpose." This means that the courts will not enforce a contract that contains a promise to violate the law or public policy. The mafia cannot go to court to enforce its gambling, prostitution, or murder contracts. Other contract requirements may be present, but the purpose is illegal. Public policy considerations reflect society's desire not to enforce contracts that harm the public welfare, health, safety or common good. For example, the courts will probably not enforce a lease that discriminates against overweight people.

Similarly an accountant cannot enter into an enforceable contract to falsify financial statements to obtain some benefit for a client. The professional could not enforce the payment of his fee in court. The purpose is either illegal or at least against public policy.

Competency

The law does not hold incompetent people to their promises. Our society recognizes that some people cannot make promises and that others should not be held to their promises because they are unable to make reasonable decisions.

People that the law considers unable to make promises are those that are mentally incompetent and have been so ruled by a court of law. Typically, incompetent people have guardians appointed who act for them. An incompetent person cannot make a contract. Any agreement signed by an incompetent person is void.

Other people may not be held to their promises because the law recognizes their inability to make reasonable decisions. This group includes minors, those who claim incompetency (without a court ruling), and perhaps those under the influence of drugs or alcohol. When a member of this group signs an agreement, it is said to be voidable, which means that the person can seek to be released from his promise if he shows minority, incompetency or other circumstance indicating an impaired mental state.

Minors, however, can make contracts that are enforceable. They do it every day. For example, children who work make contracts (e.g., babysitters make contracts), and children who buy products or services make contracts. All of these are good contracts. BUT, the law allows minors to cancel a contract at any time before they reach the age of majority. The adult in the contract, however, cannot cancel it.

When a contract is formed, we assume the other person's competency (as he assumes ours). However, he may later be able to show that he was not competent when he made the contract. He may do this, for example, by showing medical evidence of mental illness, or by showing that he was a minor. If he proves his incompetency, he can void the contract, and the law releases him from his promises. Of course, if the party cancels, both parties are released from any promises not yet completed. And, the law typically does not allow for one party to gain financially by canceling - the parties must both be left in fair financial positions.

Mutual Assent

This requirement simply means that enforceable promises must be understood and voluntarily given. Two competent parties can make an agreement, with legal purpose and consideration, and not have a mutual understanding of the facts or the subject matter. Occasionally, human nature being what it is, one party may make a misrepresentation to the other party. Or, one of the parties may make the promise involuntarily. In these situations, the law may not enforce the promises.

The basic rules for valid mutual assent are simple, but maybe a bit confusing. If both parties do not understand what they agree to do, there is no contract. If one party misrepresents the subject matter of the agreement, the other party can cancel. But if one party is mistaken about the subject matter, and the other party did not misrepresent, the contract cannot be cancelled.

Let's consider an example. If an accountant enters into an engagement contract with a client to represent him in a tax audit, and they agree to this for a set fee, the accountant has contracted to represent the client by all reasonable means. But if it turns out that the client is being investigated for criminal activity, we may have a voidable contract because neither party understood the subject of the government inquiry. Similarly, if the client lies and tells the accountant he is being audited but knows that he is under criminal investigation, the accountant has the right to void the contract on learning the truth. In these situations, there was not a "meeting of the minds" about what the parties were promising. The client cannot recover damages from the accountant for failing to perform when neither party knew, or one was misled about the real job to carry out.

An extension of mutual assent is duress. If a party is forced to enter a contract, or overly pressured to do so, he may be able to void the contract. For example if a boss threatens to fire an employee unless he buys a product from the company, there is duress. The contract could later be canceled.

Mutual assent issues should not arise, but they frequently do. Written contracts with clear language are often used to avoid misunderstandings.

Form (aka "The Statute of Frauds")

The rule of form is meant to reduce the opportunity for fraud in contracts. It requires certain contracts to be in writing to be enforceable. The types of agreements that must be in writing are those that are most susceptible to mistake, misrepresentation, or misunderstanding. Without a writing, the promises in these contracts will not be enforced.

The types of contracts that must be in writing to be enforceable include all contracts about real estate, contracts in contemplation of marriage ("prenups"), contracts for the sale of goods for more than $500, and contracts for personal services that last more than one year.

For example, a contract to perform as a professional football player for two years for a team must be in writing to be enforceable because it lasts for more than a year.

Contract Defenses

Even if a valid contract is formed, there may be grounds to cancel it. There are sometimes enforceable promises that do not have to be kept and the parties can be discharged from their obligations under a contract.

The most obvious way to escape a contract is to show that one of the six necessary elements described in the above contract elements discussion is missing or deficient. This is the most common way that contracts are contested.

For example, one of the parties might argue that the agreement was not definite in its wording and the performance required cannot be determined. Or there may be an argument that consideration was not present. As in our example earlier in this chapter, if a party promises to not compete with another, he can argue later that there was no consideration from the other party. Attempts are made to show that a contract had an illegal purpose. My favorite is the car dealer that argued that offering a car as a prize for a hole-in-one at a charitable golf tournament was illegal because it was akin to gambling (the dealer lost). Or perhaps one of the parties will try to show he was incompetent because he had too much to drink. And there is always the argument that duress or misrepresentation was present, thus defeating the mutual assent requirement.

The law also recognizes that some contracts cannot be fulfilled. This usually requires the occurrence of events beyond the control of either party. An example includes the destruction of the subject matter of the contract. If a warehouse burns down, its owner cannot deliver the goods it contained. Or something else beyond the control of the parties may prevent performance. Such "acts of God" include storms, floods, wildfires, and earthquakes as examples. Death of one of the parties may prevent a contract from being completed, as well as war, civil disruption, or infrastructure failure.

Many commercial contracts contain *"force majeure"* (meaning something beyond the control of the parties) clauses that attempt to define the circumstances that may prohibit performance under the contract. These clauses typically address "acts of God" and other unanticipated events such as machinery breakdowns or employee strikes.

In all situations where one of the parties claims an unforeseeable event as the cause for a contract to be terminated, he must show that the event prohibited his performance and that it was not due to his negligence or lack of reasonable planning. For example, a party may claim that a severe storm is a cause to cancel to a contract, but if his ability to perform was not directly impacted, he cannot escape his contractual obligations.

Whenever a contract is terminated before full performance, both parties have an obligation to restore the other party to his pre-contract financial status. If one party has partially performed before an act of God prohibits completion of the contract, for example, he may seek payment for the part of the contract he completed.

Damages

Like tort law, damages are the bottom line in the enforcement of contracts. If one of the parties breaches the contract (does not perform his promises), he must pay the other party the damages suffered. These are generally money damages that represent the "loss of the contract" - such amounts may include the cost of replacing the promises of the breaching party, lost opportunity costs, and incidental costs to make the injured party whole.

Contract damages must be "mitigated." This means that if a contract is breached, the party who suffers damages must take reasonable actions to reduce the damages as much as possible. This would include finding a new supplier or a new service provider as soon as possible to reduce the amount of loss. The party who seeks damages can only recover the amount that he could not prevent.

In some circumstances, the court may also award "equitable damages," which require the breaching party to perform or cease some activity. Equitable damages are only available when money damages cannot adequately compensate the injured party or when a particular action is required to carry out the agreement. For example, the court may award specific performance that requires a breaching party to keep a promise to sell a unique good that cannot be purchased anyplace else. Money damages, at any amount, could not provide a remedy for the injured party. All real estate is considered unique, so specific performance is available as a remedy if a party breaches a real estate sale contract.

The courts will not, however, order specific performance of a personal services contract no matter how unique the services promised. Public policy will not permit forced labor. So if a professional football player breaches a contract with his team by refusing to play, the owner cannot obtain a court order requiring his performance. The owner is limited to money damages. The player will not be compensated, and the owner may be able to recover lost revenue because he did not show for the game. Also, the player probably signed a non-compete or similar agreement as part of his contract that prohibits him from working for others if he breaches. This is the general situation for professional athletes. They cannot be forced to play for a particular team with which they are under contract, but they can be prohibited from playing for any other team in the league for the length of the contract.

The Uniform Commercial Code

Articles 2 and 2A of the UCC that apply to contracts and leases (which are contracts) do not change contract requirements, but they encourage the parties to deal fairly with each other, and they allow the enforcement of contracts when technical issues may otherwise prevent enforcement.

For example, contract law requires that all terms of the agreement be stated and understood by the parties, or there is not an enforceable contract. Under the UCC, terms can be inferred if the facts otherwise show that the parties intended to make a contract. This is commonly referred to as the "gap-filling rule," and it allows for unstated terms to be "filled in" by the court to make the contract complete. The purpose is to encourage the completion of contract agreements that may have omitted some of the details.

The UCC also allows for the acceptance of contracts with terms different from the original offer, unlike contract law that requires a "mirror image" acceptance. This means that a party can accept an offer with different terms inserted so long as these terms do not materially affect the agreement and are not objected to within a reasonable time. This allows contracts to move forward without delays.

The required signatures and written agreement required under contract law are not necessary under the UCC so long as one of the parties sends a written confirmation of an oral agreement and the other side does not give a written notice of objection within ten days.

Finally, under common law, a contract cannot be modified without additional consideration from the party wanting to change the terms; under the UCC, consideration for modification is not required. This allows business agreements to be more flexible and to change if a situation requires.

The UCC also standardizes the risk of loss. This means that if the goods are in some way damaged or destroyed before completion of the contract, the UCC identifies the party that suffers the loss. Before the UCC, state title laws frequently determined the question of loss and were difficult to apply and varied from state to state.

The above does not provide all of the differences between common law contracts and Article 2. There are also other differences all intended to make contracts among businesses easier to make and complete.

The UCC contract provisions apply primarily to commercial (business to business) sales transactions. They standardize contract rules and ease the conduct of business among merchants. Critical to the application of the UCC to contract law is the "good faith and fair dealing" standard of the statute. Good faith means that the parties conduct themselves honestly, openly and fairly, and fulfill their obligations in accordance with industry standards and practices. Deception, dishonesty and incomplete disclosure will generally cause a party to bear legal responsibility under the UCC.

In Conclusion

Contact law rules can be complex and voluminous. They are intended to make sure that the promises that society enforces are good promises, valid promises, valuable promises, and clearly stated promises. The myriad of rules attempts to remove uncertainty about which promises must be kept!

A Story from the Real

Jay was 16 years old. He completed driver's training at school and obtained a driver's license. He wanted a car. Unfortunately for Jay, his mother said no. Sound familiar?

For most teenagers, this would be the end of the story because parents, as dreadful as they may be, rule. But Jay was not accepting of such adult limitations in his life. After all, Jay worked 20 hours per week at a local grocery chain and earned $250 per week. He had saved a little over $1,000. Why shouldn't he have a car? Jay visited Rally Rob's Used Cars, a neighborhood dealership. Rally Rob had cars to sell.

Rob discussed cars with Jay. He knew Jay was 16 and he learned of Jay's job and his savings. He told Jay he could work a deal with him. Yesterday, Rally Rob was at the auto auction and purchased a beautiful 1996 Ford Tauris for $800. It was properly appointed with big 20-inch chrome wheels. He told Jay he could sell it to him for $3,000. The terms would be $1,000 down and $200 per month for two years (that's about 18% interest). Jay could easily afford that and quickly agreed to the deal. Rob and Jay signed a purchase contract and an installment agreement.

Rob immediately sold the installment agreement to his brother-in-law's finance company "Thomas Auto Finance, Inc." Thomas paid $1,000 for the two-year agreement, and of course, Rob agreed to reimburse him for any losses if Jay didn't pay.

To register the car, Jay needed a driver's license (he had that), a title (he had that from Rob with the lien properly recorded on it), and insurance. Rob helped Jay with insurance by sending him to his wife's insurance agency (Terrie Covers, LLC) that sells car policies for monthly premiums. Terrie's advice was to buy a minimum amount policy ($25,000 of liability coverage) with no collision or other coverage. The monthly rate for this policy for Jay was $80. Jay paid for one month, and with policy in hand, Rob was able to register the car in Jay's name.

So everybody (except one) was happy. Jay had his car. Rob made $1,200 in one day, Thomas would make $1,400 if Jay paid the loan, and even Terrie would make a commission of about $25 for each month Jay paid. Jay's friends were ecstatic as the group now had wheels. Mom would not be happy, but she didn't know about it - yet.

So what do you think? Can this happen? The answer is that in many states this can happen. There is, however, potential ruin in the scheme. Ruin is named Mom. Jay kept the car a secret for three months, parking it a couple of blocks from home and keeping his mouth tightly sealed. Jay knew the strategy, but his friends were not as clandestine. After three months, one of them let his parents know that Jay had a car. That was not really a serious revelation. Lots of kids have cars. Unfortunately, parents occasionally run into each other and the knowledgeable one made an offhand comment to Mom about Jay's car.

An inquisition resulted. Jay was outed, and he finally confessed to his Mom that he bought a car. He also assured her there was nothing she could do about it. Unlike Jay though, Mom knew a little bit about how the world works. She knew that although the law permitted minors to make contracts (they are competent under the law once they reach the age of reason - usually considered about seven or eight years old), she also knew that minors have the right under the law to cancel a contract until they reach majority (18 in most states). Most importantly, she knew that a parent has the legal right to cancel a contract on behalf of a minor.

Mom visited with Rally Rob and told him she was canceling the contract. Of course, she had to return the car. She also demanded that Rob return the $1,000 that Jay had put down and the $600 of monthly payments he had made. Rob knew that Mom could cancel the contract, but he did not agree that he should return the money. And the law somewhat supports him. He is entitled to receive back the value he gave when Mom cancels the contract.

So, assuming Jay put only a few thousand miles on the car, what is its value now as opposed to when they made the contract? In reality, it is probably not much different. The car was overpriced when Jay bought it, so it was not worth $3,000 then. Was it worth $800? Probably the retail value was something in between and given the age of the car, it is doubtful that a few thousand more miles would make much of a difference. After some discussion, Rob returned $800 to Mom (this was not a legal determination, but just a settlement between Rob and Mom).

What about the others? Rob gave Thomas $400 to compensate him for the remainder of the $1,000 that he paid for the note, but will now not collect. Terrie is good; she collected three months of premiums and made $75. Rob still has the car and also kept $800 cash. And Jay did have a car for three months in exchange for $800; he may or may not have thought that was okay.

The moral of the story is that minors can and do make contracts. An adult dealing with a minor though does so at his own risk because the minor can cancel at any time.

In Rob's case, he sold the car to Jay because he really could not lose. If the contract was canceled before Jay turned 18, he got the car back and could argue about the amount of money paid that he had to return. Even if Jay totaled the car, Rob was permitted to keep the value of the car. He got enough money from Jay up front to make the risk worth taking.

But just for fun, let's turn the tables. Suppose Rob and Jay discover that a famous person (e.g., the President) once owned the car. Cars owned by famous people, even though not very valuable in and of themselves, have sold for tens of thousands of dollars in the past. Rob and Jay learn that the old Ford can probably be sold for $50,000. Rob calls Jay and tells him the contract was "illegal," and he wants to cancel it before anybody gets into trouble. He tells Jay to return the car and get his money back.

Rob is not going to be successful. The contract was not illegal. Although a minor (or his parent) has the right to cancel a contract until he turns 18, the adult in the contract does not have this option and is bound by it. Jay, in this case, made a terrific deal. His mother is undoubtedly very proud of him!

Chapter 15
Warranties

(Making Sellers Accountable)

Warranty is a magic word in modern marketing. Sellers and manufacturers compete for our business by offering them, and we compare them when making major purchases. Even new homes come with warranties, some lasting ten years or more. And if the stated warranty is not enough, the sellers try to convince us that an "extended warranty (for additional cost) is exactly what we need. A warranty is something good, and we are happy that businesses give them to us.

But what exactly is a warranty? Under the law, it is a guarantee by a seller that a product or service is what it is represented to be and that its function and condition are what is normally expected. Isn't that what we all expect anyway? Why all of the hype?

Warranty law is an extension of contract law. Under the common law, products were expected to be in good order and fit for the intended use and purpose. If a product failed this standard, the buyer had a right to cancel the contract and/or to recover damages.

Warranties are now statutory, contained in the Uniform Commercial Code in all states and also contained in other statutes among the states. The law provides warranties; sellers are not giving us anything they are not required to give us.

There are two categories of warranties: express and implied. An express warranty is a written statement that the product meets an assured level of quality, reliability, and function. An express warranty usually also states the supplier's promise to repair or replace any defect in the product. Sellers do not have to provide express warranties.

An implied warranty arises under the law. The seller does not "give" it to the buyer in the contract. It comes into existence automatically with the formation of the sales contract. While in commercial transactions, sellers can disclaim implied warranties, a federal statute, the Magnusson-Moss Act, limits disclaimers in consumer sales.

Express Warranties

Express warranties can arise from the specific language in a written warranty document, from oral statements and from advertising or posted product claims. Sellers must be very careful in statements they make or the advertising they publish; they will be bound by what they say.

Typically, an express warranty is written and provided to the buyer of the product. It can be a "full warranty" or a "limited warranty" depending on its promises. A full warranty is not restricted by any conditions except length of time. Any other express warranty is considered to be limited. The law does not require express warranties. A seller does not have to provide a written warranty of any kind. For consumer sales, however, the lack of an express warranty requires clear labeling that there is no express warranty offered.

Implied Warranties

The law provides and requires implied warranties. The UCC and the older common law make them part of every sale. Because they are automatic, they are part of every sales contract. They do not have to be stated or acknowledged. They can be disclaimed in business to business contracts and in limited circumstances in consumer contracts as well, but the language must be specific and clear. The term "as is" is often used to disclaim implied warranties.

Although there are many implied warranties described in the UCC, there are three essential ones we will discuss. The implied warranty of title, implied warranty of merchantability, and implied warranty of fitness for specific purpose are the core types provided in the statute.

Implied Warranty of Title – This warranty is assumed in every sales contract. It just means that the seller is guaranteeing that he has legal title to transfer; in other words, he has the legal right to transfer ownership. This warranty gives the buyer the right to recover damages from the seller if he did not receive a clear title. Under property law, a seller cannot transfer title he does not have, and the buyer could not prevail against another who has good title. For example, a seller cannot transfer clear title to stolen property; the person from whom it was stolen is the true owner, and a buyer from someone other than the true owner does not have legal rights in it. The warranty of title, therefore, protects the buyer from title issues and gives him the right to seek damages from the seller if some other person actually owns the property sold to him.

Implied Warranty of Merchantability – This is a very powerful warranty that is automatic; it is provided by law. Merchants do not tell us about it. An implied warranty of merchantability requires the product sold to be fit for the purposes for which such goods are ordinarily used, to conform to the standards of the industry, and to meet the product specifications contained in the contract or labeling. This is a broad warranty that arose from an expectation by buyers that goods would be suitable for the purposes for which they are intended. The law assumes that the sellers of goods meet this expectation and the warranty is part of the contract.

While sellers can disclaim implied warranties of merchantability in business to business transactions with specific language, such a statement should make the buyer beware. In consumer transactions in many states, the seller cannot disclaim an implied warranty if the supplier provides an express warranty; generally, the only limitation permitted is limiting the implied warranty to the same length of time as the express warranty.

For consumer sales that usually contain an express warranty, the buyer may want to consider the express warranty as a supplier attempt to limit the implied warranty. An express warranty seldom provides coverage that exceeds the implied warranty but instead attempts to limit the warranty or provide conditions for warranty coverage. The implied warranty usually survives, particularly with the purchase of new merchandise.

Implied Warranty for a Specific Purpose – This warranty arises when a merchant gives advice to a customer about the correct product to meet a need. For example, if a customer tells a car dealer that he intends to pull a 10,000 pound trailer with his new vehicle and asks the dealer for advice, the warranty arises if the dealer recommends a particular vehicle and the customer buys it. If the vehicle's engine, transmission, or other component fails due to pulling the trailer, this warranty would be applicable, perhaps even after the express "new car" warranty expired.

The discussion above incorporates some of the provisions of The Magnusson-Moss Act. This act is a federal statute that regulates consumer product warranties. The act requires suppliers (both manufacturers and sellers) of consumer products to provide comprehensive information about warranties. It defines the terms that sellers must explain in a written warranty and the notices they must give to consumers before and after the sale regarding the warranty coverage and operation. The act also limits or prohibits the ability of suppliers to disclaim warranties.

In Conclusion

Warranties are an integral part of sales contracts. The quality of the goods is critical to the buyer, but he does not control the sourcing or production of them. Warranties guarantee that the money paid for a product obtains the money's worth. In consumer transactions, warranties play not only this role but have also become a major part of marketing products and bargaining in a sale.

Consumer protections in sales, however, are not only safeguarded by warranties. Tort law and particularly product liability law provide alternative and concurrent protection if a defective product causes harm.

Don't be impressed with an express warranty touted by a seller, and carefully consider buying an extended warranty, because the law already provides legal protections automatically. The legal protections may be better than the warranties provided by the seller.

A Story from the Real

Jewelry is a mystery to most people. If it's gold, we understand gold has high intrinsic value, but how $100 worth of gold shaped into a ring can become worth $1,000 is sometimes perplexing. But maybe most mysterious of all is diamonds. We know they are rare and we know they are difficult and expensive to find and cut. But looking at one diamond versus another and discerning the value difference can be challenging. We usually take a jeweler's word for the quality of the diamonds we admire and that we buy.

That is what a man did in Virginia. He went to a jewelry store and asked for a diamond bracelet to purchase as a gift for his wife. He was shown a bracelet and told that the diamonds were "nice." The price was also nice at $15,000. After giving it some thought for a few days, our gift giver bought the diamond bracelet. The jeweler gave him an insurance appraisal with the bracelet that said the diamonds were "v.v.s." quality - indicating a high grade.

After he had given the bracelet to his wife, another jeweler told her they were not v.v.s. diamonds. In fact, they were a much less valuable grade. They returned to the store where they had purchased the bracelet and demanded that the jeweler replace the diamonds with v.v.s. quality stones. The owner refused but offered to refund the purchase price.

The buyer sued the jeweler for breach of express warranty. He claimed that the information provided on the appraisal was a statement as to the quality of the goods that turned out to be not true. The trial court ruled against our buyer.

On appeal, however, the court reviewed the facts and the express warranty law in the state. The state had adopted the UCC warranty provisions. The parties agreed that they did not discuss the quality grade (i.e., v.v.s.) as part of the sale; the jeweler only described the diamonds as "nice." The seller, therefore, argued that the buyer did not rely on the later-learned rating in making the contract to purchase the bracelet. Since it was not part of the discussions, it was therefore not part of the representations made by the seller, nor was it relied upon by the buyer. It could not be part of the contract for sale.

The court disagreed. The justices found that reliance is not required. If the seller made a statement, it is part of the agreement. There is no requirement that a seller intended to give a warranty or that the warranty is stated. The court found that any statements made by the seller about the goods are part of the contract. If a statement is made after the contract is completed, as argued by our jeweler, the court said it is a modification of the original contract and therefore part of it. They defined the contract as the total of all statements made.

To take any statement out of the agreement requires proof by the person maintaining this position that the statement was separate. The jeweler provided no evidence that the quality statement in the appraisal was meant to be separate from the sale of the bracelet.

The court, therefore, found that the buyer was entitled to recover damages based on the difference in value between the diamonds he had received and v.v.s. diamonds.

Warranties are taken very seriously by the courts. The law sees a warranty as a guarantee that the seller delivers what he intended to deliver or what he promised to deliver. Our jeweler learned that at least in his state, the courts will give strong preference to finding a warranty when sellers make statements about quality.

Chapter 16
Banking and Securities Law

(Keeping Wall Street Upright)

Most people have bank accounts, many have car and home loans, and reports say that nearly 60 percent of Americans own investments in the stock market. The law in this area impacts nearly every person. To a certain extent, banking and securities law overlaps with contract and debtor-creditor laws. All are intended to provide for a secure and fair economic system.

There are at least two ways financial law impacts our financial lives. It provides rules for the operation of our financial systems, including establishing liability when mistakes are made, and it provides protections and government oversight for investors and other users of the system.

The UCC provides some of the rules. These rules were adopted by all of the states in the U.S. providing consistency across the country. Federal statutes and regulatory agencies provide other rules that apply nationwide. In a financial system that is blind to state borders, homogenous laws are a necessity. There are also treaties that establish rules on a global scale, again necessary in a world economy.

Financial System Operation

A starting point for this discussion is Articles 3, 4, 4A and 8 of the UCC.

UCC Article 3 – Article 3 provides uniform rules for negotiable instruments. A negotiable instrument is a document that promises to pay a set amount of money to a named person (payee) at a particular time or on demand. Negotiable instruments include checks, drafts, promissory notes like car loans, bills of lading (documents issued by carriers that describe goods in a shipment and show the person owning them), and certificates of deposits (CDs). All of these documents are promises to pay a specific amount of money.

A negotiable instrument must be in writing, signed by the maker, be an unconditional promise or order to pay, state a fixed amount of money, not require anything except payment of money, be payable at a particular time or on demand, and be payable to order or to bearer.

Negotiable instruments are substitutes for money because they can be transferred by indorsement. For example, when the payee of a check indorses to it another, that person has the rights and title of the original payee. When the original payee indorses without naming another, the document becomes bearer paper meaning that whoever holds the indorsed document is entitled to payment.

An indorser may also create special types of indorsements in which he names a specific person as the person to be paid or that limits liability for payment. The indorser can also specify conditions in his indorsement such as payment only for deposit, only if certain events take place, or limiting payment to specified circumstances. If the indorsement does not include any restrictions or conditions, each person that indorses the instrument is liable for its payment in the order of indorsement.

The indorsement of a negotiable instrument for value may make the new holder of the instrument a "holder in due course." A holder in due course is entitled to payment without regard to any other matters relative to the deal. For example, if Layne buys a promissory note from the original payee by paying him for it, she is entitled to collect the note even if the original payee of the note failed to perform some part of his obligation.

A case like this might arise when a car dealer sells a car and takes an installment note for payment. The dealer may sell the note to a third party. If the buyer of the car later learns that the car is defective, he is still obligated to pay the holder in due course even though the seller of the car breached his contract by selling defective goods.

For a holder to become a holder in due course requires that he paid value for the instrument, there was no notice of any claim or defect, and there was no evidence of forgery or alterations.

UCC Article 4 – Article 4 provides rules regarding the liability of a bank for action or non-action on an instrument presented to it for payment or collection. The location of the bank determines the law that applies, but all states have adopted the UCC, which standardizes the law across the country.

Checks are negotiable instruments in which an account owner orders his bank to pay a certain amount of money on demand to the named payee. The payee may indorse the check in blank which makes it a bearer instrument. Any holder of a bearer instrument is entitled to payment. Checks are often indorsed with conditions or to named other parties, such as "For deposit to the account of X only," or "Pay to the order of Y." Banks, of course, have a right and an obligation to assure that a holder of a bearer instrument is not committing a fraud.

Under the UCC, a bank is required to pay a check drawn on one of its accounts if funds are available. But a bank does not have to pay if it suspects fraud, legal process froze the account, a stop payment order was received, or there is some notice affecting the account such as death or bankruptcy of its owner. Banks also have the right to set off any delinquent amounts due to the bank before payment of a check.

Article 4 provides detailed rules for the actions of banks in processing checks and assigns liability for mistakes in the processing.

UCC Article 4A – Article 4A is a relatively new part of the UCC that all of the states have adopted. It provides rules for handling electronic funds transfers. The electronic transfer of money is now extremely common because of its convenience, speed and relative security. What began with a couple of million dollars per year transferred by Western Union in the 1800s has grown to trillions of dollars per day in modern commerce.

While the process is relatively simple and straightforward, there were historically no legal rules for how the process took place or who was liable if something went wrong. Article 4A divides the parties to a funds transfer into three groups - an originator who wants to transfer funds, the originator's bank and the sender of the payment, and the receiving bank that accepts the funds and places them in the recipient's account.

Article 4A provides rules for the issuance and acceptance of a "payment order" that directs the originator's bank to send the payment. There are possibilities of mistakes in the completion of the order and in the receipt by the bank of an unauthorized order. To avoid errors, the UCC mandates a security procedure that requires communications and codes. Both parties agree to these procedures. If there is an unauthorized payment order, the security agreement determines who bears the loss. If the security process is "commercially reasonable" the originator bears the loss unless he can show that the bank did not follow the procedures or some person outside of his control compromised the process. If a bank processes an erroneous order, it bears the loss so long as the originator can show he complied with the security procedures.

After the sending bank initiates the order, the transferred funds may pass through intervening banks before reaching the receiver's bank. Article 4A provides rules and duties for this intervening process that require each bank to make payment to the next bank in the string. The transfer is the movement of funds from receiving bank to receiving bank until they reach the recipient's bank. As a general rule, any errors made in the payments among the intervening banks are the responsibility of the recipient's bank unless one of the intervening banks underpays an order. In underpayment situations, the bank making the underpayment is liable for the shortage.

In the final part of the process, the receiving bank is obligated to pay the recipient. The interbank process is virtually instantaneous as each bank in the process pays the orders immediately. Actual payment is made by credit extended by each bank in the string. All of the transactions take place through electronic communication. The actual movement of funds is a second part of the process although the funds are posted in the same immediate time frame.

To summarize the process, the sender of the funds and his bank must have an agreement for placing orders. Orders must be made in a secure system that requires passwords. Mistakes made are the bank's responsibility so long as the sender followed the agreement. Mistakes in the transfer of the funds through a series of other banks are the receiver's bank's responsibility. The receiver's bank is required to pay the receiver immediately on transfer.

UCC Article 8 – Article 8 provides rules for the ownership and transfers of securities. Securities represent ownership or creditor rights in a business (e.g., stocks and bonds). There are currently at least three ways this ownership can be held.

◻ Owner possession – The owner may actually possess the stock certificates or other documents of interest.

◻ Corporate recording – The owner may be recorded on the books of the business as a non-certificated owner.

◻ Held by the broker – The owner's certificates may be held by a broker in its account with the Depository Trust and Clearing Corporation (a company owned by its users that holds and transfer securities).

Article 8 provides rules for transferring these ownership interests within the various systems and for using the interests as security for loans.

Where stocks and other financial assets are in brokerage accounts, Article 8 creates a "security entitlement" interest that includes all the rights and title of the underlying certificates held by the broker, including rights to dividends and to vote the shares. Security entitlements can be pledged as collateral for loans. The holding of securities in brokerage accounts provides an efficient way for the brokerage firms to manage and record the vast number of trades that take place among them.

The Article 8 security entitlements concept covers not just stocks and bonds, but also many other forms of business interests, including partnership interests, interests in mutual and hedge funds, commodity contracts, options, and certificates of deposit and other negotiable instruments held in broker accounts.

Regulation and Oversight

A wide array of both federal and state laws control banks and securities businesses (and insurance companies). Banking and securities statutes provide for "regulation" of the institutions by government agencies that both provide rules and conduct audits to assure that the rules are followed. Regulators have substantial authority under the laws to enforce compliance, including the power to censure and shut down operations. The regulations establish rules for management, financial security, privacy, fraud and consumer protection, and crime prevention.

Agency oversight has two primary objectives: 1) regulating "risk," and 2) regulating "disclosure."

Risk refers to the financial strength of the organizations and the actions they take to assure the safety of their deposits, investors, and customers, and to protect the economy from economic collapse.

Disclosure refers to the information that the organizations make available to depositors, investors, and consumers regarding financial positions and status so they can make informed decisions.

Bank regulation is carried out by several agencies at both the federal and state levels. At the federal level Title 12 of the U.S. Code - Banks and Banking, and Title 15: U.S. Code - Commerce and Trade provide the statutory authority granted by Congress. Within the scope of the statutes, the agencies have broad discretion to make rules and enforce compliance.

Financial regulatory agencies include: the Office of the Controller of the Currency (OCC), Federal Deposit Insurance Corporation (FDIC), National Credit Union Administration (NCUA) and the Federal Reserve Board (Fed), the Security and Exchange Commission (SEC), the Commodities Futures Trading Commission (CFTC), the Federal Housing Finance Agency (FHFA), and the Consumer Financial Protection Bureau (CFPB). There are also many other bureaus, agencies, and councils that participate in financial regulation.

Federal securities law primarily resides in Title 15 of the U.S. Code, Commerce and Trade, which grants substantial authority for industry oversight. Securities regulation is principally the responsibility of the SEC, a federal agency created by the Security and Exchange Act of 1933 after the disastrous collapse of the stock market in 1929. The Commodity Futures Trading Commission (CFTC) is another federal agency with regulatory responsibility. In addition, the New York Stock Exchange and the other exchanges implement their own rules and standards of conduct for trading. Finally, the Financial Industry Regulatory Authority, Inc.

(FINRA) is a private, non-governmental organization that regulates member brokerage firms.

What do these laws and agencies monitor and regulate to limit risk exposure to depositors, investors, and the U.S. economy? Summary lists follow.

Banks – Bank regulation assures capital (funds) adequacy, asset quality, competent management, appropriate earnings, liquidity, sensitivity to market risk, and customer protection. Some of the factors regulated include:

◻ The mix and collectability of banks' assets, which are typically loans and management services provided to customers.

◻ Banks' levels of debt and their liquid reserves to pay depositors and absorb loan losses. Banks around the world use the guidelines of the "Basel Accords" that also set standards for other facets of bank regulation.

◻ Banks' policies and procedures for interacting with customers and investors.

◻ Bank competition, interbank lending, and the incidence of high-risk behaviors in interbank transactions.

◻ Banks' and bank officials' incentives to serve one interest at the expense of another interest or obligation - conflicts of interest.

◻ Banks' policies and requirements for evaluating their investments.

◻ Banks' use of reasonable care to maintain information about customers and the products offered to customers.

◻ Banks' oversight of investment products including registration, disclosure, and consumer protection.

◻ Undue risks and weak risk management practices that may affect the stability of the federal deposit insurance system (FDIC), including a bank's sources of funds, assets, management, earnings, liquidity, and attention to market risk.

◻ Banks' standards of competence and integrity for their managers.

◻ Limitations on interest paid and early withdrawal penalties.

◘ Interbank loan relationships, including loan interest rates and standards for interest rate adjustments, disclosures, and fairness.

◘ Reserve requirements – banks' holdings of sufficient cash, short-term investments, and deposits with the Federal Reserve to meet anticipated depositor withdrawals.

◘ Banks' transaction reporting – banks are required to report all cash transactions over $10,000, or patterns of transactions that exceed this amount.

◘ Banks' lending and service practices to assure no discrimination.

◘ Disclosure standards – banks are required to disclose deposit, service, privacy and lending terms in great detail.

Public companies, brokers, and investors – The regulation of securities concerns the accurate disclosure of financial information, the disclosure of risks, and the prevention of fraud. Some of the regulated areas for public companies (companies whose stock or debt are held widely among the general public and are freely traded on the stock exchanges), brokerage companies, and other securities firms include the following:

◘ Registration with the SEC and the required detailed reports regarding the firm, its management, its financial condition, the intended use of the funds it raises and the risks involved. Accounting under Generally Accepted Accounting Principles (GAAP) is required to maintain consistency in reporting.

◘ Misleading or deceptive conduct in securities presentations or sales.

◘ Insider trading – acquisitions or dispositions of securities by any persons with information that is not available to the public.

◘ Treatment of shareholders in takeovers – all shareholders must be treated equally in any offer to take or modify control of an entity.

◘ Minority shareholder protections for access to voting, meetings, financial information, and records, dividends, and costs.

◘ The dissemination and the clarity of company information to shareholders and others.

◻ Financial standards – the preparation, timely issuance and accuracy of financial statements and the notes filed with them. This includes the requirement for third party audits of financial statements and the regulation of the auditors.

◻ Company internal controls to assure compliance with financial and accounting rules.

The regulation of banks and securities is intended to protect not only individual members of society but also to protect the economy itself. Regulation is driven by an understood objective to keep the financial system of the U.S. secure. Together with tax policy and monetary policy (the government's control of the money supply, interest rates, and inflation), a safe and stable financial system should permit growth and greater wealth production for the country.

In Conclusion

Besides just providing services to the individuals in society, our financial institutions greatly control much of our economy and through that shape our well-being. The risks they take can influence the entire national and global financial system and the strength and security of it. Financial information and its availability are critical to safe investments and fair investment decisions.

We are familiar with the problems and the excesses that financial institutions encounter. A recession in 2007 was primarily caused by issues in our banking and financial sectors as they made loans that could not be collected and thus destroyed their solvency. The securities firms played a major role by investing in the bad mortgages made by the banks. Some blame government rules and regulations for pushing banks to make these loans. Regardless of the causes, the crisis demonstrates the importance of regulation and close monitoring of this industry.

We hope the regulators, and the financial institutions themselves, are now behaving more responsibly. Have ethics improved, or is our only protection from economic collapse the attention and control exerted by the law and the regulatory agencies? Hopefully, we have both.

A Story from the Real

Loose lips sink ships - and sometimes careers. Consider the world of finance in which companies undertake deals that are sometimes worth billions of dollars to merge, raise additional capital, or change their business forms or operations. They do this with the assistance of "investment bankers" who help by serving as agents in the negotiation of terms, valuing securities, arranging borrowing, and orchestrating the issuance of new securities (stocks and/or bonds). Investment bankers typically work for large banks or brokerage firms.

Josef worked for a large brokerage firm as an investment banker. He had a very successful career working with various corporate clients that both respected and trusted him. His specialty was mergers and acquisitions (combining two companies into one new one).

Through his close relationship with a large corporate client, he was able to secure work for his firm for the buyout of his client by another larger corporation. He led the team that put the combination of the companies together, and he arranged a "deal" with substantial benefits to his client, the other corporation, and of course his firm. Completion of the deal was imminent.

Josef was approached by a major bank and offered a job with a multi-million dollar per year salary. He at first declined, but later accepted the position. He told his new employer that he could not report as soon as they wanted because he had a major project to complete. He also informed his current employer that he was leaving, but would stay to finish the project. They both agreed.

Josef was encouraged by his new employer to make contact with his new associates and team members to develop rapport and ease into his new job. He did that through personal meetings and phone conversations. One of his new associates asked him if he knew anything about an upcoming merger in the industry in which his deal was pending. At first, Josef did not provide any information, but in a subsequent conversation he divulged some of the details and swore the new associate to secrecy.

Secrecy seems to be particularly adverse to human nature, particularly when money is involved. His new associate told another member of the bank's upper management about the pending merger. The manager called Josef's client and asked if there was anything his bank could do to help. The world around Josef very quickly collapsed.

Josef was questioned by his current employer and the bank's internal investigative team because everyone immediately determined Josef had to be the source of the information that the bank possessed. Josef's current employer fired him within a matter of days; his new employer withdrew its offer of employment. The bank also fired both his new associate and the senior bank manager. Josef was then charged by the New York Stock Exchange (he was a registered member) with violations of its rules, specifically for engaging in "conduct or proceeding inconsistent with just and equitable principles of trade." The Stock Exchange held a hearing under its regulatory process.

Josef was found in violation of the rule and issued a reprimand and fined $100,000. While this may not sound like a very severe penalty in the world of money that Josef inhabited, it did far more damage than a piece of paper and a payment of $100,000. It effectively ended Josef's very lucrative career.

Under the procedures of the New York Stock Exchange, Josef appealed to the SEC. The Commission upheld both the finding of his violation and the sanctions. Josef then appealed under the rules to the U.S. Court of Appeals.

Josef's argument was that his violation was not intended to cause any harm, and in fact did not cause any harm as the deal was completed as planned. Nobody suffered any damages (except Josef and the people who were involved in Josef's conversation with his new employer). He argued that violation of the rule required either planned misconduct for financial gain or at least "bad faith" (fraud or intentional conduct that avoids a duty or obligation). He argued that his disclosure of information was nothing more than an error in judgment. He asserted that he only meant to establish a good relationship with his new co-worker and was trying to protect the deal from any interference because the new bank official indicated he was aware that a merger was pending. He said that providing him with information that the deal was already done would keep the bank from attempting to interfere with the plans.

The court said that intentional misconduct or bad faith was not required under the rule. Ethical misconduct was part of the rule and fully supported the sanctions. His conduct was unethical because he disclosed information that was confidential. He breached his duty to his client in doing this. It did not matter that no harm resulted or that his disclosure was not for his personal financial gain. The Stock Exchange hearing officer, the SEC and the court all agreed that the Stock Exchange rule centers on conduct and does not require any consideration of the member's intent or mindset.

The court discussed the role of the industry in determining unacceptable conduct and found that industry standards govern what is unethical. The court gave great leeway to the Stock Exchange and the SEC to make this determination as they represented the "industry experts." The court, therefore, sustained the violation finding.

Confidentiality is critical to the operation of a securities market. That is understood from the fiduciary (highest trust and confidence) relationship of the parties and the needs to protect the market from the release of information that is not available to the public as a whole.

Josef paid a very high price for his breach of confidence. His motives were not really bad, and he certainly did not intend to harm his client or anybody else. But this situation shows the importance of confidentiality in the financial world. Josef is no longer a participant in this realm.

Chapter 17
Debtor/Creditor Law

(The Law of Paying the Piper)

Almost everybody borrows money for one purpose or another. Just using a credit card is borrowing money, even if the balance is paid in full each month. Many of us have received calls, emails, letters or other contacts inviting us and making us attractive offers to borrow. Some of us have also received collection notices or calls; sometimes even when our loan is current and in good standing. Given the universal use of credit, the opportunity for abuse is tremendous, and this abuse can be of the lender or the borrower.

To deal with the potential for abuse, the law establishes rules for lending and borrowing money. The law has two primary roles in the relationship between borrowers (debtors) and lenders (creditors). It provides rules for protecting creditors and facilitating the process, and it provides rules for protecting the debtors from abuse and affording them relief when debt becomes oppressive.

There are laws at both the state and federal levels to address credit abuse, and the courts weigh in with rulings that can alter a perfectly legal contract if one of the parties acts unconscionably. We will discuss the law in general terms that are broadly applicable, although individual states may have statutes that are different.

Facilitating the Lending Process and Protecting Creditors

In a loan arrangement, it is the creditor that takes the risk. The risk, of course, is that the debtor may not repay the loan. The law recognizes that creditors need protection, both from a default (nonpayment) of the loan and from disputes regarding the amount and terms of the loan.

Credit Ratings – In modern lending, perhaps the best protection that lenders have is the credit bureau ratings available for all consumers. Using a complex formula that considers total debt, repayment history, defaults, and other factors, the bureaus provide a score that reflects a person's credit worthiness. Lenders both provide information to the bureaus and receive credit scores from them. The availability of credit, the terms of loans, and the costs of loans (interest rates) are heavily dependent on the score assigned to a borrower.

Creditors that make loans to low scoring borrowers understand that they are taking a greater risk of not collecting the loans. Credit granted to low credit score borrowers is commonly referred to as "sub-prime."

Businesses are also rated for credit worthiness. There are several companies that review financial information and provide ratings for many businesses. Moody's is perhaps the most well-known company that rates large businesses. Banks and other lenders also have their own scoring systems for evaluating business loans.

Contracts – It is contract law that provides the rules for forming a debtor/creditor relationship. The agreement to provide funds and to repay the funds must comply with all the necessary rules of contract law to be enforceable. Like all contracts, the description of the agreement is critical; all terms, including repayment dates, must be clearly stated. Like any other contract, the promises made by the parties can be enforced by the courts and damages can be awarded.

But contract law will not necessarily help a creditor collect what is due. And contracts may not provide creditors with the ability to assign their rights to collect the amount to others without strings. For example, car dealerships make many loans to buyers of the cars they sell, but the dealers cannot wait for years to collect them. The huge amount of loans they would have to hold would prevent more than a limited number of sales. So dealers "sell" the loans they make to banks or finance companies. The banks become the creditor entitled to collect the debt. But would banks take these car loans if they came with potential liability for defects in the vehicles? Probably not, at least not at interest rates that allow dealers to sell cars.

Negotiable Instruments – The law provides a solution to the assignment of debt issue. The negotiable instrument rules contained in the UCC solve this problem. The indorsement of a negotiable instrument for value makes the new holder of the note a "holder in due course." A holder in due course is entitled to payment on the note without regard to any other matters relative to it. See the discussions of negotiable instruments in Chapters 13 and 16 for more information regarding this.

Many loans, particularly consumer loans, are therefore made possible and expedited by the negotiable instrument protections given to the ultimate holder of the loan. So if the car you buy is a lemon, do not stop making your payments. The law requires that you go to the dealer and the manufacturer for relief, but not to the holder of your loan.

Security – The law also provides detailed rules for security instruments. Security instruments are very common in both consumer and business loans. In a secured loan, the borrower is required to transfer his interest in some property (collateral) to the lender. This transfer does not usually involve actual possession by the creditor or even any rights to use the property, but it does give the creditor the right to take possession of the property if the loan is not paid. It also gives the creditor rights to the property above any rights afterward obtained by any other creditors. It gives the lender "security" that the loan will be repaid one way or the other.

A creditor can obtain security in several ways. The UCC, Article 9, sets out the rules for obtaining security interests in goods and other personal property, including security interests in some intangible properties such as stocks and bonds or copyrights and trademarks. Security interests in real estate are commonly obtained through mortgages and leases. Other security interests can arise automatically under state law to those who provide services or goods, such as artisans, contractors, suppliers and innkeepers.

Lenders obtain security interests by following the rules established in the law. The UCC outlines the rules for the creation, perfection, and enforcement of security interests in personal property. Rules for the creation of security interests in land (mortgages) are in some ways similar, but individual state laws provide them rather than uniform rules under the UCC.

Creation of security interests – Contracts create security interests. Both parties must enter into a financing agreement that provides details regarding the property offered as security for the loan. A financing statement reflects this agreement when personal property is the collateral; for real estate, a mortgage shows the agreement. The arrangement states that the debtor and creditor agree that if the loan is not repaid, the property listed will be available to the creditor to satisfy the loan. Typical personal property pledged in a financing agreement includes the inventory and receivables of a business, furniture, equipment, securities (stocks and bonds), and vehicles. But, just about any personal property can be used. Real estate used for security consists of land and the improvements on the land (buildings, roads, etc.).

Security interests in personal property can include "after-acquired" property and the proceeds of sales of the property. This protects creditors that finance the acquisition of inventory by maintaining their security in the proceeds of goods in the normal movements through the purchase, sale and repurchase cycle.

"Perfection" of security interests – Creditors must "perfect" their security interests to obtain priority over other creditors. This usually means that the security interest must be filed or recorded in a way that puts the public (and other potential creditors) on notice that the property is security for a loan. The UCC provides that financing statements must be filed with the state to protect priority. Mortgages are usually recorded in the county where the property is located. Once a security interest is properly filed, it establishes the creditor's first right to the property against other creditors or claims. We commonly refer to this right as a lien.

Some types of property have special perfection rules. For example, vehicle liens must be recorded on the title of the vehicle. Also, perfection can be made without filing if the creditor takes possession of the property; and, for some intangible property like stocks and bonds, possession is required for perfection.

Creditors must monitor their security interests. The movement of pledged property to a different state, for example, may require a new filing. Also, financing statements have a life under the UCC; after five years, there must be a refiling to maintain the security interest.

Security interests can often cause conflicts between creditors and even buyers of goods. A secured creditor normally has priority over an unsecured creditor. Among secured creditors, the rule is simple: "first in time, first in right." This means that the timing of perfection by the creditors determines their relative priority. Buyers are in most cases protected if they pay fair value in an ordinary business purchase. However, if the payment is below market value or the purchase is not an ordinary business transaction (e.g., a bulk sale of an entire inventory), the security interest will follow the property.

Enforcement of security interests – Enforcement is available when the debtor defaults. This usually means that he did not make payment as required. Enforcement of a security interest involves taking possession of the property, selling it, and using the proceeds to satisfy the debt. Excess sale proceeds must be returned to the debtor.

Under the UCC, repossession of personal property can normally be made by the creditor without court intervention so long as there is no "breach of the peace," and so long as a personal residence is not entered without permission. If the property cannot be readily retrieved, a court intervention is necessary.

With real estate, foreclosure may require court intervention unless the debtor voluntarily conveys his interest in the real estate to the creditor by deed. A majority of states, however, do not require court action. These states set specific statutory steps that must be followed by the creditor to sell the property. Even in these states, if the proceeds of the sale of the property are not sufficient to satisfy the debt, court action must be used to obtain a judgment for any balance still due after sale of the property. Many states also allow a period of time for the person in default to redeem the property with payment after the sale.

Security interests protect creditors by providing property to back up the promise to repay the loan. No creditor wants to repossess the property, and it is done only as a last resort after efforts to work with the debtor to obtain or even settle the amount due have failed. Enforcement is a time consuming and expensive exercise.

Other creditor protections – The law also provides several other protections for creditors.

Automatic liens – Creditors receive automatic liens in several circumstances. A "purchase money" security interest arises automatically when a lender provides funds to purchase property. This security interest must ultimately be filed or recorded, but it gives automatic priority over prior security interests, such as "after-acquired property" liens.

Mechanics' liens – Certain providers of services (e.g., home repairmen) also acquire automatic mechanics' liens. These liens can apply to both personal and real property. They arise when services are performed or materials are provided, and depending on state law, take priority over all other liens that may attach to the property (including mortgages in some states). Although the law in many states allows the timing of the lien to reflect the date work began, perfection (filing) is required before the lien can be foreclosed.

Judgment liens – These arise when the creditor sues a party that has not paid a debt. The creditor must prove the amount due, the validity of the agreement and that payment has not occurred. After he receives a court judgment, it typically must be filed to be perfected. A judgment lien attaches to most property of the debtor, and once filed, it takes priority over any subsequent liens on the property (except mechanics' liens).

"Lis pendens" – When a party (including a creditor) files a lawsuit regarding real estate, most states provide that the plaintiff can record a "*lis pendens*" (suit pending) in the county where real estate of the debtor is located. This is a perfection of a future lien that may arise when the lawsuit is concluded and notifies any potential creditors or buyers of the property that they take it subject to any ultimate judgment that may be determined.

Guarantees – The law provides a set of rules for creditors to obtain guarantees of loans from third parties. Even though the third party guarantors do not receive anything personally in the agreements, the law allows the loan to the borrower to provide the necessary consideration element of a contract to bind the guarantor. Guarantors can be either primarily liable for the debt, meaning they have the same liability as the debtor, or secondarily liable, which means that reasonable efforts must first be made to collect from the debtor before the guarantor must pay.

Statutory protections – Creditors are also given protections by the various consumer lending statutes discussed below. These laws give creditors a number of rights, including the right to determine credit worthiness based on credit scoring systems and to require debtors to provide notices of fraud against their credit card or other credit accounts.

Protections for Debtors

Protections for debtors are a relatively new function of the law. In previous times, borrowers that did not pay could be subject to prison, involuntary servitude and non-judicial seizures of property. With the advent of credit reporting systems and modern security interests permitted by the law, creditors rights to "punish" defaulting debtors is long gone. While many debtors may disagree with the prior sentence, it is a fact that the law now provides creditors with the tools to avoid making loans that will not be repaid and to secure their loans with liens. Lenders who make loans to those with poor credit ratings and/or no collateral do so at their own risk. There is no way to "get blood from a turnip" in modern law.

Debtor protections are wide ranging. They place limitations on the ability of creditors to commit fraud and deception in soliciting and granting credit. They also limit forceful methods of collection, and the ability of creditors to make loans that have abusive terms. When lenders make risky loans, the law limits their ability to charge high interest and costs and to use aggressive methods to collect the amounts due. The law even provides an avenue for debtors to completely escape their debts and start over.

While a detailed discussion of all debtor protections and creditor limitations under the law is not possible in this book, we can provide some of the more relevant laws and the limitations they provide. These laws were created at the state and federal levels and may vary significantly among the states. A debtor with problems must seek the appropriate guidance under the laws of his state.

Federal laws provide protections from creditor misconduct and require disclosure of information. They also give borrowers relief when errors are made, fraud is committed by third parties, or the ability to repay changes. Some of the federal statutes that impact debtor/creditor relationships include the following:

Truth in Lending Act – This act requires that all terms of credit be clearly disclosed and it allows consumer debtors to cancel any credit contract that does not do so. Regulation Z issued under this law provides detailed requirements for disclosure. This law also contains limitations on consumer liability in the event of third party fraud. The Truth in Lending Act also prohibits the issuance of credit cards without a request or application from the customer.

Fair Credit Reporting Act – This law restricts credit reporting agencies' (such as Equifax and TransUnion) release of reports to only certain situations and requires these agencies to inform consumers of denied credit due to information in their reports. The act also requires credit agencies to provide consumers with copies of their reports and to provide a process for correcting incorrect information.

Equal Credit Opportunity Act – The Equal Credit Opportunity Act prohibits denial of credit to protected classes of individuals (race, religion, national origin, color, gender, age, or marital status) based on any factor different from others.

Fair Credit Billing Act – This provides protections for consumers from unfair billing practices and provides a process to address billing errors in credit accounts.

Federal Wage Garnishment Law – This law requires full disclosure of the terms and conditions of finance charges in credit transactions and in proposals to extend credit. It also restricts and limits the garnishment of wages.

Right to Financial Privacy Act – This act prohibits federal government access to bank and other financial accounts unless:

◘ The customer authorizes access.

◘ There is an appropriate administrative subpoena or summons.

◘ There is a qualified search warrant.

◘ There is an appropriate judicial subpoena.

◘ Or, there is an appropriate written request from an authorized government authority.

This statute provides exceptions for national security situations. The act also requires financial institutions to report financial behavior that indicates fraudulent or criminal activity.

Consumer Leasing Act – This act covers only consumer leases that last more than four months and are for less than $150,000 (this amount is adjusted yearly for inflation). This includes most automobile leases. The act provides for full disclosure of terms, penalties, and conditions in lease agreements and in the advertising of consumer leases. The act also prohibits unreasonable computations of residual values and additions of undefined amounts in lease contracts.

Note that leases not covered by the Consumer Leasing Act may be subject to the provisions of Article 2A of the UCC.

Fair Debt Collection Practices Act – This act, passed originally in 1976, is the most important federal legislation enacted to limit the activities of creditors in collecting debts. It arose from an increasingly abusive debt collection industry that some saw as harassing, unresponsive, and damaging to consumers.

The act:

◘ Limits creditors' ability to locate and communicate with debtors, and places limitations on the types of contacts permitted, including prohibitions on contacts late at night or at a debtor's place of employment.

◘ Allows debtors to stop all personal contact with debt collectors and requires creditors to speak only with a debtor's attorney if he has one.

◘ Prohibits any conduct that harasses, oppresses, or abuses any person in connection with the collection of a debt. This includes threats, obscene language, repeated phone contacts, and the publication of lists of debtors.

◘ Forbids the use of any false or misleading representation or means to collect a debt. This includes false threats of legal actions, insinuations that a crime has been committed, and using false identification, threatening non-judicial seizure or other enforcement, or implying that legal process is imminent when it is not.

◘ Requires creditors to explain debts, and allows debtors to contest debts and obtain relief from collection actions while disputes are discussed and resolved.

◘ Provides for civil remedies and penalties in the courts if a creditor violates any of the provisions of the act.

◘ Gives the Federal Trade Commission (FTC) the authority to administratively enforce the creditor limitations in the act through its regulatory power.

Curiously, federal law contains no limitations on loan interest rates. Most states have "usury laws" that limit interest rates (about 30 percent is common). But a combination of federal court cases and laws (e.g., Depository Institutions Deregulation and Monetary Control Act) not only do not specify limitations, but actually exempt many banks and other lenders from the limits set in state usury laws.

Bankruptcy

Bankruptcy serves both the creditor and the debtor, but the Bankruptcy Act is no doubt the most well-known protection from creditors given to debtors by the law. But we must understand that bankruptcy in the U.S.

has two purposes: to provide relief to debtors who cannot repay their debt and to provide a fair means of distributing their property among the creditors.

Under the U.S. Constitution, only the federal government can provide for bankruptcy. The founding fathers understandably recognized the danger of allowing states to grant bankruptcy protections that might prejudice creditors in other states. Current bankruptcy law is contained in The Bankruptcy Reform Act of 1978.

Bankruptcy is a highly specialized area of law and "bankruptcy attorneys" are typically employed to assist persons or businesses that must file.

Bankruptcy is a legal process for dealing with insolvency or an inability to repay debts. When a person or entity has more debt than assets or cannot repay his debt, bankruptcy allows for the removal of debt, the distribution of assets to creditors, and a fresh start for the bankrupt. Some forms of bankruptcy also allow for a court ordered and supervised repayment of debt, or for the reorganization of a business entity to reduce debt by substituting new equity for old debt, or by restructuring its debt to make it more payable.

There are several types of bankruptcy. The three most common are:

Chapter 7 – This type provides for complete liquidation of the debtor's assets and payment of any proceeds to the creditors. The remaining debt is discharged.

Chapter 11 – This bankruptcy provides for business reorganizations. It allows the bankrupt business to continue to operate under a court approved plan that may allow for new borrowing with priority repayment, the restructuring of debt into more favorable terms, and/or allow the bankrupt to cancel or modify existing contracts, including collective bargaining agreements. If a business has debt greater than its assets, it may propose a plan that leaves the owners (stockholders) with no value and makes the creditors and/or new investors the equity owners of a newly organized company.

Chapter 13 – Chapter 13 provides for the retention of assets and a court supervised repayment of debt, usually at a lower payment level that the debtor can afford after living expenses. This chapter is available only to individuals.

Bankruptcy begins when a person files a voluntary petition in the bankruptcy court, or when a creditor files a petition seeking the appointment of a trustee to take and administer the debtor's assets. When a debtor files a petition in the bankruptcy court, an automatic stay stops all collection actions by all creditors. After a bankruptcy filing, there are several common steps that take place:

Trustee appointment – The court appoints a trustee to take possession of the debtor's nonexempt assets.

Filing of claims – All creditors must timely file claims. If a claim is not filed, creditors without a security interest in property have no right to participate in the distribution of any assets of the debtor.

Creditors' meeting – The creditors hold a meeting under court supervision. At the meeting, the creditors have the right to question the debtor under oath regarding any assets and the locations of them.

Proof of claims – Creditors must prove their claims if challenged by the trustee. This may require the introduction of evidence supporting the claim such as contracts, billing statements or account records.

Secured interests – Secured creditors have first rights to the property on which they hold valid security interests (those perfected by proper filing or other legal action) and have the right to foreclose on and sell the property.

Collection and sale of assets – Under Chapter 7, the trustee sells unsecured assets and distributes the proceeds according to priorities listed in the bankruptcy statute. Some claims, such as unpaid wages, have super priorities and are paid before any other creditors.

Discharge of debts – Under Chapter 7, unpaid debts are discharged but see the discussion below regarding nondischargeable debts.

Debtor plans – Under Chapter 11, the debtor submits a plan for the reorganization of the company (in some cases, the creditors may become the new owners) and/or adjusting of the debts. Creditors vote on acceptance and the court must approve the plan. Under Chapter 13, the debtor submits a plan for repayment of debts.

Discharge or approval of plan – After assets are sold and the proceeds distributed under Chapter 7, the debtor is discharged from any remaining debt. Under Chapters 11 and 13, after the court approves the plan, the debtor continues to pay his debts in accordance with the plan. Under Chapter 11, a business remains in operation.

All steps are subject to contest by either side and are under the strict supervision of the court.

Exempt Property – Some property is exempt from the bankruptcy proceedings, meaning that the property is not subject to sale for the satisfaction of debts. These exemptions are provided by state law and vary among the states. In more debtor friendly states, personal residences, automobiles, retirement accounts, and work tools are all exempt. Debt secured by these assets is not discharged, and repayment must continue, but nonsecured creditors have no rights to the exempt assets.

Nondischargeable Debt – Nor is all nonsecured debt discharged in bankruptcy. Some of the debts that cannot be discharged include: debts incurred after filing of bankruptcy, most taxes, student loans and many other government obligations, child and spousal support obligations, money owed on a judgment for damages as a result of injury caused by operation of a vehicle while intoxicated, and any debt that resulted from a fraud committed by the debtor.

Debtors can keep property subject to secured loans if they agree to new loan arrangements. Otherwise, secured property may be repossessed or foreclosed on by the creditor.

A final note is that bankruptcy provides both good reasons and many avenues for fraud to be committed. Debtors can hide or misrepresent assets or value, and creditors can file false or exaggerated claims.

Because the debtor is surrendering all of his property, and perhaps his livelihood, and because a creditor is likely not to be repaid all that he provided to the debtor, the propensity for dishonesty is extreme. The law provides severe penalties for any violations of the bankruptcy statute, fraud, or concealment.

In Conclusion

Credit has long been controversial and prone to disputes. The major religions of the world, including Hinduism, Buddhism, Judaism, Islam and Christianity (which make up about 75 percent of the world population) all contain teachings about the abusive nature of credit and interest. Some religions forbid interest completely. Perhaps a good summary of sentiment is contained in The Bible - "the borrower is the slave of the lender."

While worldwide viewpoint seems adverse to the concept of borrowing and paying interest, it has become a primary driver of successful economies. The world's wealthiest countries (with a few exceptions) are awash in private and government debt. It has become a way of life primarily because it allows economic expansion and the creation of wealth ahead of society's ability to save the capital necessary to grow.

Once we accept that debt is part of our economy, we can understand that most societies find it necessary to regulate and control the borrowing process through laws. While these laws originally seemed to favor the creditors as a means to protect them from ruin if debts were not repaid, in more recent times, the law has taken a much more active role in protecting debtors. As credit became more common and acceptable in consumer activities, the law in the U.S. and in much of the developed world progressed rapidly to protect us from ourselves and from those who may prey upon us.

A Story from the Real

In the last 75 years, the U.S. rapidly added laws protecting consumers from credit abuse. As explained in this chapter, they impose numerous restrictions on lenders and require detailed disclosures and explanations. But sometimes, even when a lender crosses every "T" and dots every "I," there may still be serious abuse. And, our courts are then called upon to render justice.

Take the case of the Jones. Mr. & Mrs. Jones were immigrants on welfare. They did not have a good command of the English language. They were visited by a door-to-door salesman who convinced them that they needed a freezer. He readily sold them one on an installment contract.

The freezer had a retail value of $300. The contract terms amounted to a total price of over $1,200 including interest, fees, and credit life and other insurance options which the Jones fully agreed to by signing the contract. Needless to say, the Jones had difficulty paying for the freezer. After they had paid over $600 of the contract, the balance due was still more than $800 due to late charges and extension costs.

The Jones and the credit company that had acquired the contract ended up in court. The Jones alleged that the contract was unconscionable meaning that it was so unfair as to shock the conscious of the community. Based on the unconscionable character of the contract, they argued that it was not enforceable. The credit company argued simply that the contract spoke for itself. There was nothing in it that was unusual or not clearly stated. Further, it argued that the high charges in the terms were necessary to compensate for the very high risks of default. Without such harsh terms, it could not offer credit to people like the Jones.

The court could have simply ruled under its common law authority that the contract was morally unacceptable and would not be enforced (i.e., it violated public policy). The common law had allowed such leeway for many years in contract enforcement.

But the court looked to the statutes and applied the UCC to cancel the contract. The UCC contains language that allows a court to find a contract or any clause in it to be unconscionable and to refuse to enforce the contract or to limit its enforcement to the parts that are acceptable. The UCC allows the offending party the opportunity to explain the clause and provide evidence to support its commercial purpose.

The UCC does not require that courts find evidence of fraud or even factual support for injustice. There is no requirement that damages or dissimilar treatment be shown. Courts simply have the authority to look at all of the facts and determine that contracts are unconscionable.

After finding the terms of the contract unconscionable, the court reformed the Jones' contract to require only the payment of the $600 already paid. The court then ruled that the remaining contract amount was not enforceable.

The courts will seldom interfere with contract terms. Don't let this case give you even a fleeting hope to escape the contracts you entered! We are all expected to understand the terms we sign or to seek help in understanding them before we enter the agreement. The age old contract expectation is that the "buyer beware" as he will be held to the terms he signs.

But this situation shows how a court will intervene when it finds the relative bargaining power of the parties to be manifestly unequal, and one party appears to take advantage of the other. The terms here were unquestionably beyond normal commercial standards, and the court exercised its role as the conscience of the community.

Chapter 18
Wills, Probate and Trust Law

(The Law's Role in Who Gets Your Stuff)

We have already discussed taxes, and now we will deal with the other certainty in life. That, of course, is death!

The law of wills, probate, and trusts is not exclusively about death or dying, but it does have its origins there. This law deals with the disposition of property (and debts) of people not only when they die, but also during life, perhaps in preparation for death.

First, we need to define the terms.

A **will** is a written directive for the distribution of a person's property upon his death. For a will to be legally binding, it must follow the statutes of the state where it is created.

Probate is the judicial process for administering a will, or if no will, to dispose of a decedent's property under the laws of the state. If a person dies without a will, he is said to die "**intestate.**"

A **trust** is a legally enforceable arrangement in which one party (the trustee) agrees to take property from a second person (grantor) to hold for the benefit of a third person (beneficiary). A trust created before death can avoid a probate of the decedent's estate in court.

At death, property passes to heirs in essentially five different ways:

◻ Will
◻ By operation of law
◻ Intestacy

◘ Escheat

◘ Trust

Let's discuss these.

Wills

References to the concept of wills, or the right to dispose of one's property after death, appear throughout history. The Bible makes reference, ancient Greece adopted the idea, and Roman law embraced it. English law, which is the basis for U.S. law, developed the concept based on this history and enacted the Statute of Wills in 1540. This statute allowed land owners to devise their holdings to whomever they preferred. Modern wills are very much derived from thousands of years of human history.

There are just four requirements needed to create a legally enforceable will:

◘ A person who is competent to make legal decisions and expresses the wish to dispose of his property at death.

◘ A written expression of that person's wishes for the disposition of his property.

◘ His signature.

◘ The signatures (attestation) of mentally competent witnesses (most states require two).

If one of the above requirements is missing, a court action may be necessary to validate the will before any property is distributed.

The purpose of a will is to direct the disposition of property upon death. Although this may seem like a morbid idea and if given some thought, a radical suggestion, our law does indeed allow us to control the future.

Properly executed wills are perhaps the most absolute legal documents that our system enforces. Once duly signed and attested, a will can only be revoked by action of the person who made it. Revocation requires either a new will revoking the old or the physical destruction of the will by the maker. Only a "codicil" that must be signed and attested the same as the original can change a will. A properly executed will can be contested after death, but only by proving fraud or undue influence on the maker. Proving fraud or undue influence is very difficult. Our legal system favors wills.

Wills, however, can sometimes be disputed. In most states, a spouse cannot disinherit the other spouse. State laws provide for a right to take against a will (traditionally this right was called dower). Today, this is commonly available for both men and women. If a spouse is excluded from a will or left a small portion of the property, he or she has the right to take a share of the estate even though contrary to the terms of the will. This share is typically between one-third and one-half of the property depending on the state law and the presence of children. This is an election, and the spouse does not have to elect the share. The election is voluntary.

A will leaves property in several ways. A devise directs the disposition of real estate. A specific bequest leaves a specific piece of property or amount of money to a named person. A general gift is usually money that does not identify a specific source of the funds. And a residuary gift is the amount of the property left after payment of the specific and general gifts. No property can pass to an heir, however, until after the payment of the debts of the deceased and the costs of administering the estate.

A will controls only the property of a person at the time he dies. Property that has already transferred by gift, or that transfers by operation of law or trust, is not included in the probate estate (the amount of property that must be transferred through the probate court).

If a person dies with a will, it is normally necessary to file a petition in the state probate court to administer the will. The court will appoint an executor, often named in the will, to administer the estate. The court oversees the gathering of assets, the determination of debts and the distribution of the property by the executor. An executor is entitled to payment for his services.

If a person dies with little or no property that passes under his will, most states have an abbreviated process for finalizing the estate and distributing the property that does not require the formal filing of a petition in the probate court. These processes are court supervised, but simply require the filing of a schedule of assets, debts and expenses. If burial expenses exceed the amount of assets, the court will typically allow the executor to use the assets to pay them.

Operation of Law

At death, some property passes by operation of law. This means that the property passes outside of the will and automatically under the terms of contract law. Some examples include property held jointly with the decedent - the balance or title passes automatically to the surviving joint owner at death (e.g., a joint bank account). Life insurance and pension accounts typically pass automatically to the named beneficiaries. And property held in a trust passes to the designated beneficiaries under the terms of the trust.

Many people with substantial wealth die with little or no property passing under their wills. In the absence of fraud or a security interest, the property passing outside of the will by operation of law is not subject to the payment of the decedent's debts.

Property passing by operation of law is not subject to court procedures or processes. No probate court action is required. A person dies, and upon death, the property automatically belongs to the beneficiary or joint tenant as determined before death.

Intestate

If a person dies without a will and has property that does not pass by operation of law, he is said to die intestate. In this situation, heirs are determined by state law, which vary considerably. In most states, a surviving spouse is entitled to the property unless there are children. If the deceased has children, the spouse may receive one-half to two-thirds of the estate and any surviving children share the rest equally. If there is not a surviving spouse, the children receive the property in equal shares. If there is no spouse and no children, the law looks first to descendants (i.e., grandchildren), and then ancestors (i.e., parents) and then to brothers and sisters and the children of brothers and sisters.

If no living relatives are located, the property goes to the state (this is called "escheat").

An important element of inheritance law is the concept of *per stirpes* versus *per capita*. This concept applies to both the transfer of property by will or by intestacy. *Per stirpes* means that heirs receive property based on the share that their parents would receive. *Per capita* means that heirs receive equal shares.

For example, if a person dies intestate without a spouse, parents, or descendants (children, grandchildren, etc.) surviving him, his property would pass to his brothers and sisters, or if they are deceased to his nephews and nieces. But what would each receive?

Under *per stirpes*, each nephew and niece would receive a share of what their parents would have received. If there were two brothers, each with two children, but only one of the brothers survives the decedent, the remaining brother would receive one-half of the property, and each of the children of the deceased brother would receive one-fourth of the property (one-half of the share of their deceased parent). Under *per capita* distribution, each surviving relative receives an equal share. In the example, the surviving brother and each of the children of the deceased brother would each receive one-third.

Most states require *per stirpes* distribution if a person dies intestate. Wills can and do provide for either, depending on the wishes expressed in the will by the deceased.

As suggested in the simple example above, if state law controls the distribution of an estate, there may be problems. The law, the distribution, and the process itself can be very complicated (and expensive). Administering the estate, filing the probate action, determining living relatives and their location, and gathering the information necessary to distribute the estate can be mind boggling. If there are many prior close relative deaths and large families, the difficulties can become monumental. Wills significantly reduce these challenging complications.

Trusts

As stated above, a trust allows a third party, the trustee, to hold property for the benefit of a beneficiary or beneficiaries. Trusts serve many purposes, including as a vehicle to pass property to heirs at death.

Trusts do not require any action in probate court. Heirs can, therefore, receive property more quickly and without the public display of assets and names as required in a probate proceeding. Trusts are confidential; while probate records are available to the public. For the very wealthy, trusts also provide for potential death tax savings.

Trusts are also used as vehicles to control wealth both before and after death. They can restrict the access of heirs to property after death, and limit the liability of the person creating the trust both before and after death by removing title and control from him or his estate.

A trust is normally established by a written agreement in which the creator (grantor or settlor) grants a third person (trustee - who may be an individual or a corporation (e.g., a bank)) legal title to property that he transfers to the trust. In the trust document, the trustee is given specific directions and authority for managing and distributing the property. The persons entitled to the benefit of the property (its income and its ultimate distribution) are the beneficiaries. The trustee has a fiduciary relationship to the beneficiaries. This means that he must keep their interests paramount. The trustee is liable to the beneficiaries personally for any errors or omissions beyond normal business decision results.

Trusts can be created during the life of the settlor (*inter vivos* trust) or at death (testamentary trust). This means that a settlor can transfer his property to a trust at any time during his life, or he can cause some or all of his property to pass to a trust created in his will. Property can also be transferred to an *inter vivos* trust at death by will or by operation of law (for example, life insurance proceeds can be paid into a trust that was established before death).

Inter vivos trusts can be revocable during life; the settlor can retain the right to cancel the trust and take back his property, or modify the trust at any time before he dies (sometimes these are called "grantor trusts"). Trusts can also be irrevocable meaning that once they are created, they cannot be terminated or changed.

A revocable trust is commonly used to allow assets to pass to heirs without probate. The grantor retains full rights to the property because he has the power to terminate the trust any time. The trust may call for income to be distributed to the grantor as well. This type of trust, while effective to eliminate probate, essentially is treated as though the property belongs to the grantor until he dies. For example, all income is taxed to the grantor. Under this type of trust, the property is normally distributed to the beneficiaries as soon as possible after death.

Irrevocable trusts permanently remove property and the control of it from a grantor, while limiting the property's use by the beneficiaries. This type of trust effectively removes assets from a person's estate before he dies. The goal may be to reduce the amount and value of property subject to death taxes. It must be noted, however, that when property is transferred to an irrevocable trust, it is considered a gift to the beneficiaries and may be taxable as part of the grantor's estate as such.

Revocable trusts can also become permanent and irrevocable upon the death of the grantor. The trustee may be directed to keep and invest the assets until some future time. After the death of the grantor, such trusts can control wealth for a long time into the future. Although trusts traditionally could not last indefinitely (the general common law rule was that they can last for the life of any beneficiary plus 21 years), this rule has been modified by many states. Under some states' laws, trusts for some purposes can now last forever.

Why would a person want to control his property after death? This is a very legitimate question that anybody considering a long-term trust may want to contemplate. Some common reasons include limiting access to the property for those felt incompetent to handle it, maintaining a business enterprise, providing for specific other persons (e.g., spouses) during their lives, or preserving property for future generations.

Besides serving as vehicles to transfer or retain post-death control of property, trusts serve many other purposes in business and individual property management. They are used to hold business entities allowing the owners to give management responsibility and the liability of ownership to the trustee. They can provide temporary custody of property to a trustee while awaiting delivery to a third person. They can provide funds for the care and protection of a disabled person that is separate from the funds of the grantor that may suffer later bankruptcy or insolvency. They can even be created by law to protect property that comes into the possession of a third party by some accident or fraud. For example, if a person embezzles money from his employer and uses it to buy a house, the courts may find that the embezzler holds the house in trust for the employer.

State laws regarding trusts can be very different, and a person considering a trust must make careful decisions. He must be aware of the particular law in the jurisdiction where he forms the trust and consider his intentions relative to it.

In Conclusion

When death occurs, the property of the deceased must be transferred to somebody. It cannot just continue to exist without ownership. The laws of wills, probate, and trusts provide the mechanisms for transferring property to the right persons according to the wishes of the deceased, or if he has not made his wishes formally known in a will or trust, according to the distribution determined by the state. Many people do not have wills or trusts, perhaps because their property is minimal, but if there is property, the law allows and assists us in passing it to those we want to have it.

A Story from the Real

The wife of a man who had accumulated substantial wealth passed after 53 years of marriage. The couple had two children and four grandchildren at the time of her death. The surviving spouse was alleged to have suffered from severe depression, heavy drinking, outbursts of crying, and hallucinations after his wife's death. A few months after her death, he moved back to his small hometown after living in another state for many years with his family.

Apparently, he quickly recovered his composure and found new love in the old setting. After a three month courtship, he married another woman. This was within six months of his first wife's death. A month later he died. We could say all's well that ends well. But this story did not end well.

One week after his new marriage, the new wife met with her attorney and had a new will drafted. She then had her husband sign it. As you might suspect, the will left everything to his new wife of one week. His children received nothing.

His two children filed an action to set aside the will claiming undue influence and lack of mental capacity. To support their position, they offered evidence of his bizarre behavior after his first wife's death. To support undue influence, they showed the new wife's apparent pressure on him and that her attorney had prepared the new will at her direction and without their father's involvement.

Interestingly, the new wife produced witnesses that claimed the man had not changed, did not drink, and was very happy and content in his new relationship and marriage.

The trial was held before a jury, and the jury ruled in favor of the children setting aside the new will. The new wife appealed. She argued that the children provided insufficient evidence to support either deficient mental capacity or undue influence.

The appeals court discussed a somewhat muddled history of law regarding undue influence and mental capacity. Different facts had produced different rulings regarding these. The court explained that the courts firmly uphold a decedent's intentions as stated in his will and that having insufficient mental capacity is more than just odd behavior, age, infirmity or forgetfulness. It requires that the person making the will does not have an understanding of his property, the people that would normally receive his possessions, and his relationship to them.

Further, the court said that to set aside a will based on undue influence requires evidence that shows that someone acquired such control over the deceased person's mind that his free will was removed.

These are very powerful standards to overcome to set aside a will. But the court also found that a combination of factors can lessen the stringent requirements. If undue influence is shown in combination with an altered mental state, that may be enough to nullify a will.

The court ruled that since there was evidence presented of both questionable mental capacity and undue influence, the validity of the will became a factual matter for the jury to review and decide. Here the jury accepted the evidence presented by the children, and considered the relatively short relationship of the decedent and his new wife. Given the facts presented, there was no legal error in the trial court, and the ruling in favor of the children was affirmed.

This case illustrates that overturning a will is a difficult process. Evidence must support any alleged invalidity. Juries are not permitted to consider whether a will is fair or if its distribution of property is customary. A decision to set aside a will must be based on evidence that there was a defect in the mental state of the will maker, or that some strong influence beyond mere affection, kindness or argument influenced his decisions.

Chapter 19
Societal Protection Law

(Big Brother Comes Through For Us)

We are all victims of others in our society. A neighbor driving his car pollutes the air that I breathe. A factory in town may release toxins into the water. The gas stations in my locale may collude to raise prices. My friend may use body chemicals that cause coughing or difficulty breathing. The meat at the corner market may be full of bacteria. I may lose my job and have no food. We need protection!

As used in this chapter, societal protection means laws intended to protect and provide for the well-being of people in our society. While all laws are intended to serve that purpose in some ways, there are others directed specifically to our protection. Other chapters of this book cover some of the protections we receive from the law. For example, tort law, employment law, and debtor/creditor law provide many protections.

This chapter includes others that do not fit into these categories. We will specifically look at business crimes, consumer protection laws, rules to encourage competition, environmental laws, and social well-being laws

Business Crimes

Businesses sometimes commit crimes. When they do, it impacts not only the owners, but may also affect the customers, suppliers, and employees of the business. Many times there are large numbers of others in society affected as well. Investment losses, pension fund failures, defective products, and corruption can negatively change the lives of thousands or even millions of people.

We know that crime refers to intentional behavior that offends society. The state prosecutes crimes; convictions for business crimes usually result in fines, loss of licenses, or loss of business charters. The burden of proof requires the government to meet a high standard - beyond a reasonable doubt.

In addition to business behavior being potentially criminal, many laws and regulations also provide for "civil" consequences if businesses violate them. Civil consequences are not criminal penalties. They require a lower standard of proof - a preponderance of the evidence - and they are less harsh in impact. They do not require a court conviction and are often levied by regulatory agencies. Civil fines and penalties are levied to encourage proper behavior, as well as to punish bad behavior. While the definitions of civil and criminal violations are academically distinguishable, they are sometimes difficult to differentiate. But the payment of civil fines may carry far less stigma than a criminal conviction. Most businesses on occasion are subjected to civil penalties.

Business crime is a vast topic. Corporations and other business entities can commit many of the same crimes as individuals - for example, business entities have been convicted of theft, assault, conspiracy, criminal trespass, fraud, and even homicide. Obviously, a corporation cannot go to jail, but it can receive heavy fines and be barred from many business arrangements and licenses that forbid felons. Businesses, however, also have a unique set of crimes that are business related.

Making false statements in financial and governmental investigation matters violates criminal statutes. Some examples include false statements to banks, false statements in financial reports, false tax returns, or false statements to any government agency investigator. Bankruptcy crimes fall into this group. While we usually think it is debtors that attempt to defraud the bankruptcy court, creditors that submit false claims or obtain inappropriate preferential arrangements with debtors also commit crimes. For example, a false proof of claim filed by a creditor could easily contain an extra "0" at the end of the number, increasing the potential payment from the bankruptcy by tenfold.

Government funding and government reimbursements also lead to many business crimes. Defrauding the government, with $2,000 hammers or false Medicare claims, is a significant criminal activity that many companies justify because the government somehow cannot be harmed. But these crimes are regularly pursued and prosecuted.

Besides traditional crimes and criminal prosecutions, the regulatory environment of our government is vigorously involved in addressing business crime and dangerous activities. Instead of waiting for wrongdoing to occur and then punishing it, laws and regulations now dictate acceptable behavior and address noncompliance before damage can occur. It appears that many regulations have positively changed bad business conduct, but not without the sometimes very high costs of compliance and enforcement.

Consumer Protection Law

Outside of the spheres of contract law and tort law, there was historically little law devoted to protecting the rights of consumers - those who trade with commercial businesses. Perhaps there was this omission in the law because historically businesses were small and business was typically conducted with neighbors and others on a local and personal scale. In the past 100 years, however, this view of commerce has changed dramatically. Products and services are still provided by small local businesses, but most come from very large, even worldwide business operations that are far removed from daily interactions and relationships. This change in the world of business is one of the primary drivers of our now expansive consumer protection laws.

Consumer protection laws protect from overreaching and abusive behavior by commercial enterprises. That sounds harsh, but we know it happens and it is the reason we have these laws. The laws set standards for what is permitted behavior and provide penalties for failure to follow these standards. Let's discuss some of the laws that protect us from bad business practices.

False advertising, bait and switch advertising, and tele-marketing and electronic abuse – Many federal and state laws protect us from false advertising, bait and switch advertising, and telemarketing and electronic abuse. These laws do not require that actions of a business harm anybody.

The Federal Trade Commission Act – This was perhaps the earliest of the consumer protection laws. It was passed in 1914 and created the FTC. The act gave the FTC the authority to regulate advertising. The FTC challenges deceptive advertising, not only that which is false, but also that which is based on supposition, half-truths, and unreliable research or data. The FTC has issued thousands of pages of regulations that define what is acceptable and what is not in advertising, covering topics from EPA mileage estimates to product endorsements made by celebrities.

In 1968, the FTC issued guidelines for "bait and switch" advertising that requires advertisers to have the product advertised in stock and available for the advertised price.

The FTC has the authority to fine violators, and to issue "cease and desist orders" to stop deceptive advertising. It can also impose sanctions on the offending company, including orders to advertise that prior advertising was false!

The Telephone Consumer Protection Act of 1991 (TCPA) – This act prohibits electronic dialing and prerecorded voice calling. It requires identification of the seller and the products for sale. It also gives the consumer the right to be removed from contact lists. Penalties of $500 per violation are available to consumers that take action under the statute. Is this law being violated?

Labeling of goods – The federal government similarly has enacted several statutes that regulate the labeling of products sold to consumers.

The Fair Packaging and Labeling Act – This act requires that labels on products be truthful, contain certain defined information about ingredients, and accurately reflect size and contents.

The Nutrition Labeling and Education Act – This law mandates standardized information regarding the nutritional content of foods. The FTC and other agencies that enforce these provisions are struggling today to regulate packaging labels. The recent trends regarding food health and purity claims, such as "natural," "gluten-free" and "organic," are not easily defined. Rules distinguishing these terms have been difficult to develop.

Consumer health and safety – Consumer health and safety rules cover a broad range of product content, production and handling standards, and product safety.

The Food, Drug, and Cosmetic Act – This statute establishes federal controls on the production, creation, and labeling of all foods, drugs and cosmetics. This is a comprehensive statute that creates and gives authority to the Food and Drug Administration (FDA) to regulate and oversee just about every product meant for human consumption or use on the human body. The regulations under this law are voluminous and control everything from the butchering of meat to the introduction of new prescription drugs.

The Consumer Product Safety Act – This act established a comprehensive regulatory mechanism for protecting consumers from defective or dangerous products. It regulates both design and content. The Consumer Product Safety Commission (CPSC) created by this act oversees product safety through testing and maintaining records of product performance. This agency has the authority to ban the manufacture and sale of goods found to be unsafe.

As we discussed in other chapters, federal law also provides a vast array of consumer protections in credit and employment situations. There are also laws in every state that supplement the federal regulations. These state laws often provide even greater protections.

Rules to Encourage Competition

An entire area of business regulation reflects society's rules for fair competition. These laws are generally categorized as antitrust or monopoly laws, and anti-price fixing laws. The laws are intended to assure open and free trade. The Sherman Act makes certain restraints of trade and monopolistic acts illegal. The Clayton Act regulates business mergers and prohibits certain exclusive dealing arrangements. The Robinson-Patman Act prohibits price discrimination, and the Federal Trade Commission Act prohibits unfair methods of competition. FTC responsibilities include regulating, investigating, and enforcing anti-competition laws. And, numerous court decisions interpret, apply and explain the statutory rules.

Restraint of trade – The Sherman Act and subsequent statutes make monopoly, territorial agreements, and exclusive market arrangements illegal. Any effort to control a product market or be a sole provider is suspect. Monopoly limits competition by eliminating a market for competing products.

Several years ago, Microsoft faced a monopoly suit by the federal government. What had Microsoft done to limit competition? The government allegation centered on Microsoft's combination of operating, browser, and other software in a way that required Microsoft systems to run only Microsoft software products, and combining this exclusive matching in its arrangements with computer hardware manufacturers. Most hardware providers agreed to install Microsoft operating systems on their machines. Microsoft operating systems allowed easy use of Microsoft software programs that were designed to run on them. Essentially, other developers of other operating systems and software were slowly being eliminated from the market.

The trial court actually ruled that Microsoft be split into separate companies that made operating systems or program software. After a reversing appeal, a settlement was reached in which Microsoft agreed to share its software for a period of years.

From a society standpoint, why would it be a good thing to challenge and potentially break up a highly successful and innovative company like Microsoft (or AT&T as was done in 1982)? The answer to is to improve competition which we assume leads to better product development and pricing. Although the outcomes are not always easily measured, some would say that computer technology development has slowed in recent years as manufacturers (and software developers) have become more concentrated. What's new since Microsoft Word?

Price fixing – The Sherman Act also contains anti-price fixing laws. The law prohibits both vertical and horizontal price fixing. Vertical price fixing refers to prices enforced by producers down the line to retailers.

Horizontal price fixing means agreements among competing producers or sellers to maintain agreed upon prices. Both of these arrangements deter competition and increase prices in the market. Price fixing schemes do not have to be formal arrangements - any parallel pricing method may raise suspicion, even those in which a price leader sets market pricing that others follow. How about the gas stations where you live?

All price fixing, however, is not illegal. There must be anticompetitive conduct and results. The courts have applied the "rule of reason" to evaluate price fixing schemes. The test is whether the arrangement has an adverse impact on competition as viewed from a reasonable person standard. Often it is a jury decision.

Unfair competition – This category broadly encompasses any activity that may restrict competition. Some of the activities that may be illegal include territorial agreements that limit sellers and/or enforce prices, price discrimination, industry rules that restrict new competition, and "closed market" arrangements that prohibit outside competition.

A perfect example of a closed market arrangement is professional sports leagues. They control the number, location, and conditions for teams that can compete in the leagues as well as the availability of players. They also negotiate as a "pool" representing all of the teams for television broadcasting contracts. (Clearly a monopoly, but several court challenges, as well as specific Congressional legislation, have provided major league sports with an exemption. Society apparently does not want to limit the anti-competitive behavior of these multi-billion dollar businesses.)

Price discrimination is also a common, but illegal practice. Large buyers obtain better prices than small buyers, for example. How does this impact competition? The smaller buyers cannot sell to customers at the same price as large buyers and may be eliminated from fair competition.

Similar to price discrimination is predatory pricing. Under this arrangement, a large business can cut prices on some products to drive out competitors that only sell the product. Selling for less than cost is possible for the length of time it takes to eliminate the competition. Selling below total cost is suspect and may be illegal depending upon the circumstances and the impact on competition.

Environmental Law

Environmental law as we know it today is relatively new. While the common law long provided remedies for specific environmental destruction or pollution, it was not until the last 50 years that significant federal and state laws were put into place and the Environmental Protection Agency (EPA) was created to regulate and enforce environmental protection. There are now both criminal and civil sanctions for polluting or damaging the environment.

Common law provided (and still does) several ways to address environmental harm. Nuisance law allows for tort suit against any person that unreasonably interferes with another's right to use or enjoy property by polluting the environment. The tort of trespass provides a cause of action for pollution damage to another's property. And the torts of negligence and strict liability may apply to any polluter that violates a duty of care.

These causes of action are real and can be effective, but they require a person to initiate the suit, bear the costs of the suit, and prove damages. While class actions are possible, they are difficult to arrange. These common law actions could eventually stop pollution by making it very costly to the producer of it, but they are slow, difficult and expensive to pursue. Most importantly, tort law cannot provide relief until after pollution has occurred. In reality, before specific statutes were in place, polluters did not face a very strong opposition.

Modern environmental laws powerfully prohibit pollution as opposed to just punishing it. There are at least a dozen statutes at the federal level alone. And there are numerous state statutes that often apply stricter standards. These laws impact almost every business in some way. Many of the environmental laws at the federal level are administered by the EPA, which is an agency created by an executive order of President Richard Nixon.

Environmental law has had a dramatic impact on polluters and pollution in the environment. Water, air, and ground are much cleaner than they were just 50 years ago and natural environments are growing and becoming more protected.

The laws that created this good, however, also cost huge sums of money to implement and enforce. And they interfere with the operation of businesses, even those not polluting. This money comes from tax revenues and the economy as a whole as we all shoulder the costs of new technology, cleaner machinery, and cleanup efforts through higher prices.

Air – The Clean Air Act allows the federal government to limit polluting emissions from vehicles as well as from factories, power plants, and other stationary sources. The EPA was empowered to regulate emissions released into the atmosphere. It does this by setting standards, usually in terms of parts per million that a source can legally emit. Any emissions that exceed the standard are illegal.

The EPA enforces compliance through fines, injunctions, and by closing the offending sources. For the most part, the standards apply to businesses, and not to individuals. Therefore, automobile manufacturers must produce vehicles that meet the standards. Many states, however, have follow-up programs at the individual level that require periodic testing of cars. And, the EPA can require such local enforcement if pollution levels rise to unacceptable levels.

Under the Noise Control Act, the EPA also sets standards for acceptable noise levels and prohibits devices or activities that cause noise in excess of the limits.

The power of the EPA to accomplish its goals of restricting emissions into the air is substantial. The courts have consistently upheld the regulation standards, as well as the monitoring methodologies such as vehicle inspection stations and plant shutdowns in severe circumstances.

Water – The Federal Water Pollution Control Act empowers the federal government to regulate the discharge of pollutants into waterways and protects water oriented environments such as wetlands from modification without prior Army Corps of Engineers approval.

Other federal statutes also protect water and water environments. The Safe Drinking Water Act empowers the federal government to set maximum levels for pollutants in public water systems. The Ocean Dumping Act regulates the transportation and dumping of pollutants into ocean waters. The Oil Pollution Act creates liability for damages to natural resources, private property, and local economies caused by the discharge of oil into navigable water or onto adjoining land.

Toxic and hazardous substances – Several federal statutes control the production, use, and disposal of hazardous materials. All impose criminal and civil sanctions for violation and are enforced by the EPA.

The Federal Insecticide, Fungicide, and Rodenticide Act (FIFRA) requires the registration of all pesticides and herbicides before sale. They must be certified and used for approved applications only, and used only in limited quantities on food crops. The FIFRA also imposes strict labeling requirements.

The Toxic Substances Control Act requires manufacturers, processors, and users of chemicals to determine their effects on human health and the environment. The EPA requires informative labeling, limits uses, and sets production standards. In some cases, the EPA may entirely prohibit the use of a product.

The Resource Conservation and Recovery Act allows the EPA to determine which waste materials may be hazardous to human health and to monitor and control their use and disposal.

"The Superfund", is a common shorthand name for the Comprehensive Environmental Response, Compensation, and Liability Act of 1980 (CERCLA). It may be the most well-known hazardous materials statute. CERCLA provides for the cleanup of polluted sites. It also imposes liability on the polluters for the cost of the cleanup.

When a toxic site is identified, the EPA attempts to determine who caused the pollution. Polluters may include the source of the polluting agents, those who transported the pollutants, and the owners of the site. All of these parties are jointly and severally responsible for the costs. This means that each of them is individually liable for the entire cost of clean-up. The government can pursue any or all of the parties to collect the costs. Because these costs can be tremendous, this liability can be and has been a destroyer of businesses. And it has curbed pollution!

Hazardous waste disposal is expensive and applies to many everyday business products and by-products. Compliance with the laws for the use, storage, and disposal of these products is critical. The penalties and costs of non-compliance are enormous.

As discussed in Chapter 8, the government levies excise taxes on many hazardous chemicals. Manufacturers pay these taxes. The tax funds offset the costs incurred by the various activities of the EPA to control them.

Environmental laws are very encompassing and are intended to strictly control pollution and hazardous waste disposal into the air, water, and land environments. They impact every business because all businesses produce some waste or pollutants of varying quantity and danger. A simple illustration may best make the point.

Assume that we know the owner of a McDonald's restaurant. The used oil in his deep fryer is a hazardous, carcinogenic waste product. He must carefully dispose of it. If he decides that the cost of licensed disposal with proper return manifest is too high, and decides to use unlicensed disposal or even does the job himself, he takes on very substantial risk.

If he disposes of the product in an unauthorized site, or his unlicensed hauler does so, he faces felony criminal charges and/or civil penalties if the EPA discovers his unauthorized disposal. If the dumpsite is later declared a Superfund site under CERCLA, he will be liable for the entire cleanup of the property - in full. The site owner and the hauler will also be fully liable. But even if his used oil made up only a tiny fraction of the waste dumped there illegally, he could bear the entire cost - many millions of dollars - alone if the other parties are not able to pay!

Social Well-Being

There are many laws at both the federal and state levels that provide assistance and benefits to individuals in need. These laws offer an overwhelming number of programs designed to help. Numerous agencies at the federal and state levels devote substantial funds and other resources to operating them. At the national level, these programs comprise one-half of all federal expenditures (a total exceeding $2.5 trillion). Let's discuss some of the most well-known.

Social Security – This system requires individuals and their employers to both contribute a part of salaries to fund it. It provides retirement benefits, as well as disability insurance and survivorship insurance. The retirement benefit is just one part of this system. Every working person who participates in the Social Security system also has the right to income if disabled, and his surviving children also have the right to payments of support if he dies before they reach age 18. Social Security is not voluntary; every worker and every employer must participate with a few limited exceptions. The system collects and distributes hundreds of billions of dollars each year.

Medicare – Medicare is a federal health insurance system that pays benefits to those over 65 years of age. Both employers and employees fund the system with taxes collected as a percentage of wages paid. When a person reaches the age of 65, coverage begins. Medicare coverage is not, however, complete. It pays 80 percent of many health related costs but does not cover drugs and many other ordinary medical expenses. Medicare offers supplemental plans, for additional fees, which cover additional costs for other charges. Many people also have private backup insurance to cover all or part of the costs not covered by Medicare. Medicare covers about 17 percent of Americans.

Medicaid – Medicaid is a health care system supported jointly by the federal and state governments. It is operated by the individual states, and each has its own program. Medicaid provides medical services for low income individuals who do not have other coverage. The services provided are basic and usually only available at limited locations. If a person qualifies for Medicaid, he essentially has no-cost healthcare provided by the government. He is not eligible for Obamacare as presented below. Medicaid covers about 16 percent of Americans.

The Patient Protection and Affordable Care Act (commonly called **"Obamacare"**) – This law provides for a federal health care program intended to make healthcare available to all Americans. It accomplishes this by creating a system in which private insurance companies offer insurance products to all members of the public. Those who did not qualify for private insurance in the past due to pre-existing conditions, age or other factors must be included in the coverage offered. Those who cannot afford the premiums (as determined by standards in the statute) are entitled to supplements from the federal government to cover the costs. The IRS administers the supplements. All supplemental payments under the system are monitored and in some instances paid through the tax returns of the individuals. Under Obamacare, every American is required to have health care coverage, and every employer of more than 50 persons is required to provide insurance. It has been successful at increasing insurance coverage, but there are still a significant number of Americans that do not have health insurance coverage of any kind because they choose not to comply with this act.

There are many federal and state programs that provide assistance to low income individuals and families. Some of them are described below.

The Supplemental Nutrition Assistance Program (SNAP) – This program provides prepaid food cards to low income families that help them purchase groceries.

The Temporary Assistance for Needy Families (TANF) Act – The U.S. Department of Health and Human Services administers the programs under this act that provide cash payments to various indigent persons, mostly those with dependent children. The states operate this program, and the benefits and conditions vary significantly among different states.

According to the Department of Health and Human Services, nearly 15 percent of Americans receive SNAP benefits and nearly 25 percent of Americans, and 38 percent of Americans under the age of five, receive some kind of welfare benefits.

The Housing and Urban Development Act of 1965 – This act increased federal government involvement in providing and managing housing. The agency oversees a large number of programs that provide rent assistance, housing improvement grants, veteran's benefits in obtaining mortgages, grants for the construction of infrastructures such as sewers and water facilities, and urban improvement grants for parks, reconstruction, and community centers. The act created a cabinet level position and agency called the Department of Housing and Urban Development (HUD). This agency administers a broad range of programs.

The Housing Choice Voucher Program (Section 8) – Section 8 is the largest federal housing program. It is a voucher program run by state agencies. Under this program, indigent persons receive vouchers that can be used to obtain housing. A complicated formula that takes into account family size and the local real estate market determines the amounts of the vouchers. HUD must approve all housing paid for with the vouchers. Although HUD helps low or no income people pay for it, the availability of housing under the program is severely limited in most cities and there are long waiting lists for participation.

And, many others – There are also many other social welfare and public assistance programs available, including at least 91 major programs at the federal level alone. These include child care assistance and enhanced educational opportunities (such as Head Start and numerous special training programs), energy cost assistance, education payment assistance (including federally backed student loans), school lunch programs, adoption and foster care assistance, and various other programs to provide health and nutrition services to children and families. In addition, the military and the VA administer many programs providing health and welfare services to military families and retirees.

In Conclusion

The government and our law take very good care of us! In the last 100 years, the federal and state governments enacted thousands of laws that very actively assure our health, safety, and well-being. The government shields us from abusive enterprises. The products and food we purchase are inspected and determined safe. Our air and water are now much cleaner. Big Brother provides help and assistance to those that fall on hard times. And, medical services are available to all. We are protected!

A Story from the Real

Our cell phones have become our communication links with the world. The access to information and communication offered by the cellular telephone is incredible with libraries, news, unlimited data, and global connection in our pockets and purses. But with this convenience comes substantial interruption and intrusion in our lives.

Consider an individual who received six calls on his mobile phone within a two week period from a large bank. The bank calls were about mortgage payments that were delinquent. A "robodialer," a machine that dials numbers by the thousands, made each of the calls. If someone answered, the system transferred the call to a person. If nobody answered, the autodialer just went to the next number. In addition to the problem with the frequent calls, the receiver of the calls did not have a mortgage with the bank and advised the person connected to the calls of this. The autocalls continued.

The person receiving the calls sued the bank alleging violations of the TCPA. He sought a court order for the bank to stop the auto calls, and he sought monetary penalties as provided by the TCPA. Interestingly, the bank had paid $4.5 million to settle a prior TCPA class action case just one year before this case was filed.

The TCPA specifically prohibits the use of autodialers to make any call to a wireless number in the absence of an emergency or the prior express consent of the called party. Prior consent is considered granted only if the cell number is provided to the creditor by the consumer at the time the debt originated. Also, the FTC that administers the TCPA, published a regulation that banned autodialer credit and collection calls unless the recipient had expressly consented to such calls.

The case was filed as a class-action. This means that all persons who may have received the robocalls were included as plaintiffs. The court certified it as a class-action. Damages, therefore, could be computed by measuring the number of robocalls made and multiplying that number by the $500 per call penalty provided by the statute. Discovery could easily determine the number of calls by requiring the bank to provide its records of the calls made. The bank would have to prove which calls were expressly authorized by the consumers.

Obviously, the amount at issue here was enormous due to the many thousands of calls that were made using the automated system. Any attempt by the bank to prove that it obtained consent for the calls would also be a monumental task. And, certainly many of the customers had not consented. Also, the bank really had no idea how many calls were like the ones made to the person who brought the action. Those calls were made to wrong numbers.

The bank again settled for a very large sum of money and agreed to stop the autodialed calls. It seems very peculiar that a large business like this would continue to make the calls even after they had settled a case just a year earlier based on similar allegations.

There are many of these cases brought against banks, retail outlets, medical and health care companies, cable and wireless companies, and many others for the same violations of the TCPA. The calls continue to be made notwithstanding the many cases brought, lost and settled. These companies have paid hundreds of millions of dollars.

If any company makes calls to cell phones, autodialed or not, which promote goods or services, or for any commercial purpose, and there was no consent given to receive these calls, there may be a cause of action under the TCPA.

Another Case from the Real

It is common practice for automobile dealers to advertise "genuine X parts" where the "X" is the manufacturer of the vehicle. We have all heard this in advertisements. We see it posted in dealerships. Is it okay?

At its heart, the statement is intended to obtain the goodwill of customers. Customers may feel more secure in knowing that the manufacturer produced the parts, or at least tested and approved them to be of good quality. Aftermarket parts have developed a reputation, founded or not, of being inferior and substandard.

But, what if a manufacturer demands that its dealers use the parts it supplies and charges them higher prices than are available from other suppliers? And, what if the manufacturer limits the number and kinds of new vehicles delivered to the dealers if they purchase parts elsewhere? Does this sound like an illegal restraint of trade and competition?

An independent supplier of parts for foreign automobiles thought that it sounded a lot like anticompetitive behavior. A German automobile company required its dealers in the U.S. to buy all of their replacement parts from the company. The franchise agreements with the dealerships contained specific language forcing it. This effectively eliminated competition from any other supplier of parts.

The independent supplier filed suit under the Sherman Act. This Act, first passed in 1890, provides that "contracts... in restraint of trade or commerce among the several States, or with foreign nations, are illegal..."

The Clayton Antitrust Act, passed in 1914, specifically identifies "tying arrangements" as impermissible activities. Further, the Clayton Act allows the recovery of damages by any person who suffered damages as a result of a violation of any antitrust act, including the Sherman Act. It is significant that not only do these statutes provide for criminal penalties and injunctions to stop the anticompetitive behavior, but they also allow any individual or business to bring suit in federal court.

The independent supplier argued that the arrangement the manufacturer had with it dealers presented a clear violation of the Sherman Act. He showed that the agreements were in place with all dealers, the agreements limited competition, and that they affected interstate commerce.

The "tying arrangement" that tied the dealership franchises to the purchase of only manufacturer parts controlled the parts businesses of the dealers. The supplier provided evidence that the manufacturer was using automobile allocations to the dealers to enforce the provision. He also provided testimony detailing the damages he had suffered from lost business after the manufacturer began to enforce its franchise agreements with the dealers.

The manufacturer claimed that the issue was not that clear and that it had a reasonable business purpose in its tying arrangements. It cited a previous U.S. Supreme Court case in which an American car manufacturer was sued for a similar parts tying arrangement with its dealers. That manufacturer had been allowed to continue because the arrangement was "reasonable" and was not shown to inhibit competition.

Our manufacturer argued the same basic points made in the previous case. Its arrangement was intended for valid business purposes. It ensured the quality of the replacement parts that its dealers were selling. It fulfilled customer expectations of receiving quality parts. And, it prevented fraud by dealers that might return non-manufacturer parts under warranty claims to the manufacturer.

The jury in the trial court, however, did not accept the manufacturer's arguments. It found a violation of the Sherman Act. The jury awarded the full damages sought by the independent supplier. In fact, it awarded triple damages under the special damages provisions of the Clayton Act.

The manufacturer appealed. The appeals court did not readily accept the prior Supreme Court ruling as guidance on the law. While recognizing it, the appeals court found that it was primarily an approval of the jury's findings of fact. In that case, the person seeking to recover damages had not provided sufficient evidence to rebut the American manufacturer's claims of reasonable business purpose.

Our supplier, however, met his burden to show that the arrangement was not reasonable. The quality of the parts was shown to be identical, often provided to both the manufacturer and the supplier by the same German companies. The argument about customer preference was simply set aside by showing that there was nothing to prevent a customer from asking for and receiving manufacturer supplied parts if he so desired. Finally, the argument about fraudulent conduct by its dealers was shown to have much more simple remedies available that did not require restraint of trade.

The German manufacturer lost the case. Dealers can still buy and sell only manufacturer parts, but they cannot be forced to do so without the manufacturer showing a good business reason. Good business reasons that might allow tying could include a showing that aftermarket products have a high rate of defects or that they damage the vehicles when installed. Lack of proper functionality or difficulty in installing the parts may also provide a basis. But if a manufacturer attempts to force competitors out of business by placing business pressure on its dealers without good cause, it does so at substantial risk.

Chapter 20
Property Law

(What Exactly Do You Own?)

"Property" is a fascinating concept. We all have it, but can we define it? What is property? The usual answer is "something I own." But what does it mean to own something? Defining property without the presence of law must come down to possession. And possession can be maintained only by strength and force. It's not a pretty picture when we really consider it.

Fortunately, we have the law that defines property for us and protects our ownership of it. The law provides "rights" to property, and the law allows those rights to be enforced in the courts. Property is conceptually defined as a "bundle of legal rights." We don't need physical strength to protect our property; we have the law.

The U.S. Constitution contains the following words in Amendment 5:

> "No person shall…be deprived of life, liberty, or property, without due process of law; nor shall private property be taken for public use, without just compensation."

The document that is the foundation of our government recognizes that property is a right protected by the law.

The discussion that follows walks through the law that creates our property rights.

Types of Property

Property can take three forms: tangible, intangible, and money. Tangible property is that which we can feel and touch (e.g., a table, an automobile).

Intangible property is something of value that is not represented by a physical presence (e.g., a stock certificate that denotes ownership in a corporation, a copyright). Money is intangible in that the paper itself has little value. But money is a separate form of property because in and of itself it has value backed by the government.

We also divide property into three groupings defined by its mobility. Real estate is land and anything permanently attached to it (e.g., a house). Personal property is movable property, or anything not attached to land. A third grouping is fixtures. This group includes personal property permanently affixed to real estate (e.g., a furnace in a building). While fixtures are movable, they typically are not moved; they remain with the real estate to which they are attached.

Acquiring and Passing Title to Property

The very core of property is obtaining the legal right to it. There are many ways we acquire property; some of them are obvious, and some are perhaps surprising.

Purchase – The most obvious way we obtain property is to pay for it. We take title from the previous owner in what is essentially a contractual transfer. All the elements of a valid contract must be present to obtain legal title in this way - agreement, consideration, competent parties, legal purpose, proper form, and mutual assent or understanding.

The person that sells the property must have title himself for the purchaser to obtain title from him. For personal property, a bill of sale (or the contract) is evidence of title, unless state law requires recorded titles such as for automobiles, boats and mobile homes. Contracts for personal property can be oral. For real estate, title comes from a deed given by the prior owner. State laws provide for the recording of deeds, usually in the county where the property is located.

Abandonment – If the rightful owner of personal property abandons it, the first person to take possession obtains title and is the new owner. Abandon means the owner intentionally gives up all rights to it. For example, if property is put out for trash pickup and another takes it from the curb, the taker now owns the property. A trespasser, however, cannot obtain title. Interestingly, real estate cannot be abandon. Ownership of real property remains with the last person to whom it was transferred by deed and the owner cannot dispose himself of it without somebody else taking it. But see adverse possession below.

Possession – In the opening of this chapter, we said that possession does not define ownership. But possession may be legal ownership if no other ownership interest exists and nobody else asserts ownership. The legal taking of a wild animal, for example, creates a property right in the animal taken. Once there is possession of personal property, only a person with a prior legal title can claim ownership of it.

Adverse possession – In many states, title to real estate can be claimed by occupying and openly demonstrating ownership by use of a property for a period of years (i.e., usually seven years). If the true owner does not contest the occupation and use of the property, the person in possession can file a court action to obtain a deed. This is not a simple process. And, the courts may question an adverse possession claim when the original owner paid the real estate taxes on the property.

Production and accession – Property can be produced, constructed, made, or increased in value by labor or materials (accession). A person can obtain materials or make materials and construct them into property. For example, trees can be cut and fashioned into a table. The table is now property owned by the creator. His legal title rests in his possession of something that did not exist before. Therefore, no one else can claim ownership. A person can also obtain at least partial title by adding value to the property of another by improving it or otherwise adding to its value.

A person can also create property with intellectual effort. For example, artistic creations, inventions, and music are created basically out of nothing but human effort. Some created property (e.g., copyrights, patents) requires registration or recording for the creator to establish ownership. Also, consider that a person who starts a business may create intangible property in the new value of the business entity itself.

Gift – Property can be gifted without a sale from one person to another. Such a transfer requires "donative intent" on the part of the person transferring the property. Donative intent can be shown by a written document making the transfer or from the conduct of the parties. A gift also requires delivery and acceptance of the gift. A gift cannot be forced. When a valid gift is completed, the recipient takes the title of the previous owner.

Will or inheritance – Property can be transferred at death by will, operation of law (e.g., joint property), trust, or by intestacy under state law. The heir takes the title of the decedent. Will and inheritance transfers also cannot be forced. An heir has the right to refuse to take the property.

Lost property – If property is lost or mislaid, the owner retains title to it. "Finders keepers, losers weepers" is not the law. A finder of lost property may assert ownership, but in many states, he cannot claim title until he attempts to find the true owner. Also, many states require that all or part of the found property be ceded to the state. Real estate cannot be "lost," but see adverse possession above.

Ownership Interests in Property

Both real and personal property ownership come in several forms. If personal property is owned by one person who has all legal rights to it, the ownership is called "individual." That means that the person has sole and exclusive rights to the property. Similarly, an old English term "fee simple" describes the individual ownership of real property.

Property can also be owned together with other persons and ownership can be limited. There are several types of ownership interests available with co-owners or limitations:

Tenants in common – This means there are two or more owners and each owns an undivided fraction of the property. Their interests may be 50/50, or different fractions, such as 40/60 or 70/30, but they each have an interest in the entire property. The interest of a tenant in common can be sold, inherited and otherwise transferred to another. Tenants in common title can be broken only by one of the tenants receiving all of the interest from the others (e.g., by sale), by court action, or by agreement to separate the interests if possible. An heir takes the place of a deceased tenant in common. Creditors of one tenant in common can judicially acquire the rights of a tenant in common debtor.

Joint tenants – Joint tenants hold undivided interests in the entire property and upon the death of one joint tenant, the entire interest and title pass to the survivor. Joint tenancy can be broken in the same ways as a tenancy in common, and a creditor can assert its rights against a joint tenancy.

Tenancy by the entirety – This is a special ownership by a husband and wife that is available in many states. It is a survivorship tenancy like joint tenancy, but neither spouse can transfer his or her interest separately during life. A transfer of the property or any part of it requires both parties. Tenancy by the entirety is generally protected against attachment by creditors as well, although states may have different rules regarding this.

"Community property" – Community property is not an ownership form like those described above. It is a legal structure in nine states that makes all property acquired during the marriage the property of both spouses. Each spouse holds an undivided one-half interest in it. Each community property state has its individual set of laws, but generally, they recognize separate property as property acquired before marriage or acquired during marriage by gift or inheritance. Other property acquired during marriage by either spouse is deemed to be half owned by each spouse. Community property is not joint property in most community property jurisdictions. It is subject to the claims of either spouse's creditors. Community property can only be separated by divorce, death, or creditor initiated judicial action.

Life estate – Property can be held for the life of a named person. When that person dies, the ownership interest ends. The remainderman designated by the original owner obtains ownership after the life tenant dies. A life estate may be measured by the life of the person owning the interest or by some other person. For example, at death, a man may leave a life estate to his spouse, with the remainder to his children. Or, he may leave a life estate to his wife measured by the life of his mother who lives with them. In the first example, the wife's interest ends when she dies, but in the second example, the life interest ends when the mother dies.

When the life interest ends, the remaindermen take the full interest (the children in the example).

Leases – A lease is an agreement by the title holder of property (lessor) to allow the use of the property by another (lessee) for a period in exchange for a charge. In a lease, the person who leases the property in effect becomes the owner of the property for the term of the lease. He acquires most rights of ownership. Lease agreements may spell out the rights and responsibilities of each party and limit them, but without such limitations, a person having a lease has only the duty to return the property in the condition he received it.

Conditional – An ownership interest can revert to the prior owner if a stated condition fails. For example, a person may sell his farm to another with the condition that it be farmed for another 50 years and not used in any other way. If the new owner stops farming the property, the title will "revert" to the original owner.

Easements – An easement is the right of a person to use another person's real property. Easements are ownership interests that are evidenced by deeds. They are recorded like deeds. Typical examples of easements include a driveway across a neighbor's property, a right given to a utility company to run wires or pipes under the property, or hunting rights. Easements can be permanent or temporary.

Limitations of Property Ownership

Although the Constitution guarantees the right to property without government interference or confiscation, there are legal exceptions that can limit the ownership or use of property.

Statutory prohibitions – Statutes provide many restrictions to ownership rights for many types of property. This means it is illegal to own or possess them. Examples of these include certain types of guns, military equipment, drugs, and chemicals. How can the government prohibit ownership of property? The courts have ruled that the government has an overriding interest in protecting the public health, safety, and welfare. The police powers of the state can be exercised to safeguard these interests even if the government denies other rights in the process.

Eminent domain – This is the process by which the government can take private property for public use. The Constitution recognizes this governmental right and only requires that fair compensation is paid. While we commonly think of eminent domain as the government taking land for highways or parks, it can also be used to take personal property in time of national need (e.g., airplanes and even factories during a time of war). The important principle of eminent domain is that the taking must be for the public good.

Zoning – Local governments have the authority to limit the use of real property in their areas. Zoning does not require compensation for affected landowners unless it causes a severe restriction of use that has the same effect as confiscation. Normally, zoning is meant to foster neighborhood development and aesthetics and maintain separation between business and residential areas. It is considered an exercise of the government's police powers to preserve the public welfare.

Restrictive covenants – These are private limitations on the use of land that are attached to the deed of the property and "run with" the property (they remain with a property even if it is transferred to another person). They are very common today in both commercial and residential areas. For example, many communities have restrictions that homeowners' associations monitor and enforce. These restrictions may require stated sizes, colors, and styles of homes and may limit outbuildings, street parking and decorations. Because these covenants are part of the contract to purchase the title, they are enforceable unless they violate the law or public policy. A restriction on the nationality of the residents, for example, would be illegal and not enforceable.

Systems of Property Ownership Recording

The narrative above makes several references to proper format and recording of property ownership. All states have detailed systems of preparing and recording titles and deeds to real estate and many types of personal property. These systems are designed to protect the owner of the property from claims against it as well as to protect creditors who loan money using the property as collateral (see Chapter 17 on Debtor/Creditor Law).

As a general rule, owners of all interests in real estate record their deeds in the Recorder's Office of the county where the property is located. While the actual paper deed is still prepared in all jurisdictions, many now record these documents electronically. In many states, all deeds and other interests in real estate (including mortgages and liens) are available from a home computer.

Similarly, titles to vehicles, airplanes, boats, trailers, mobile homes, motorcycles and some other personal property are recorded. Again a paper title is prepared and recorded by the state, either in the county where the property is located or at a central location in the state. These records too are mostly available online.

Ownership of intellectual property is evidenced by copyrights, patents, trademark registrations and in some instances original possession (meaning nobody else can show prior possession).

Ownership of business interests and debt may be shown by corporate stock certificates, bonds, or similar documentations, and in the official records of the company.

When we eliminate real estate filings, registrations, and other legally titled items, the evidence of ownership of the remaining personal property is primarily the responsibility of the owner to prove or a claimant to disprove. As previously stated, invoices, warehouse receipts, bills of lading, and payment receipts provide the documentation for ownership of many items. Possession, without evidence of prior legal title, is the final determination. If nobody can prove previous ownership, the law will typically grant the possessor title.

In Conclusion

Property law allows an owner to enforce his property rights in the courts. If a person has possession of property, and the ownership is challenged and proven by another person, the person holding the property will be required by the law to turn it over to the rightful owner. He may also have to pay damages for any use or destruction of it.

Property ownership like this is a unique part of modern law. In the U.S., our system is highly developed, and we resolve property ownership interests civilly. The right to property, although guaranteed by the Constitution, is almost assumed in our society. There is still plenty of property crime, and there are legitimate disputes over property ownership and rights, but we all understand the concept of lawful ownership and the available legal actions to protect it.

Americans and the citizens of other countries with fully developed property law systems are fortunate. In many parts of the world, such laws do not exist. Without property protections, many of the privileges we take for granted cannot happen. For example, without a reliable and functioning real estate recording system, buying a home with a mortgage loan is not possible.

A Story from the Real

Just 60 years ago, grade school science books contained pie chart graphs showing the valuable elements in a human body. The total value of all of the elements on the graph (e.g., gold, silver, and other metals and minerals) was 98 cents. Today, estimates place the value of a body, without restriction on the use of its parts, to be as high as $46 million. There has been inflation in the past 60 years, but medical science has changed much more than the value of a dollar. Today, body parts could be hugely valuable. One estimate places the value of bone marrow alone at over $20 million.

The law, however, strictly regulates the "selling" of human body parts. It is, for the most part, illegal, although we do allow compensation for blood, hair, and a few other renewable items. But what happens if somebody else sells our body parts? Can it be done? If so, who is entitled to the proceeds of that sale? Several situations have occurred in which the ownership of body parts created legal questions. Let's look at one of the first.

A man had leukemia and sought treatment at a university hospital. The doctors did extensive analysis of his blood, bone marrow, and other bodily fluids and tissues. They recommended that he have his spleen removed to slow down the progress of the disease. The patient signed a consent form for the surgery, and the doctors removed his spleen.

It turns out that the doctors knew that his white blood cells were unusual. They produced unusually large amounts of a certain protein that has potential healing ability. Laboratories can sometimes grow proteins like these once the structure of the protein is identified. Our patient's cells produced large amounts of the protein, allowing easier identification of the protein structure. The cells had commercial value if they could be converted to a "cell line" that would grow indefinitely in a lab.

The doctors used parts of his removed spleen and the fluids they obtained from him to develop such a cell line. They acquired a patent on the cell line and sold it to drug companies for research. They made substantial money, more than $1 million.

Our patient later learned that his cells had been used to produce the cell line without his knowledge (or participation in the profits). He sued. Among other issues, the patient alleged that his "property" was converted, meaning that it was stolen from him. Under the tort of conversion, a plaintiff is entitled to recover any profits made from the use of his stolen property.

The case went to the state supreme court after contradictory rulings at the trial and appeals court levels. The supreme court found that the plaintiff had no claim under the tort of conversion. The court ruled that privacy rights may exist, but that such rights did not require an ownership interest. Also, there was no statute supporting his claim that body parts were "owned" and could be subject to conversion, and the court was unwilling to make such law. The court specifically said that granting a property right in body parts should be undertaken by the legislative branch of government, not the courts.

Further, a state statute specifically directed that "anatomical parts, human tissues, anatomical human remains, or infectious waste following the conclusion of scientific use shall be disposed of by interment, incineration, or any other method determined by the state department of health to protect the public health and safety." This language denied ownership or any property rights to the person from whom the parts were removed. Without a property right in the cells, there could be no tort of conversion.

This was one of the first cases to address the ownership of our body parts after they are removed. Other courts have used this case as precedent in deciding their cases. Today, it seems that we do not own our bodies, at least in a property sense, because the law gives us no ownership rights in them. This case demonstrates an extreme example perhaps of the definition of property. We have no property unless we can find the legal right to it in the law.

Note: Please do not be offended by the result of this case. The court did find that the doctors breached their fiduciary duty to the patient by failing to disclose their commercial interest in his "parts." The court reasoned that if the doctors had disclosed all of the facts, the patient could have refused consent for the removal of the spleen unless the profits were shared with him. He ultimately did get at least part of the profits!

Chapter 21
Agency

(The Law of Representation)

What is an agent? Musicians and actors have agents. Professional sports figures have agents. When selling a house, real estate agents are involved. The government has a lot of agents. Are you an agent?

The word "agent" has more than one meaning. A real estate agent may be an agent of her broker, but in many states, she is not the agent of the buyer or the seller. Similarly, an athlete's agent may or may not have the authority to act as a legal agent. And government agents are often just law enforcement officers who have no real agency relationship to the government. So what is an agent?

Agency is a legal relationship in which one party (the principal) and another party (the agent) agree that the agent will have the authority to act for the principal, binding the principal to contracts with third parties. The legal rules of agency arose and were developed under the common law and were critical to the expansion of business. Agents allowed businesses to seek customers, contract for supplies, and sell goods without the owner being personally involved. Without agents, business owners would be required to conduct all business themselves, severely limiting growth potential. With agents, the amount of trade conducted is almost unlimited.

Agency is therefore essential to the understanding of the legal rules that affect business. Today, nearly every large business has agents, and in many situations, employees are agents of their employers. As employment law developed, it relied on many of the legal principles that developed in agency. A review of agency and employment law shows that employers owe employees the same duties as they owe agents, and conversely, employees owe similar duties to their employers.

Agency is an overt and agreed relationship. If no agency exists, the purported agent's contracts with third parties are not binding on the principal. But, agency by estoppel is applicable when a principal causes a third person to believe that another person is the principal's agent. For example, if a business owner allows another person to buy goods on his behalf and always pays for the goods, he has sent a message to the seller of the goods that this other person is his agent. Therefore, the seller's actions in dealing with the person are in reliance upon the business owner's words or actions and the seller's reasonable belief that the person has authority. This "estops" the business owner from claiming that no agency existed. But the implied agency has limits. If the apparent agent does something different or excessive, there may not be an enforceable estoppel based agency. The seller should have realized the agent's actions were not reasonable.

Agent's Duties to the Principal

Upon creation of an agency, the agent owes certain fiduciary duties to the principal.

These duties are:

Performance – Perhaps this duty is obvious, but an agent has a legal duty to do the work he was hired to do and to do it well. If an agent decides not to perform his work, the principal can recover lost profits from him.

Notification – The agent has a duty to disclose to the principal any facts or information he obtains that is pertinent to the subject matter of the agency.

Loyalty – The duty of loyalty is a fundamental concept of the fiduciary relationship. The agent must act solely for the benefit of the principal, and never in the agent's own interest or the interests of other persons. For example, an agent employed to sell cannot compete with the principal by selling on his own behalf. When an agent breaches the fiduciary duty owed to the principal by becoming a seller himself, the sales contract is voidable at the election of the principal and any profit made belongs to the principal.

Any information or knowledge acquired through the agency relationship is confidential. It is a breach of loyalty to use or disclose such information after termination of the agency.

Obedience – Because the agent is acting on behalf of the principal, a duty is imposed on the agent to follow all lawful, clearly stated instructions of the principal. Whenever an agent deviates from these instructions, the agent is in breach of the fiduciary duty owed.

Accounting – The agent must account to the principal for all property or money received by the agent on behalf of the principal. This duty also requires the agent (in the absence of an agreement) to maintain separate accounts for the principal's funds and his own funds. Any funds received by the agent because of the agency belong to the principal. It is a breach of an agent's duty to secretly retain benefits or profits. Funds so retained by the agent are held in trust on behalf of the principal.

Principal's Duties to the Agent

The principal also has duties to the agent. These are:

Compensation – A principal has a legal duty to pay the agent for services performed.

Reimbursement and indemnification – The principal has a duty to reimburse expenses and pay for damages suffered by the agent in the performance of his services. This duty includes the requirement to pay for negligent acts committed by the agent while performing his job.

Cooperation and assistance – The principal must provide the information and other requirements to do the job, and make sure that the agent has instructions, directions and specific objectives. This may include a duty to provide training, samples, transportation, and the tools necessary to do the job.

Safe working conditions – Even under the common law, a principal has a legal duty to provide safe working conditions. The Occupational Health and Safety Act (OSHA) has enhanced this duty in the modern work place.

If either the principal or the agent breaches a duty, a legal cause of action arises that allows the party injured by the breach to sue for damages.

In Conclusion

Agency is a critical part of business transactions. It creates business expansion and economic growth by allowing entrepreneurs to have others represent them. This gives businesses much greater access to markets and customers.

Because agency law covers the representation of others, it also applies to corporate officers and board members as they are the agents of the owners (stockholders). Likewise, partners in a partnership are agents of each other allowing them to represent the interests of the entire business and potentially creating greater profits (or losses) for the other partners.

Agency also provides much of the foundation for employment law that we have today.

A Story from the Real

We started our agency discussion by asking what it means to be an agent. The discussion above should provide a better understanding of what an agent is and how an agency relationship is formed. The law sets out rules, but that does not mean they cannot be twisted. Consider a tree trimmer.

Homeowners contracted with a gardener to trim a large tree. The tree had a 20-inch branch that hung over a neighbor's house. The neighbor was present when the agreement to trim the tree was made with the gardener. He expressed his concerns that the large branch might fall on his house.

When the gardener performed the work, the homeowners were not present. The neighbor was home working in his garage. He kept watch on the progress of the work and questioned the gardener several times about the methods, safety measures, and other aspects of the work. When the gardener started to trim the large branch, the neighbor took an even more active role.

The gardener was high in the tree without an adequate safety line using a chain saw. The neighbor questioned him about the lack of a safety line, but the gardener told him there was not sufficient room to attach one. The neighbor held a rope tied to the large branch while the gardener began to cut it off with the chain saw.

According to the gardener, the neighbor pulled the rope unexpectedly causing the gardener to fall to the ground. The fall caused severe injuries resulting in paraplegia.

As might be expected, the gardener sought compensation from somebody for his injuries. He tried to allege he was an employee of the homeowners and therefore entitled to recover for his injuries from them. The court did not accept that argument and stated that the facts clearly showed he was an independent contractor not entitled to any damages for his self-caused injuries.

More interestingly, however, the gardener argued that the neighbor was an agent of the homeowners and that because the "agent" was negligent, this negligence should be attributed to the homeowners. This would require the homeowners to pay for the damages caused by his agent. While the assertions about the liability of a principal for the negligent acts of his agent are correct, the court was highly suspect of the existence of an agency relationship.

First, an agency relationship requires an agreement between the principal and the agent that the agent will act on behalf of the principal. Although the neighbor had provided unrelated services to the homeowners in the past for compensation, the court found that this association did not result in an agency regarding the tree trimming. A person who is an agent for one purpose is not an agent for all purposes.

Second, there can be an implied agency if the actions of the principal indicate that another is his agent. For example, if a business owner regularly pays the charges of an employee to the business owner's account at a store, the store may assume that a valid agency relationship exists and be able to collect charges from the business owner that the employee makes without authorization. But to have an implied agency (agency by estoppel), there must be acts of the principal supporting it.

The court found that even though the neighbor was present during the negotiations to make the contract to trim the tree, and was on site the day of the trimming, and was actively interacting with the gardener, he was doing so only to protect his own interests. He was not representing the homeowners, nor was he doing anything on their behalf. The homeowners were not present, did not know of the neighbor's involvement, and did not ask him to watch over the work. The neighbor acted solely on his own behalf.

The court, therefore, found that no agency existed, either actual or implied, as a matter of law. The facts were undisputed, and the only question for the court was whether or not the facts supported agency. They just did not.

Chapter 22
Employment Law

(The Legal Labyrinth of the Workplace)

Dislike your boss? Fed up with employees who don't show up for work? Long hours and no appreciation make unhappy days. Or, maybe you and the boss are colleagues and friends. You love your job and find real satisfaction in your accomplishments. There are many miserable stories from the workplace. There are also many good stories of harmony, reward, and even fun. But the working relationship has a lot of rules, and they impact almost all of us. Only the self-employed can maybe avoid employment law.

Society created laws for employment that affect both employers and employees. In recent years, the law has provided ever more restrictions on the actions of each. Many businesses have employees, and almost every employment situation creates disputes that the legal system must resolve. Employment law is rooted in agency law - employers and employees have rights and duties similar to those found in an agency. Today, fairness and balance are becoming the guiding principles in employment relationships.

What is an Employee?

The discussion of employment law must begin with the definition of an employee. People who work for a business in roles other than employees do not have the same relationship to the business and are normally not protected by employment law.

An employee is a worker that provides effort and/or knowledge to an employer. The employer controls the work through expectations, directions and oversight as to how the job is done. An employee typically has no financial risk in the business, and the employee's work is an integral part of the continuous business operation.

Many businesses today classify some workers as "independent contractors." Independent contractors are individual businesses that complete work based on results, not on methods. The employer may have control over the work that is performed, but not over how it is completed. Independent contractors have financial risk, meaning they can lose money in operating their businesses. They are also typically hired to complete specific tasks or jobs that are not part of the continuous operations of the employer.

Some employers attempt to treat employees as independent contractors to avoid employment law issues and costs. In particular, independent contractors are not entitled to employee benefits and are not covered by workers' compensation, unemployment insurance, or employer contributions to social security.

While the impacted workers may believe they are being paid more as independent contractors that is seldom true. They are responsible for paying for many costs ordinarily paid by the employer, in particular the entire amount of social security taxes (see Chapter 8). They also do not have the legal right to enforce employer duties such as reimbursement and indemnity.

Employers may see independent contractors as less expensive and much easier to manipulate. Independent contractors can be terminated without any of the restrictions discussed below. And, none of the employment laws that follow apply to them.

Suffice it to say that numerous state and federal agencies can and do intervene in the workplace to determine and correct employee classification. These agencies include the IRS, the Department of Labor, the Social Security Administration, state and federal unemployment tax examiners, and state workers' compensation agencies. The government has an interest in assuring that taxes are properly collected and that people working as employees receive the benefits the laws provide.

Employment-at-Will

Employment-at-will is a two-sided concept intended to avoid involuntary servitude. An employee has a right to quit at will, and an employer has a right to fire at will. The mutual right to terminate the employment relationship at any time was intended to create freedom in personal service contracts. Over time, however, the power of the employer to impact employee welfare, and the power of employees to harm the employer's business through unrestrained freedom, required checks to ensure fairness.

From an employer perspective, employment-at-will is limited by several restraints. These include employment and union contracts, implied contract, public policy, breach of the duty of good faith, and antidiscrimination laws.

Employee freedom is also limited. Employee freedom of employment is restrained by contract, non-compete clauses, the duty of loyalty, and the duty of accounting relative to employer trade secrets, customers, and intellectual property infringement. We will discuss some of these areas as they affect the overall employment relationship.

Employment Contracts

Employment contracts are common. They are formal, written agreements that describe the terms of the relationship including items such as compensation, duties, and termination rights, as well as terms for severance packages, non-compete provisions, and even methods for dispute resolution.

Like all contracts, employment contracts must meet the legal requirements of offer and acceptance, consideration, legality, competence of the parties, proper form, and mutual assent. They are enforceable in terms of money damages only. The courts will not enforce personal service, but the courts may enforce a limitation on employment by others.

Non-compete Agreements

A non-compete agreement is a contractual limitation of future employment. Under its terms, an employee in exchange for consideration (that may include current employment) agrees to not work for someone else, or work in the same business, for a given number of years and within a stated area. These agreements are enforceable so long as the time, geographic area, and scope of the restrictions are reasonable considering the terms of the entire agreement.

Generally, the agreements can restrict other employment for time frames of one to five years and restrict geographic areas to the business territory of the employer. The scope of the agreement refers to the kind of work prohibited by the employee after separation; the contract can limit similar work, but not all work.

Implied Contracts

In most states, courts will imply contracts of employment in various circumstances, some based on practices in the industry or a particular company, and others based on written company policies that may suggest a contractual relationship. For example, a company may have a remedial process outlined in its human resources manual. Or, it may have practices that it used consistently in the past. The practices or processes could include things like a 60-day improvement period, additional training and coaching, or opportunities in other jobs before termination. The courts may find that these processes are contractual in nature because they are known and expected by both employers and employees. Such established practices, which are viewed as offered and accepted as a condition of employment, may cause the courts to deny an employer the right to terminate without following the process.

Human resources manuals that are in place in many companies provide a substantial basis for an implied contract. A review of the manual of your company will provide a broad range of "contractual obligations." These might include hiring and termination procedures, medical and other insurance commitments, vacation time, and other benefits. If an employer attempts to change these rules unilaterally, some courts may consider the violation a breach of the employment contract.

Public Policy and Good Faith

In almost all states, both employer and employee behavior are subject to scrutiny based on public policy and/or a duty of good faith. This means that the courts will review conduct and determine if the parties acted in a way that upholds the principles of law and if they acted fairly and reasonably under the circumstances.

The duty of good faith also requires fair disclosure and accounting. For example, if an employee contacts customers of his employer to solicit business for a new employer or himself, he may be acting in bad faith, especially if his only knowledge of the customers came from his employment. Such an action could also create liability under intellectual property law and violate any nondisclosure limitations he has related to his employment. He could be liable for an accounting and damages. Similarly, if an employer allows a confrontational or hostile work environment caused by managers or even other employees, it may be found liable for a breach of the duty of good faith, for breaching the employment contract by violating public policy, or by violating criminal or civil statutes.

Discrimination

Perhaps the greatest employment threat to a business today is a claim of discrimination. Almost all of us have experienced or witnessed discrimination actions. Title VII of the 1964 Civil Right Act is the basis for most discrimination allegations, although subsequent laws such as the Equal Pay Act, the Pregnancy Discrimination Act, and Americans with Disabilities Act also prohibit discrimination.

Title VII lists specific categories of discrimination: race, color, religion, sex, age, and national origin are protected categories. It is important to note that this law does not prohibit discrimination for any other reason (although other laws, public policy and breach of duty may be used to challenge other discrimination). It is also important to understand that discrimination is not limited to particular races, colors, religions, sexes or national origins. Reverse discrimination is a misnomer - discrimination is discrimination no matter the victim's identification.

Discrimination laws were passed to force equality. The law itself does not favor, but only prohibits disfavor. The Equal Employment Opportunity Commission (EEOC) is the federal agency created to regulate and enforce workplace equality, and Title VII provides the authority for its mission. The process of pursuing a discrimination complaint is complex and requires a series of administrative investigations and actions by the EEOC before it can be brought into the courts.

The stigma attached to discrimination complaints and the potential for substantial money damages has led most companies to very carefully comply with equal employment opportunity rules and strictly discipline non-compliance. Settlements are sometimes made to avoid publicity even when a complainant cannot prove discrimination.

Discrimination can be direct or indirect. Direct discrimination refers to unequal treatment as the explicit result of the victim's protected status. (For example, management saying there is no place for females in the company). Indirect discrimination refers to a process or environment that less obviously excludes a particular group but is evidenced by their absence or under-representation in a company or a certain category of jobs. A mere absence of the group may prove indirect discrimination.

Affirmative action is a court-approved process to rectify circumstances that show indirect discrimination. The process provides a dedicated program to increase the underrepresented group in the employee category that is underrepresented. Quotas and numerical goals have been found discriminatory toward other groups. But, the courts generally approve programs to recruit, train, educate, mentor, and even favorably consider members of the underrepresented groups. Advantageous weighting factors that consider race or one of the other protected designations in the selection process have also been approved as a way to increase representation. Affirmative action plans generate substantial contention and litigation under both discrimination and equal protection arguments.

Sexual harassment is a form of discrimination that targets gender or lifestyle. In its most obvious form, it may take the form of "quid pro quo" sexual solicitation, which refers to exchanging sexual favors for some type of job advantage or promotion. This type of sexual harassment is clearly illegal.

Sexual harassment can also include unwelcome sexual advances and other verbal or physical contact of a sexual nature. Sexual harassment does not include offhand comments, bantering or joking, or efforts to initiate a romantic relationship.

Harassment is illegal when it is repeated or pervasive and offensive, and unwanted. It is then said to create a "hostile work environment." Because a hostile work environment can include any person in a work relationship, and not just those who can offer job enhancements, it can be found among all levels of employees and even with visiting customers or contractors. Inappropriate behavior among employees may also cause a hostile work environment for others in the workplace that were not involved in it directly.

In almost all cases in which a management employee is involved in sexual harassment, the employer will be liable. When two employees are involved, however, the employer must know about it and fail to stop it. If the employer takes immediate action, he will have a defense.

Other Federal Statutes

Besides Title VII and the other antidiscrimination statutes, Congress has enacted a number of other laws that apply to employer-employee relationships nationally. Some of the more important statutes are discussed below.

Fair Labor Standards Act of 1938 (FSLA) – This law sets the minimum wage and hours of work, and provides for overtime pay for work in excess of 40 hours per week. While there are over 30 exceptions in the law, especially for "professional" and managerial employees, many issues arise regarding this statute in the workplace. Common disputes involve whether or not an employee falls within one of the exceptions and which hours count as "work hours" for computing the 40-hour limit. Employers may attempt to classify workers into one of the exceptions when in fact they are not included.

Family and Medical Leave Act of 1993 (FMLA) – This statute prohibits large employers (over 50 employees) from terminating employees that seek to leave work for their own medical reasons or for those of a close family member. Employees are permitted up to 12 weeks of unpaid time off to take care of personal and family medical issues.

OHSA – This well-known statute requires safe and healthy work place environments. The Occupational Health and Safety Administration (OSHA) was created by the statute to implement and enforce regulations to make workplaces safe and free from bio and chemical hazards. OSHA carries out its responsibilities by establishing standards for safety and health risks. The agency has the authority to inspect workplaces, without warrants, and to order corrections, levy fines, and even close businesses that violate the standards.

This statute is often cited as an extremely successful government intervention in commerce. Since enactment of the statute in 1970, workplace injuries, deaths, and illnesses have dropped dramatically.

The Employee Retirement Income Security Act (ERISA) – This statute and several others provide rules and accountability for employee pension and retirement plans. These statutes not only provide greater safety for employee funds, but also require businesses to follow strict investment rules and to provide annual financial information and disclosures to employees.

Employers and pension plan administrators are personally liable for any violations of their duties to protect and properly invest the funds. ERISA also created the Pension Benefit Guaranty Corporation (PBGC) that insures retirement funds in the event they are unable to pay promised payments. Employers with retirement plans must pay premiums to support this insurance system.

Obamacare – The Affordable Care Act requires employers with more than 50 employees to provide health insurance for their employees. Failure to provide the insurance results in a penalty of up to $3,000 for each employee. The penalty is apparently not high enough as many employers have chosen to pay the penalty rather than pay higher health care premiums.

Many other federal statutes protect and provide benefits for employees and protections for employers. Some of these are discussed in Chapter 8, Tax Law, including workers' compensation, Social Security, and unemployment insurance.

State Statutes

The federal statutes discussed above are written so that states are encouraged to implement their own laws to supplement them. Many states have chosen to pass laws, and create administrative agencies to enforce them, that have stricter rules and standards. For example, minimum wage amounts exceed the federal standard in at least 29 states.

Even the definitions of employees subject to overtime rules vary widely among the states. While the federal rules have many exceptions, state laws have narrowed these. For example, some employees previously considered "professional" have filed class action suits in state courts against large employers such as the Big 4 accounting firms challenging their classifications. Accountants who are not licensed as Certified Public Accountants (CPAs) have challenged their status in several states.

States have also enacted statutory rights to breaks, lunch periods, paid vacation and holidays, and hours of work that are stricter than federal statutes. There are also substantial variations is state antidiscrimination laws. For example, discrimination based on sexual orientation is not expressly prohibited under the federal legislation, but many states have provided protected class status to gay or other sexually divergent groups.

Unions/Right-to-Work

Employee rights are most evident in unionization. The history of unions in the U.S. is one of uneven favor. The law treated unions harshly when employees first formed them. Employers convinced courts that they were engaging in illegal acts, breaches of the peace, breaches of contract, and even anti-competitive behaviors.

With the passage of the National Labor Relations Act (NLRA) in 1935, employees received the legal right to unionize. The act firmly established the right of unions to bargain for and represent employees. The NLRA also created a federal agency - The National Labor Relation Board (NLRB) - to oversee union and union-management activities.

Unions quickly became a powerful force in employment law. Employees by majority secret ballot, conducted by the NLRB, can elect union representation. Employers are required to negotiate with unions for pay, working conditions, and hiring, promotion and termination rules. The agreements are enforceable contracts.

The NLRB established a dispute resolution process that allows for the filing of unfair labor practices by either side to deal with violations of the law or the contracts. The courts have uniformly upheld the rulings of the NLRB. The NLRB also has authority to enforce workplace issues in non-union businesses. Although infrequently used, the NLRB can address and correct any employer restrictions that impact the free discussion of workplace matters among employees, including restrictions about discussing wages.

Today, the status of unions is in flux again. The changing economy and the nature of jobs have significantly affected the traditional employer - employee relationship. We can expect unions to adopt and seek new constituencies, and in some industries to lose their importance in employment relations.

Right-to-work refers to the laws of individual states that allow employees of a unionized workplace to not join the union and not be subject to the payment of union dues. Other states may require all employees of a unionized workplace to be members of the union and pay dues. Twenty-eight states are right-to-work states in 2017. The federal workforce, although not everybody knows that its workforce is highly unionized, is right-to-work. The laws of right-to-work states generally require non-union employees to be paid in accordance with union contracts and be provided with the job protections available in that contract.

In Conclusion

Employment law encompasses an extensive body of rules, regulations, and good intentions. An employer is charged with knowledge of the law and must comply or face prosecution, fines, or suit.

Many federal and state agencies regulate and monitor employment relationships. A partial list of just federal authorities includes the Department of Labor, the NLRB, OSHA, EPA, ICE, IRS, and the EEOC.

Employers' rights are dramatically limited, and their responsibilities greatly expanded by the FSLA, Title VII, the ADA, the FMLA, ADEA, health and safety laws, union contracts, common law duties, and a myriad of other federal and state laws and regulations. From the employer perspective, the concept of employment-at-will is in practice now very limited in many states. Society has decided to look after workers and provide a system of protections and safeguards.

Employee responsibilities also have expanded through contract and intellectual property laws that provide more limitations on employee actions and disclosures. And some employee behavior is limited through statutes and regulations. For example, some disclosure and all insider trading are prohibited by law.

A Story from the Real

The U.S. has many employment laws that protect employees from harm, abuse, discrimination, and minimal wages among other things. Because of the world economy in place today, U.S. citizens work in many countries, and U.S. employers operate in many countries. Sometimes overseas U.S. companies hire local workers, sometimes they hire U.S. workers, and sometimes they hire both. How do U.S. employment laws impact these workers in foreign countries?

The simple answer is that U.S. employment laws do not apply in foreign countries. But they do apply if Congress explicitly states in the statutes that they do. Confused? Perhaps it is still relatively straightforward. Let's look at a situation where this question was presented.

A naturalized U.S. citizen was working for a U.S. company in a foreign country. He transferred there from a U.S. location at his own request. The employer terminated him while in the foreign country.

The worker alleged that he was terminated because of his race, national origin, and religion. He filed a complaint with the EEOC as required by Title VII of the Civil Rights Act of 1964. Title VII prohibits employers from discriminating against employees based on sex, race, color, national origin, and religion. The EEOC investigated and accepted his claim.

The employer refused to resolve the matter, so the EEOC filed an action in the U.S. District Court at the company headquarters' location in the U.S. The district court dismissed the action because it did not have authority to hear the case. The court said that Title VII did not apply to U.S. citizens employed overseas by U.S. employers. The EEOC appealed, and the U.S. Court of Appeals upheld the dismissal. The EEOC appealed to the U.S. Supreme Court.

The Supreme Court found that U.S. legislation does not apply to activities in foreign countries even when conducted by U.S. persons unless Congress explicitly states in the statute that its provisions apply outside of the U.S. The rule of law has long held that the power of law only extends within the borders of a country. The rule not only respects the laws of other nations but is intended to avoid confrontations between the laws of different countries.

Title VII states that it applies to companies engaged in "commerce," which the EEOC argued must include all commerce in and outside of the U.S. Second, the EEOC relied on a clause that specifically excluded aliens outside of the states from coverage. It argued that by specifically excluding aliens outside of the country, the language must mean that the statute applied to U.S. citizens outside of the states. Finally, as in all administrative agency cases, the EEOC argued that its interpretation of the statutory language should be respected and enforced.

The Supreme Court rejected all of the EEOC positions, primarily because the law has always applied boundaries on law enforcement. The Court said that the limitations were critically important to the maintenance of international relationships. In past cases, the courts required very precise language from Congress to require compliance outside of U.S. territory.

The Court accepted the EEOC's contention that the language regarding commerce and the alien exclusion clauses could be interpreted to mean that Congress intended international application. But the Court also found that the language could have other legitimate meanings unrelated to an overseas application. For example, the alien exclusion clause meant that aliens only had statutory protections within the 50 states and not in U.S. territories outside the states. The term "commerce" did not imply worldwide application; several courts had already found that word did not expand the reach of other statutes internationally.

Finally, the Court stated that while the courts respect and usually approve the interpretations of statutes by federal agencies, Title VII granted no rulemaking authority to the EEOC. Its interpretations were just opinions without any force of law. The Court also stated that even though agencies' interpretations are generally accepted, they are not absolute. Here the Court found no persuasive language in the statute to support the overseas application.

Companies operating overseas are not subject to U.S. laws, employment or otherwise. Labor and wage laws, health and safety laws, and even discrimination protections do not automatically apply even to U.S. citizens working for U.S. companies in other countries. This is an interesting and important intermix of employment law and international law. The borders of a nation limit its legal authority allowing companies operating outside of their home borders to be constrained only by the laws of the locale of their operations.

Note: After the Supreme Court decided this case, Congress modified Title VII so that it applies to U.S. employers employing U.S. citizens worldwide. The required specific language was inserted.

But it is important to recognize that the protections of Title VII still do not apply to foreign persons working for U.S. companies abroad. And, almost all other employment laws in the U.S. are not applicable in foreign country operations.

Chapter 23
Business Entities

(Business Form is a Big Deal)

In this chapter, we explore a crucial area of law for business and business owners - the organization and conduct of business entities. Business operation is critical to the success and welfare of our society. Our laws provide both rules and safeguards to assure that success.

Businesses operate in several different forms - some of them are familiar, and some of them are relatively new. We will discuss the following types of entities:

◘ Sole proprietor

◘ Partnership

◘ Limited partnership

◘ Corporation

◘ Limited liability partnership (LLP)

◘ Limited liability company (LLC)

We will also briefly consider how agency law allows many of these business forms to operate efficiently. And, we will see that franchises allow successful business practices to be shared.

Each of the different forms can be defined simply:

A **sole proprietor** is a business owned and operated by a single person.

A **partnership** is two or more persons who join together to operate a business for profit.

A **limited partnership** is a business form created by state law in which there are two classes of partners - the general partner(s) that manages the business, and the limited partners that are simply investors with limited liability.

A **corporation** is a "legal person" created by state law to conduct business on behalf of its shareholder/owners. Its owners are separate persons that do not have personal liability for its obligations.

An **LLP** is a business entity created by state law that operates as a partnership, except that all partners have limited liability and have personal liability only for their personal acts.

An **LLC** is a corporation-like entity created by state law that operates and is taxed much like a partnership.

A **franchise** is not a business entity form. It is a contract in which one party permits another party to use its trade name and business processes in exchange for a fee.

Agency Relationships

Agency, discussed in Chapter 21, is the basis for the conduct of most business. It creates a relationship between two persons in which one (the agent) acts for the other (the principal). It is easy to see that almost all larger businesses have persons acting for others - employees act for employers, partners act for other partners, and officers act for a corporation and the shareholders.

The law establishes duties and obligations for both parties:

◘ The agent is required to carry out the activities; the principal is required to pay for the service.

◘ The agent must follow directions, keep the principal informed and act solely for the principal; the principal provides needed information and assistance to allow performance and a safe working environment.

◻   The agent is expected to account for all profits, and the principal is expected to reimburse the agent for all costs and expenses.

Agency creates a "fiduciary duty" between the parties. This is a very high standard of trust and loyalty between them. Breaking this duty by either party will potentially cause injury to the other. If injury results, the law allows damages to be recovered.

In a business relationship, this set of duties and responsibilities is critical to successful and efficient operation. A sole proprietor can carry out his business without agents. He can personally sell his product or his service directly to customers. But if a business wants to expand beyond what one person can accomplish, the owner must act through others. Once this acting through others occurs, agency law sets the rules.

Not only does agency law apply to people representing a business, it also applies to the relationship of people functioning within the business. Partners in a partnership are agents of each other. The board of directors and the officers of a corporation are agents of the stockholders. And, LLC management members are agents of all members and the members may be agents of each other.

This agency relationship creates the fiduciary duty between the parties that requires them to deal with each other with extreme care and good faith. This duty requires that they put the interests of the others first in any transaction. Failure to exercise this duty subjects them to personal suit for damages.

As this discussion suggests, agency plays an important role in business form. Almost all business entities create agency relationships among the owners and/or between the owners and those running the company.

How Does a Business Decide the Form?

When starting a business, some important questions must be addressed. The answers to these questions will help determine the business form that is best. These questions include:

◻   Where will the business obtain funds to start up and expand?

◘ How will the business obtain operating funds and distribute the profits and losses?

◘ Is the business expected to present significant liability risks to the owner(s)?

◘ Are there plans for adding more owners?

◘ What is the expected impact of taxes on profits?

◘ Which management structure will provide the most efficiency in operating the business?

◘ Is there an accounting or legal limitation that may require a particular form?

◘ What costs are associated with different business forms?

Let's explore each of these questions as we set up a new business. Let's imagine that I am starting a plumbing business. I determine that I will need $100,000 to buy my equipment. I will also need $50,000 to cover expenses for the first few months of operation. Which business entity will work the best?

Where Will the Business Obtain Funds to Start Up?

Let's say I have $150,000 in the bank. If so, start-up funds may not be a factor in the decision. I can select any form and invest my money. If I have personal assets, such as a house or stocks, I can use them as collateral to borrow the funds I need. But if I do not have the capital or the assets, I will need investors.

Investors want a return on their money, and they want protection from liability. The return they expect is based on the risk of the business - the higher the risk, the higher rate of return they expect. Simply loaning the money to me is one possibility. But usury laws, or the limitations of my projected business income, may prevent the repayment of high enough return to satisfy the risk involved. The investors may demand to share in the profits, and perhaps in the management to protect their investment. They may have to be made "owners" in exchange for their money.

We can use a partnership in which I contribute expertise and labor, and the investors contribute money. We share in the profits. But the investors would also share in the losses and liabilities and be required to contribute more money if something goes wrong.

A limited partnership may work. I contribute expertise in exchange for the general partnership interest, and my investors become limited partners entitled to some share of profits, but without liability for future contributions.

I can form a corporation and sell stock to my investors, and I can take stock in exchange for my expertise. Now we can share in the profits, and the investors' future contributions are limited to voluntary amounts.

We can form an LLC or an LLP and obtain some of the same benefits as a corporation without the formality. In most states, however, LLPs are not available to me because they are limited to professional businesses such as lawyers or accountants. An LLC, however, might work. It allows for the sale of ownership interests to raise funds and protects the owners (called members).

If I can raise the money myself, a sole proprietorship works well. If I need investors, a limited partnership, corporation or LLC may be better.

How Will the Business Obtain Operating Funds and Distribute Profits?

As above, if I have money, this is not much of an issue. As a sole proprietor, I put in the money needed, and I withdraw the profits.

But if I need investors, this becomes very important and there may not be an easy answer.

In a partnership, we share the contributions of funds and receive the profits equally unless we have a written agreement. If we have a written agreement, we share according to the terms in it. Additional needed funds must normally be contributed by all of the partners ratably.

In a limited partnership, the limited partners do not make additional contributions of funds, and the agreement establishes the distribution of profits.

An LLC is much like a limited partnership in this regard - no additional funds are required to be contributed, and the LLC operating agreement determines how the members share profits.

In a corporation, the owners/investors are much more separated from the business. The shareholders do not contribute additional funds, and they are not entitled to distributions of profits (dividends) unless declared by the Board of Directors.

Raising additional funds for operating expenses or for business expansion must be considered. Partnerships require that each partner contribute additional funds as needed by the business. My investors will probably not like that requirement. Limited partnerships, corporations, and LLCs protect the owners from additional mandatory contributions. Additional funds in these entities must be raised by selling more ownership interests or retaining profits in the business. But, selling more interests may present additional problems because current owners must approve the sales, and there may be substantial expenses involved in making the sales.

From a simplicity standpoint, a partnership would be the easiest form to use because profits are distributed by agreement and additional funds must be contributed as needed. But my investors will probably not agree to the additional contributions requirement. Limited partnerships and LLCs also distribute profits directly, but the investors are not required to contribute additional funds.

The investors would want profits distributed to them in some established form, and not be automatically subjected to additional contributions of money. The decision here must be a split one - the investors will want a limited partnership or LLC because of their profit distribution structures. But these forms will potentially make it more difficult to raise new capital for the business.

The bottom line is that an LLC or limited partnership wins out. While still somewhat difficult, it is easier to sell additional limited partnership interests and memberships in an LLC than it is to sell additional shares in a corporation, and a corporation has an indirect profit sharing limitation.

Is the Business Likely to Present Significant Liability Risks to the Owner?

Liability is always the issue immediately raised when considering business form. It may not always be the most important, and the protections provided by the various forms may not apply if the rules are not carefully followed, or if gross misconduct occurs. But the avoidance of liability for errors and negligence of the owners or employees is a significant entity choice concern.

For any new or ongoing small business, debt liability is not the issue. Almost any bank or other creditor will require the personal guaranty of the owner(s) to assure repayment of debt. An entity form will usually not relieve liability for debt for a small business owner.

But tort, contract, employment law, and agency liability are very real concerns depending on the type of business. Consider our plumbing business:

The business will be doing somewhat dangerous work in personal residences, construction sites, and commercial buildings. Activities involve sometimes difficult manual labor, handling of dangerous materials and toxic wastes, and digging and working underground. Work can be in many locations where people, furnishings, and equipment are present, and there may be risks of water and construction damage to property. This business carries a substantial risk of tort liability.

The business will also need to order supplies and equipment, provide estimates for work sought after, and enter into numerous contracts. Employees, co-owners, and other agents may be involved. There may be considerable potential liability for the commitments of agents. For example, an employee may be authorized to order pipe and may enter into a contract to purchase $100,000 of pipe that is not needed. Who will be liable for payment of this contract?

Employees in a business always have the potential of creating liability. Any event that causes employee injury will create potential liability, wage and hour issues can arise, large employment tax liabilities will occur, and the many employee protections statutes like OSHA, Title VII, and Obamacare generate potential risks of lawsuits and agency penalties.

Finally, all businesses enter into many contractual relationships, from hiring employees to arranging sales of goods and services. Contract law tells us that if a contract is breached, the party who does not keep his promises must pay damages to the other party. If my plumbing business fails and I have many incomplete contracts - for employee pay, jobs not completed, or supplies ordered - who will pay the damages?

The correct business form can minimize these potential liability exposures. A sole proprietorship and a general partnership provide no protection. The owners are personally liable for any of these potential damages. When a sole proprietorship or a partnership fails, a common result is the personal bankruptcy of the owner(s).

But liability can be limited. A limited partnership provides liability protection to the limited partners, but not to the general partner. A corporation and an LLC provide liability protection to all of the owners. Only the business assets of these entities are available to claimants for damages caused by the business. And, even if there are no other owners of the business, I can form an LLC or a corporation with just one owner!

An LLP provides a special kind of liability protection. While this business form could not be used for my plumbing business because it is available only for certain professionals, it is important to discuss the protection it provides. State law does not usually allow for liability protection for professionals because society wants them to be responsible for their malpractice. Corporations and LLCs are generally not available to these businesses.

But in large professional businesses, with many partners (in some, there can be thousands of partners), each partner is exposed to personal liability for the malpractice of his/her many partners. This is an enormous responsibility. So the law provides a compromise with LLPs. In LLPs, professionals obtain partial personal liability protection. They are each personally liable only for personal malpractice - each partner is personally responsible only for his/her own mistakes. Although firm assets are subject to the malpractice of any partner, the other partners' personal assets are protected.

After reviewing my options for liability protection in my relatively high-risk plumbing business, a corporation or LLC will work best. While a limited partnership will protect my investors, I see no reason to subject my own personal assets to liability as the general partner. The best choice is to avoid liability for everybody.

Are There Plans for Adding More Owners?

If I have plans to add others to the business venture in the future, the business form can be changed at that time. Or, I can plan ahead, and use a form that allows new owners to enter. As discussed above, we may need to add new owners to raise additional funds.

A sole proprietorship obviously does not work - by definition, it has just one owner.

A partnership can be structured to allow new partners, but bookkeeping matters can become complex. The same applies to limited partnerships - new limited or general partners can be added, but it requires amendments to the legal documents and significant accounting matters.

Corporations and LLCs also allow for new owners. New stock (corporations) or member interests (LLCs) can be issued now and sold later, or the company can buy back its own stock from current owners and sell or give it to others. It may be costly to issue and sell new stock, and it requires approval of the other shareholders, but it can be accomplished. LLC agreements can be drafted to allow for additional membership interests with less formality.

Another form of bringing new owners into a business is to distribute stock or LLC member interests to employees as incentives or awards. This will require a plan either included in the LLC agreement or established by a corporation after it is formed.

Considering all of the issues, an LLC, with the issuance of additional membership interests when it is formed, and proper language in its operating agreement, can probably accomplish new owners most efficiently.

What is the Expected Impact of Taxes on Profits?

Tax ramifications often play a significant role in the decision of business form. This aspect of the decision process, however, may be overstated. Sole proprietorships, partnerships, and LLCs generally require that each owner picks up his share of profits on his personal income tax return. Owners must include those profits in their incomes even if they are not distributed to him. For example, the profits may be retained in the business to fund operations and growth.

With most small incorporated businesses, all or most of the profits are paid to the owners through salaries. If they are not distributed to the owners, however, there are different tax results from the entities described above.

If the owner of a corporation withdraws profits as salary, he again reports this income on his individual tax return(s). The impact of this, without a technical discussion of tax law, is that the bottom line tax paid is essentially the same no matter what form is selected. If the profits are not paid to the owner as salary, however, there can be "double taxation."

With that said, we should consider tax implications. A sole proprietorship's profits are directly taxed to the owner on his Form 1040. He has no withholding and must also pay both his income and his Social Security taxes on his personal tax return. This creates a very large and often unplanned liability for the business owner. Even without considering state and local income taxes, the federal share alone may easily exceed 40 percent of profits when income tax and Social Security taxes are added together.

Partnerships, limited partnerships, and LLCs are all treated the same for tax purposes. The entity files a tax return but pays no tax. All profits are allocated to the partners/members according to the agreement. Each partner includes this amount on his/her personal tax return and pays the income tax and Social Security taxes due. There can be arrangements for withholding, but generally, the partners, like sole proprietors, are individually responsible for paying in their tax liabilities.

Corporations are different. They are taxed as "persons" themselves. They must file a tax return and pay income tax. After-tax profits that are distributed to the owners (dividends) are taxed again on the owners' individual tax returns.

But, because salaries paid to officers and employees are deductions in arriving at a corporation's taxable income, they are not taxed twice if the income is just paid to owners as wages. In most small businesses, the owners take all or most of the profits out as salaries, and there is no double taxation. However, if there are investors who want to share in the profits, or if some of the profits are not distributed, owners may be subject to double tax when the profits are paid out.

For my plumbing business, taxation is not a major factor because I anticipate that most of the profits will be paid to me as salary. There can be complicating factors, however, if I have investors who do not work for the company. As stated above, they may have double taxation when profits are distributed to them. Therefore, the LLC would work better if I have investors.

What Management Structure Will Provide Efficiency in Operating the Business?

Management structure may be important in some business circumstances. If there is one owner and he is the sole investor, it really does not matter much which business form is used because the one person will manage the business. But, when there are multiple owners, or when investors require a management role, the form of the business is more important.

Different forms have different management structures. A partnership allows each owner an equal voice in management; but, a written agreement can modify this. In the limited partnership form, only the general partner(s) can have management authority.

In an LLC with more than one member (owner), the members typically elect a managing member or management team. Otherwise they have equal voices in management like a partnership.

And, in a corporation, the shareholders elect the Board of Directors that hires the officers to manage the operations. As noted above, corporations can have one owner, who would be the sole shareholder, a member of the board of directors, and most likely the chief operating officer.

In all business forms, management has a fiduciary duty to perform for the benefit of the owners. This means that general partners, managing members, directors, officers, and other managing owners all owe the highest standards of loyalty and trust to the other owners. They are required in all of their actions to look out for their interests.

For my plumbing business, if I have co-owners or investors, the best choice would be an LLC or corporation because it allows for more orderly management, especially when investors are not working in the business. They can control the management (probably me) if they own a majority of the business through elections of managers or board members. If unhappy with the business progress, they can change management without being involved in day-to-day operations.

Is There an Accounting or Legal Limitation that May Require a Particular Form?

There are many different accounting, legal, and/or bookkeeping rules that can dictate a business form. Some examples: Many franchise agreements require the franchisee to be incorporated to provide liability protection for the franchisor. Banks may require certain business forms as part of loan or credit arrangements. Some businesses, such as professional services companies cannot limit their malpractice liability and therefore cannot be traditional corporations or LLCs in most states.

Whenever there are investors and/or co-owners, the agency relationship of the parties requires careful maintenance of books and records and proper accounting. While in a sole proprietorship my bookkeeping can be less formal, any other entity form that involves co-owners or investors must maintain correct accounting records. And with corporations and

LLCs, there are statutory requirements for maintaining records of shareholder interests and notifications, meetings, and financial data.

The plumbing business may want to consider the various requirements of each entity form, and the conditions set by accounting and legal rules. And, I must be aware of the entity requirements if I decide to franchise (e.g., Roto-Rooter), enter into a contracts with other investors, or want to obtain bank funding.

What Costs are Associated with Different Business Forms?

This is perhaps the least considered aspect of business organizations. But it is important. Different business forms have significantly different costs, particularly for small businesses.

Some entities have relatively low costs. A sole proprietorship has only the costs of formation, business accounting, and licenses. A general partnership has additional legal costs for a partnership agreement and formation, and accounting and additional tax preparation costs because a separate tax return is required. Partnerships may also have different state level tax requirements and costs.

Other entity forms have higher costs. Limited partnerships, corporations, LLCs, and LLPs all have state formation requirements and filing charges to start up. They have yearly renewal filings and fees. Corporations, and LLCs in some states, have considerable additional expenses for state tax filings, tax payments, and annual organizational responsibilities and filings. Bookkeeping requirements, such as minutes of meetings, and separate accounting requirements, may also add costs. Legal and accounting fees can be substantial. A small business can easily incur additional expenses exceeding $5,000 per year for a corporate or LLC organization form.

It is necessary to consider these costs because they come directly from profits, and they are absolutely mandatory. If the entity does not meet state requirements, it loses its status, and all liability protection evaporates.

My plumbing business may have to pay these costs to obtain the protections of a corporation or LLC because of the relatively high liability risks of the business. The costs should be considered in light of insurance costs and the extent of personal wealth that may be at risk.

Summary of Entity Choice

It is evident from the discussion above that I should consider either a corporation or an LLC to form my plumbing business, particularly if I need investors. An LLC seems to have the overall advantage because of the flexibility in profit distribution and taxation, and its lower level of legal formality.

We have limited facts in my example, and it is important to understand that each situation must be evaluated differently and independently with all of the facts known.

In Conclusion

The example in this chapter discusses many of the factors to consider in selecting a small business form. It is apparent that liability protection can be a major factor in the decision-making process.

Remember, however, that even with liability protection in a corporate, LLC or LLP form, the business assets are subject to the claims of those injured. If anyone associated with my business commits a tort, breaches a contract, or otherwise causes injury, agency law requires the business to pay. As the owner, I will lose the business if considerable damages are caused. I may protect my personal assets with the proper entity form, but my business will be gone! When a business is a livelihood, as most are, this is a drastic result.

How do businesses, no matter what form they adopt, protect from this? Business insurance provides protection. All businesses, from small sole proprietorships to large corporations should carry insurance to protect the business from mistakes and negligence. It is an additional business expense that must be considered. The business form selected should only be a backup protection.

A Story from the Real

Partners sometimes believe that individual efforts to further the partnership business deserve extra compensation. It is really not unusual to ask for payment for services rendered in a business. Most would agree that payment is appropriate for extra work. But consider a partner that wanted to be paid for his day-to-day services on behalf of the business.

Three individuals formed a partnership to operate a commercial building that rented its space to various tenants. One of the partners was a limited partner, and two were general partners. The limited partner owned 50 percent of the partnership, and the general partners had one-third and one-sixth interests respectively. They had a written agreement that called for the division of profits based on interests owned. All were required to complete any necessary work for the benefit of the partnership.

The business operated for several years with no problems. The partnership agreement provided that a property manager could be hired and they had one for a time. The limited partner and one of the general partners both spent considerable time managing the business and eventually they terminated the property manager.

The limited partner died, and his partnership interest passed to his daughter. Immediately upon his death, the general partner who was already actively engaged in the business stated that he would manage the business for compensation. The other general partner agreed, and they determined reasonable compensation. The two general partners shared the agreement with the daughter of the former partner, and she did not protest.

A year later, the two general partners agreed to increase the compensation of the partner managing the business. The daughter objected, but the general partners implemented the pay increase anyway.

The daughter sued the general partner receiving the compensation to recover the amounts paid. She alleged that he breached the partnership agreement because it allowed no compensation to the partners. Further, the agreement required the approval of 75 percent of the partnership interests for any changes to it. Since she did not agree, the compensation payments were not approved by the required percentage. She also alleged that the compensated partner had breached his fiduciary duty to the partnership.

The court looked to the terms of the written agreement. It clearly stated that the partners were not entitled to compensation beyond their individual shares of profits for performing services. In fact, the agreement required them to provide services as needed in support of the business without compensation.

The court also found that the agreement could be modified by the parties if 75 percent of the ownership interests agreed. Even though the two general partners agreed to the compensation plan, they together held only 50 percent of the interests. The court noted that the partnership statute in the state required that an amendment to the partnership agreement could be made only with the consent of all of the partners unless the partnership agreement provided otherwise. The question for the court, therefore, became whether or not at least 75 percent of the partners approved the change to the agreement.

The court found that the daughter was informed of the first agreement before it was implemented and did not object. Therefore, the court considered this to be an implied agreement allowing the first arrangement for the payment of compensation to stand. However, the court also found that when she objected to the second arrangement, she specifically did not agree to it. So there were not sufficient interests approving the second compensation amendment.

The compensated partner had to repay to the partnership all of the compensation he received after the first year.

Partnership agreements and partnership law are strictly enforced when there is a duty violation among the partners. Here, the compensated partner was withdrawing funds for his personal benefit in breach of his agreement not to receive payment for services rendered to the business. He not only breached the partnership agreement by this, but he also breached his fiduciary duty to protect the interests of the other partners.

Note: The court pointed out that the limited partner who was providing management services to the partnership, even without compensation, had surrendered his limited partner status. Limited partners are prohibited by law from participation in management. There were not necessarily any damages caused to the other partners or anyone else; in fact, it probably provided them with a benefit. But by participating in the management of the business, the limited partner lost his liability protection for any actions brought against the partnership!

Chapter 24
International Business Considerations

(Business in a Near Legal Void)

This book discusses the rules our society established to maintain order and resolve disputes. There are tort rules of responsibility when people do wrong or act carelessly. Under contract law, we enforce promises. U.S. businesses also have legal relationships, duties, and liabilities that arise under agency and employment law and that are imposed by numerous regulatory agencies. These rules apply to our society in the U.S. We know them, and we expect others to know and follow them.

But business is now global, and we interact with different societies with different rules. Do our rules apply when we are selling products in China, or building factories in Bangladesh? Do the Germans and French have the same expectations for keeping promises? Do workers in India and Nigeria respect the same duties of agency that we apply?

The answer to all of these questions is a resounding "NO."

Each society has its own set of rules and its own laws to enforce them. Each has its own court systems and rules of dispute resolution. Understanding, accepting, and operating within these rules is critical to overseas business success.

U.S. laws and the laws of other countries deal with the differences among countries in several ways. There are both legal doctrines for respecting the law of other nations, and there are international rules that various countries have agreed to follow.

These include:

- ◘ The Comity Doctrine.

◻ The Act of State Doctrine.

◻ Sovereign immunity.

◻ Treaties.

◻ International conventions and agreements.

Comity Doctrine

This doctrine states that the courts of one nation will respect the decisions of courts in other countries. This gives full force and effect to the resolution of legal disputes made in the courts of foreign countries. It discourages repeated hearings of the same case. U.S. courts require, however, that the decision of the foreign court must not violate public policy or basic rights recognized in the U.S.

If a Japanese court hears a contract dispute, for example, and the Japanese court renders a decision under Japanese law, U.S. courts will respect the decision even if the rules for contract law are different in Japan. However, U.S. courts would not likely accept and enforce a contract decision from Japan that violated U.S. law or public policy. For example, a U.S. court would not enforce a discriminatory contract award of a Japanese court.

Act of State Doctrine

The courts of one country will not review or rule on the acts of a foreign government. This rule prohibits U.S. courts from interfering in the political processes of other countries. For a business operating overseas, this creates a significant hazard, particularly in countries that are politically unstable, or where the government controls business operations. If a foreign government chooses to tax local companies differently, allow unequal trade practices, or interfere with communications, transportation, or even property rights, U.S. courts cannot be used to challenge the decisions.

In reaction to the expropriation of property by the Cuban government, however, Congress enacted legislation that allows U.S. companies to use the courts to seek compensation for property confiscated by foreign governments. But this legislation also allows the President to stop such an action if it is harmful to U.S. foreign policy.

The Doctrine of Sovereign Immunity

Generally, foreign governments are not subject to suits in the courts of other countries. This follows from the Act of State Doctrine described above. Nations are immune from lawsuits.

But as worldwide business expanded and many foreign states became the parties to business contracts, this rule proved unfair and inappropriate under modern trading practices. Many governments enter into contracts for the purchase of goods and the provision of services with private companies. An unlimited right to breach contracts would greatly harm business concerns and international trade.

The Foreign Sovereign Immunities Act (FSIA) allows U.S. businesses to bring suit against foreign nations in U.S. courts if the action is based on commercial activity, such as contract enforcement. This permits businesses to seek redress in the courts when a foreign nation fails to perform under a contractual arrangement.

Treaties

The Constitution provides for treaties with foreign governments. Treaties, in fact, are among the highest laws of the land. They are negotiated by the executive branch of government and must be approved by two-thirds of the Senate. They supersede any conflicting statutes of the U.S. or any state government. Foreign governments give treaties similar force and effect.

The U.S. has entered into hundreds of treaties that impact foreign business. NAFTA, the North American Free Trade Agreement, is an example. This treaty and others with similar provisions remove trade tariffs and other barriers to international commerce. They provide for favorable trade relationships among the signing nations. Other treaties deal with issues like taxation, property rights, law enforcement, and intellectual property.

International Conventions and Agreements

The U.S. and many other governments around the world have joined in international organizations that allow businesses to operate freely within the variety of rules imposed by different cultures and societies. These agreements are often entered as part of treaties. Some of these agreements also provide rules for dispute resolution as well as mediation and arbitration forums.

The United Nations has many member organizations that promote trade and financial harmony. The World Bank and International Monetary Fund are two examples. The World Trade Organization (WTO) provides a forum for its 164 members to enter into trade agreements that reduce barriers and disputes. Regional organizations such as the European Union, OPEC, NAFTA, and the Organization of African Unity all provide for standardized trade rules that encourage business development.

International dispute resolution bodies help businesses cope with differing rules and laws. The International Court of Justice (aka the "World Court") is the court of the United Nations. It does not hear disputes between private parties, but does rule on trade and other disputes between nations. While participation in the world court is voluntary, its authority is becoming more recognized as a fair and broad-based resolution forum.

The WTO is primarily concerned with resolving trade disputes between its 164 member states. It provides a number of dispute resolution forums, including a semi-formal judicial process.

Finally, 157 countries are signatories of the United Nations Convention on the Recognition and Enforcement of Foreign Arbitral Awards of 1958 (the New York Accords). This agreement provides for international arbitration of business disputes and for domestic enforcement in national courts. And, over 75 countries have adopted The UNICITRAL Model Arbitration Law, which provides a model law for arbitrating international disputes. U.S. courts will enforce the arbitration decisions determined by this body.

In Conclusion

Overseas markets provide a very lucrative opportunity for business expansion. The world market is huge. But different societies follow different rules and customs. Many foreign governments and legal systems are unstable and may change frequently. The values of foreign currencies sometimes change rapidly and dramatically. Property and individual rights are not uniformly recognized. Avarice and contempt for successes and wealth can impact many day-to-day business activities. And taxation, financial instability, and confiscatory laws can turn success into failure very quickly.

While the international community is working to establish more trade agreements and dispute resolution methods, the world is still a very difficult to place to conduct business.

The critical rule for a successful overseas business operation is understanding and preparation. Understanding requires local expertise and thorough planning taking into account local laws, customs, and accounting requirements. Local religious values and practices can also be important.

Preparation includes a realistic assessment of business climate and risk and an anticipated return that is great enough to overcome occasional failures. A U.S. financial model will not usually work. An expectation that U.S. legal principles will apply is almost always incorrect. Although improving, uniform international legal dispute resolution is not yet in place.

A Story from the Real

The above discussion should indicate that global rules for business practices are still developing. While many organizations are in place to deal with differences in the many laws around the globe, businesses must be very wary of foreign investment and operation. International legal expertise is an absolute necessity, and local country knowledge is critical.

The following story has a very somber message.

A company, which was very successful in the U.S., purchased several entities in several western European countries to expand its operations. Its products, services, and methods were all very well managed and successful in the U.S. The company initially invested $50 million in the European expansion, mostly by acquiring on-going businesses. Market research indicated that operations like the company used in the U.S. would be successful in other countries.

The company acquired in-business companies but intended to install its own managers within a short time frame. It planned to consolidate functions among the acquired companies and reduce employees through automation and efficiency. It planned to implement its successful marketing and sales methods. It intended to fully integrate the European companies into the U.S. financial and management model.

The company did not understand the culture or business practices of the European societies.

It first learned that employees in these countries could not be terminated without cause and that very expensive separation payments were required by local law. The local management could not be replaced as planned, and the planned consolidations and employee layoffs could not proceed. The U.S. parent company could not adjust staffing, could not move plants, and could not change operations if the actions impacted employees in any way.

Local financial practices were different. Accounting information was not available in time for U.S. SEC and tax filing requirements. It was prepared based on local accounting standards and in local currencies. Recognition of income and expenses, depreciation, and many other aspects were very different. U.S. management had difficulty determining profitability.

Sales practices in Europe were found to be much less product oriented, and much more relationship oriented. In other words, potential customers were at least as much interested in the people they were dealing with as they were in the products they were purchasing. Without controls in place, the management in Europe very quickly failed to meet business objectives.

The authority for corporate officer actions and the customs under which the officers operated were much less formal in Europe. European officers borrowed funds from several banks without U.S. knowledge and often failed to repay them timely. The European banks again relied on relationships and did not press for repayment until the businesses had all but failed.

The final blow came when the U.S. company decided to exit the European market. It could not close or sell the companies there until they were proved solvent. This meant that assets had to be appraised, and loans paid off before any sale, even for very little payment, could be completed. After five years of misery, the U.S. company left its European adventure with a loss of over $100 million.

Consider that the above example took place in Western Europe, a society culturally very similar to our own. Certainly, these countries share similar values and financial concepts, and their laws are based on the same objectives of fairness and responsibility. Even in a similar culture, doing business is very different.

Expanding operations to different cultures is even more challenging. Some societies, for example, recognize bribery, embezzlement, and personal favors as acceptable means of supplementing income and demand them in everyday business. It is illegal under the Foreign Corrupt Practices Act for any U.S. company to pay bribes. How does a U.S. company compete in that environment?

International expansion has a lot of "risk" attached to it. Businesses do it to expand operations and revenue, find lower cost resources, and to open new markets for their products. But they must and do recognize the inherent risks and act accordingly.

A foreign operation must have projections that show very substantial opportunities for growth and profit; enough to overcome the risk.

Fini

Our journey comes to an end. I hope you enjoyed this book and have learned more about what our law means and how it affects you and our society. The law provides guidance and rules of behavior that we are expected to follow, and there are consequences if we chose to find our own ways outside of the law.

We know some people take that route and we sometimes even romanticize their behavior. But we also know inside that without the law, all of our fates would be much different and unpredictable. Law allows for an organized and productive society in which we can flourish and feel protected (at least some of the time). It deserves our respect and our contributions.

Our law also provides us with many safeguards. It rights wrongs committed against us, it requires that promises be kept, it establishes and enforces duties, and it spends huge amounts of money to give us a personal and societal safety umbrella that is second to none.

Having traveled to many other countries, some with more advanced legal systems than others, and observing and sometimes participating in their legal systems, I consider the U.S. to be very fortunate. Our law is stable, consistently applied, and reflects our morality. Most important, perhaps, is that it works very well when compared to many other places. The stability and functionality it provides for society and business are truly remarkable in our complex world.

Now that law is more familiar to you, please discuss it with your friends, co-workers, and family. We need to share our thoughts about it, and we need to contribute to the decisions that must be made every day regarding the law in our lives. Correct misunderstandings and contribute to discussions about the law, and be an advocate for the changes that you see necessary. Recognize that we are the law, and it is what we want it to be. If it does not reflect our values, let's convince a majority that it needs to be changed. If we agree with all of our laws, let's celebrate its reflection of us.

Made in the USA
Lexington, KY
04 January 2018